PETER E. DIETZ,
LABOR PRIEST

PETER E. DIETZ,
LABOR PRIEST

by **MARY HARRITA FOX**

with a Foreword by Aaron I. Abell, Ph.D.

197319

UNIVERSITY OF NOTRE DAME PRESS
Notre Dame, Indiana

Library of Congress
Catalog Card Number
53-7348

Foreword

In the pages of this book is unravelled a fascinating and instructive story, that of the Reverend Peter E. Dietz who was the key figure in the American Catholic social movement during the first quarter of the present century. The Dietz story well deserves telling. With a few contemporaries, notably Monsignor John A. Ryan, Dietz channeled the Catholic labor movement into its modern course whose ever-widening stream has given the Catholic Church an influence in the field of labor which many deplore but all concede. Earlier, during the 1880's and the 1890's, Catholic wage-earners with the help of forward-looking clergymen like Cardinal Gibbons had established their moral right to join even militant labor organizations whose means and ends were not anti-Christian. But the more difficult task of positively advancing the labor movement along constructive lines devolved upon the men and women of the succeeding generation, among whom Father Dietz was preeminent for journalistic and organizational activities. The author stresses Dietz's role in the Central Verein and the Social Service Commission as groundwork for the National Catholic Welfare Conference whose brilliant piloting of Catholic social action since World War I is acknowledged by both friends and foes of the Church. More important, Dietz divined the future direction of the maturing labor movement. Unlike Ryan and others who stressed producers' cooperation and co-partnership as desirable solutions of industrial strife, Dietz lacked faith in these historic social reform panaceas, insisting that the generic remedy lay in the growth and progressive development of trade unionism with whose great leaders he was on terms of closer intimacy than any other Catholic clergyman. Recent labor history attests the accuracy of his insight.

Although he lived until 1947, Father Dietz was not active in the social movement after 1922, and his amazing career was largely forgotten until the writer of this Foreword called attention to it in "The Reception of Leo XIII's Labor Encyclical in America, 1891-

1919," *Review of Politics*, VII (October, 1945), 464-495. Besides exploring Dietz's contributions to social service in all their ramifications, the author amply demonstrates that conservative distrust of his friendliness to labor, displayed chiefly in his pioneer Catholic labor school at Cincinnati, forced his premature retirement from the social movement and denied the country the benefit of his experience and wisdom in fixing labor's new status under the New Deal. As likely as not, her scholarly study will bring him the fame he justly deserves.

The author of this full-length biography is assistant professor of history in Mundelein College. The completeness of the book — its sweep and scope, its vividness, its richness of detail — stems as much from the author's insight into the character and aspirations of Father Dietz as from the wise use made of the priest's voluminous letters and papers, all of which apparently have been preserved. There is scarcely a Catholic social attitude that is not illumined by this work which is at once the story of a dynamic personality and a significant contribution to the social history of the Catholic Church and to the evolution of the American labor movement during the great Era of Progressivism in which Father Dietz was privileged to expend the most fruitful years of a long and useful life.

— AARON I. ABELL

Preface

To a generation that takes for granted the existence of over 100 Catholic Labor Colleges, the work of many "labor priests," and the magnitude of Catholic professional social work, the deeds of one who helped "blaze the trail" are enlightening and challenging. Too often overlooked are the contributions of those pioneers who struggled and suffered to make their dreams prevail.

The Reverend Peter Ernest Dietz was such a pioneer. As a young man he saw with alarm the effects on American society of the rapid industrialization of the country. The problems of the working man won his sympathy, and he yearned to play a part in the solution of those problems. His ordination to the priesthood gave goal and purpose to this desire.

Coming on the social scene in 1904, he found an incipient Catholic social movement. He identified himself with the German Catholic Central Verein and the American Federation of Catholic Societies, trying to weld American Catholics into an articulate group, which, forgetting national and local prejudices, would adopt a common program to advance a national Catholic movement for social reform.

Father Dietz claimed no originality in his program. His life's goal was "to bring *Rerum Novarum* to the people *in practice.*" In this Encyclical which Pope Leo XIII addressed to the universal Church in May, 1891, Dietz found the blueprint for his solution of the social problem in the United States. He agreed with the Holy Father that a just and practical program of reform lay somewhere between the two extremes of economic thought — the revolutionary school of Socialism and the individualistic school of *laissez-faire.*

Fundamental in such a program, Leo XIII declared, was the inspiring and sustaining power of religion — the bond which should unite employer and employed in harmony. The teachings of religion provide the only true basis for the dignity and integrity of personal relations. The Holy Father in no wise ignores human means toward this end. Workingmen's associations, when properly organized and controlled, increased, he noted, the bargaining power of labor and helped the working man to help himself. The Pope deemed it imperative that the state protect these associations and supplement their inadequacy with "public remedial measures."

Father Dietz's study of conditions in America convinced him that the social problem was basically the problem of labor. The labor movement must hold true to its Christian heritage and fight free of Socialist domination. This it could accomplish, he believed, through the Catholic members of the American Federation of Labor. To this end he organized Catholic trade unionists into his Militia of Christ for Social Service. His American Academy of Christian Democracy, begun as a training school for women in social service, evolved into a National Labor College where labor leaders were imbued with Christian principles. Whenever the opportunity presented itself, Father Dietz allied himself with those agencies promoting the "public remedial measures" to which Leo XIII referred.

Father Dietz was not the first American priest to take an interest in the working man, but he was the first to take literally the exhortation of the Holy Father to devote "all the energy of his mind and all the strength of his endurance" to implementing the papal program. He resigned his pastorate to become writer, editor, lecturer and organizer in the cause of trade unionism.

This study was prepared originally as a dissertation for the degree of Doctor of Philosophy at the University of Notre Dame. Dr. Aaron I. Abell, Associate Professor of History, whose enthusiasm for the work of Father Dietz inspired the selection of the subject, directed the study. His patient counsel assured its completion. The Reverend Thomas T. McAvoy, C.S.C., Head of the Department of History, Dr. William O. Shanahan, Dr. Marshall T. Smelser, and Dr. Thomas Downey, members of the Department of History, read the manuscript and made pertinent suggestions for its improvement.

The author gratefully acknowledges the valuable assistance of the Very Reverend Frederick C. Dietz, M.M., Secretary-General of the Society of Maryknoll and brother of Peter Dietz, who put the intimate family papers at the discretionary use of the author. His interest, encouragement, and material help made possible the publication of this manuscript. Theresa Dietz of Oberlin, Ohio, his sister, supplied innumerable informative letters.

Special recognition is due the inestimable aid of Frederick P. Kenkel, K.S.G., Director of the Central Bureau of the German Catholic Central Verein. His prodigious memory of persons, places, and events filled in the gaps in the Dietz story; his constant challenging of the value of the work of Father Dietz helped keep the study objective.

Other busy people generously contributed their memories of Father Dietz. Chief among these were the Reverend Raymond McGowan, director of the Social Action Department of the National Catholic Welfare Conference, the Right Reverend Monsignor Edward A. Freking, national secretary of the Catholic Students' Mission Crusade, and the labor leaders, Philip Murray, Matthew Woll, John P. Frey, and Daniel Tobin.

Finally, the author acknowledges the interest and encouragement of the Superiors of her Congregation, the Sisters of Charity of the Blessed Virgin Mary, and the valuable aid of those members of the faculty of Mundelein College who read and criticized the manuscript.

MARY HARRITA FOX

Mundelein College

Table of Contents

List of Illustrations

Chapter One

EARLY YEARS:
Discovering the
Church's Social Program

TWENTY-EIGHT YEARS after Pope Leo XIII wrote his famous Encyclical *Rerum Novarum* the American Catholic hierarchy issued what is now known as the "Bishops' Plan of Social Reconstruction." To hold with one writer "that no attempt had ever been made to solidify nationally the forces of American Catholicism"[1] before 1919 is to ignore the years of labor of a few zealous and far-sighted bishops, priests, and laymen, who recognized the existence of grave social injustices and devoted their energy and talents to the cause of social reform. To arouse American Catholics to the same realizations, to educate them in the Catholic principles underlying the correct social order, particularly as enunciated in the social encyclicals of Leo XIII and Pius X, and to organize them for concerted action, was, of course, a difficult and discouraging task. This study deals with one who devoted most of his priestly life to doing just that.

Peter Ernest Dietz was born July 10, 1878, on New York's East Side, the second oldest of a family of ten. Both of his parents were born in Germany. His father, Frederick Dietz, was a native of Forst, a small town famous for its wines, near Lufwigshafen in the Palatinate; his mother, Eva Kern, came from Leidersbach and Hessental, villages in the charming Spessart region of Bavaria near Aschaffenburg. They first met and were married in New York City.[2]

In his *Diary,* begun when he was twenty-three, Peter recalls the poverty of his boyhood.[3] Because his father, a varnisher by trade, was frequently unemployed, other members of the family had to

1

work to supplement the family income. As a newsboy Peter earned two or three dollars a week and also helped his mother with the slippers she made under contract with a shoe dealer. These experiences conditioned him for his later work. His interest in the labor movement, likewise, dated from these early years when he occasionally went to the union office to pay his father's dues. "Even then," he recalled later, "the commotion and excitement that goes into a labor union intrigued me greatly. My heart was with the movement."[4]

Since the Dietz family lived in a Redemptorist parish, Peter received his early education at Holy Redeemer School.[5] The influences here formed his attraction for the priesthood, but, because he was only twelve years old when he announced his desire to become a priest, his father insisted that he wait until he was older. For three years, consequently, he was apprenticed to Ernest Heise, a paperhanger and painter. This "Heisean Period," as he called it, ended in the fall of 1894 when he matriculated at St. Mary's, the Redemptorist College in North East, Pennsylvania.

For a time all went well at school. Peter made friends, succeeded in his studies, learned to play the cornet and bass violin, and was generally interested in sports. During his second year at St. Mary's, however, a change came over him. He neglected his studies for a complete absorption in poetry and gradually developed an anti-social and melancholy outlook on life. He wrote of this "sad melancholy" that it "bore dire fruits and brought influences to bear on me which shall endure as long as I live." Because of ill health, he discontinued his studies and in the summer of 1896[6] he returned to New York.

Under the devoted kindness of his mother and sisters, Peter's health improved sufficiently for him to take up again the work of a paperhanger and painter. Gradually the melancholy left him and he joined the Gesellen-Verein and made many friends. Through these associations he met Brother Homobonus of the Society of the Divine Word and Father Godfrey Schilling, O.F.M., *praeses* of the New York branch of the Gesellen-Verein. The latter became his spiritual director and life-time friend.

2

REV. PETER E. DIETZ

Desiring to continue his education, Peter matriculated as a day student at the College of St. Francis Xavier in Manhattan in the fall of 1897. In his *Diary* he pays tribute to the fine class of boys at St. Francis and to the piety and learning of the faculty. On Saturdays and holidays he continued his work as a painter, earning enough to support himself and on occasions even giving a "lift" to his parents. His carefree life during these two years, full of the normal enjoyments of the young, did not interfere with Dietz's interest in the needs of others. He joined the St. Vincent de Paul Society and according to Thomas Mulry, president of the Superior Council of New York, became an "active and zealous" worker.[7] His penchant for organizing, characteristic of his later life, also found early expression in the "St. Paulinus Lyceum" with its constitution and *Journal,* which Dietz founded for the bell ringers of Holy Redeemer Church. Even after he left New York, Dietz contributed an occasional article and poem to the *Journal.*[8]

As the course at St. Francis Xavier's would end in 1899, the more serious question of the priesthood came again to the fore. Absorption in other affairs had made Dietz wax hot and cold on the idea, but now, at twenty-one, he would have to decide. In May, 1899, he applied for admission to St. Joseph's Seminary, Dunwoodie, New York, but because he had not completed his classical course he was not eligible. The authorities permitted him, however, to take the entrance examination, which he passed satisfactorily.[9] To make up his deficiency in the classics, he matriculated at St. Bonaventure College in Alleghany.[10] His year here passed successfully from a student's point of view; he joined the band, the James Dolan Literary Association, and was elected assistant editor of the *Laurel.* Even here Dietz was mindful of the social problems existing in the world outside his student life. In a paper on the influence of inventions on labor, he wrote:

> [They] almost invariably favor the rich who by their installation are enabled to decrease the number of their employees, and often as a consequence to reduce wages. To this source we trace strikes. . . . It is rarely that they succeed . . . and once [the strikers] perceive their failure, a lost position and a

5

dark future ahead they are often driven to desperation and in such a condition are capable of doing anything. Hence such scenes as the 'Brooklyn strikes' and the mine troubles in Homestead, Pa.

Such situations, coupled with the hiring of women and the crowded conditions of labor, create the social problem whose importance is

> vital and increasing daily. Many solutions have been proffered [sic] but none has been found practicable and we look ahead into the future with ever-increasing alarm. There is, however, one practicable solution which has been offered by the Holy Father, Leo XIII, but the world is not ready to receive it; still we live in expectation of the day when the world will accept the solution of the Catholic Doctrine convinced that it contains a remedy for every social evil.[11]

But the main purpose of his coming to St. Bonaventure he accomplished only partially, for, although Dietz completed the Classics, he did not take the course in philosophy, as the Reverend E. R. Dyer, rector at Dunwoodie, had advised.[12] This meant that he would have to take first year philosophy at Dunwoodie if he entered that seminary. For some reason, Dietz was not willing to do this and turned to a consideration of the Society of the Divine Word. He had been associated with members of that Society for some time and had accompanied two priests to Alleghany when he returned after the Christmas vacation in 1899. He relates in his *Diary* how listening to them tell of their experiences "I found myself enthusiastically swayed in favor of a similar vocation." Through Father John Peil, whom he had known in the east, and who was then located at Schermerville (now Techny), Illinois, Peter came in touch with the Father General in Steyl, Holland, and on September 8, 1900, sailed for Europe to begin his studies at St. Gabriel, Moedling, Germany, near Vienna.

The two years at Moedling were turbulent in many respects. Dietz complained of frequent headaches and nervous disorders which kept him alternating between the depths of despair and the heights of optimism and exultation. Frequent difficulties with authority added to his disturbances, but the Reverend P. Gier, S.V.D., guided him through these trying times.

6

During the summer vacation Dietz traveled, visiting his relatives in Germany. His eagerness to know the German people, particularly the common people, was coupled with a desire to familiarize them with American ways. Accordingly, on March 17, 1901, he organized the Anglo-Saxon Alliance among the students at St. Gabriel's for the purpose of studying the English language and the procedures in organizing societies (*Vereinswesen*) in America and England. The society debated in English the first year, but the next year Dietz reorganized the Alliance into the St. George's Council of the Society of St. Vincent de Paul, and, as its first president, delivered a series of lectures on the charitable work of the Church.[13]

Although he entered the novitiate and received the habit on September 15, 1901, Dietz became restless. In an analysis of his state of mind he questioned, first, the purity of his motive in coming to St. Gabriel's. Had he come, perhaps, because he was unable to enter the seminary in America, or because he thought he could finish sooner at Moedling, rather than because of any special vocation to the Society of the Divine Word? Too, the routine of novitiate life, with its long devotions and meditations at appointed times, its lack of diversion in games or enjoyments (even smoking was forbidden), and the restricted activity—these things, he feared would dull his spirit and weaken his ambition. He longed to go freely about the crowded tenements to console the poor, the sick, and the afflicted.[14] Father Gier, his spiritual director, encouraged him by promising to shorten his studies by a year, or to make it possible for him to finish his studies in America. The latter plan appealed to Dietz for several reasons: he found the climate at Moedling disagreeable; he wanted to be near his parents so he could help them; but especially, he saw the work he longed to do for the Church in America:

> I must *master* the English language, literature, theology, and character of the people. I want to penetrate the nature and the spirit of the developing American in order to be able to understand him *correctly* from the very beginning.
>
> It cannot be denied that the American realizes the social problems of the present with greater facility and thus far has

7

solved them best, although it is generally known that the final solution is still far distant. According to my opinion this solution depends not in the least part on the activity of the Catholic clergy. We all know that in the intellectual sphere America has not achieved anything beyond mediocrity. This is for the time being but natural, because America is still in its youth; nevertheless the native energy gushes forth spontaneously everywhere. To be permitted to cooperate in giving direction to this energy is a grand task.[15]

Preparation for this work could best be made at the Catholic University of America, for Dietz felt that from there American Catholic life and striving would finally take its direction. He still had no thought of leaving the Society of the Divine Word. Rather he wanted to make the Society and its work better known at the Catholic University.[16]

Gradually, however, as the time for the taking of vows drew near, Dietz was convinced that the rules of community life were too restrictive for the work he intended to do. An entry in his *Diary* for March 10, 1902, refers to a letter he wrote to a friend in New York in which Dietz described how he would make the Society of St. Vincent de Paul solve the social question. "Sometimes," he wrote, "I feel the fire of enthusiasm almost consuming me; it is so much worse when I realize that I am tied down for good with no show of doing anything." As this sense of mission grew, Dietz's plans evolved. At first he and his close friend, Gerhardt Schmitz, talked of offering themselves to some diocese still undeveloped, perhaps in Montana or Oregon, where conditions would be rugged and the work for souls challenging. Because the writings of Bishop John L. Spalding had influenced his thinking, Dietz wrote him of this plan.[17]

Before anything further developed, however, Dietz turned to formulating plans for a new Congregation, the "Militia of the Divine Will," an association of laymen and priests following the rules of the Third Order of St. Francis and the Society of St. Vincent de Paul.[18] Appealing mainly to the laity of the "middle and lower classes," it would

gather in a group of like-minded young men, who aglow with

8

enthusiasm for the Church and the Republic and deeply imbued with the spirit of Christianity, should boldly champion truth, goodness, beauty and justice in the practical walks of life.[19]

Centralized in a beautiful country area, but near some well populated center, a faculty of specialists would make available in a summer school plan the best of the Catholic past, a sort of modern *Summa* for the solution of the present social problems. They would neglect no phase of Catholic life. The ideas expounded here at the center would be diffused through a newspaper, *The American Catholic,* and by lecturers trained at the center, who would travel throughout the country speaking at colleges, seminaries, and meetings of Catholic societies.

Some of the uncertainty about the future ended when Father Godfrey, since transferred from Washington to Cairo, Egypt, invited Dietz and his friend to visit him. They took permanent leave of the S.V.D. novitiate on October 6, 1902. Father Godfrey listened to their plan for a new Congregation and, though struck by its boldness, agreed to help them locate in some diocese. Eventually they decided on Scranton as the most desirable place. From Cairo the two journeyed to Italy, where they enjoyed the sights of the Eternal City. Providence, they felt, directed them to Monsignor Lorenzo Cecchini, a personal friend of Bishop Michael J. Hoban of Scranton. Cecchini evinced great interest in their plan and agreed to give them a letter of recommendation to the Bishop.

While waiting for their cause to develop further, Dietz and his friend decided to spend the interval before their return to America at the University of Bonn. Here they enrolled in courses in theology, spending the rest of the school year and the summer session at the University. During their free time they travelled through West Germany. On one of these trips, Dietz was invited to address a labor organization in Neudorf.[20]

In the meantime, friends in America looked for a bishop who would be willing to adopt Dietz and Schmitz. Both Father Godfrey and Father Walter Elliott, C.S.P., rector of the Apostolic Mission House in Washington, tried to interest Bishop Hoban in their cause.

When the Bishop did not respond favorably, the priests suggested that Dietz and his friend return to America where the matter could be more easily arranged.[21] The pair arrived in New York on October 8, 1903, and, after a short visit at the Dietz home, went on to Washington, where Father Elliott had invited them to be guests of the Paulists until their affairs were straightened out.[22] Dietz enjoyed his sojourn at the Catholic University. The two young men lived in Keane Hall and took courses at the University. Besides a course in mission apologetics from the Paulists, Dietz studied dogmatic theology, history of education, and sociology. He met many important people at the University, including Dr. Charles P. Neill, who was to give him valuable advice later, and Dr. William Kerby. The latter especially encouraged Dietz and gave him confidence in his ability to accomplish his desired mission of reform.

This happy interlude ended abruptly when Bishop Ignatius Horstmann of Cleveland, who had agreed to adopt the two young men, ordered them to St. Mary's Seminary, Baltimore, to complete their studies for the priesthood. Again the restraint of seminary life had its effect on Dietz. His *Diary* recounts his difficulties with Father Dyer, now rector of St. Mary's. Recurring nervous attacks put him in the hospital in April, 1904. Reluctant to return to St. Mary's, Dietz received permission to recuperate in North Carolina while helping Father Thomas Frederick Price, later co-founder of Maryknoll, in his work among the non-Catholics there.[23] This permission was not unusual since Father Price frequently brought seminarians from the north for the summer vacation to help him in his North Carolina Apostolate.[24] Dietz tells in his *Diary* of his many satisfying experiences in North Carolina. His ability to play the cornet attracted crowds, which could then be instructed.

Returning to the seminary in October, Dietz completed his studies in time to be ordained by Cardinal Gibbons on December 17, 1904. Shortly before ordination he wrote to his Bishop:

> For my part, I realized from youth that the workingman's difficulties and possibilities prompted and sustained my vocation. To deal at all with the problem technical equipment is indispensable and therefore, I would gladly take up again and

finish the course in sociology, I had begun last year. . . . I aspire to qualify myself in the course of years for the 'Apostolate' of your diocese, especially that branch of it that deals with socialistic trends; in fact I have occasionally thought I would like to get in with Father Kress at once on the basis of my own observations from books and from surroundings, especially in Germany, the help I got from Dr. Kerby and Father Elliott, and the experience I had with Father Price, who candidly told me that I would make a good missionary.[25]

Though Bishop Horstmann was kind and sympathetic, he did not grant the request, but made Father Dietz assistant pastor of St. Mary's Church, Elyria, Ohio, with Oberlin as a mission.[26]

By the time Father Dietz was ready in 1904 to begin his work of social reform, the Church in America had already laid the foundations of a social program. Conditions arising from the rapid industrialization and consequent urbanization of the country following the Civil War focused the attention of leaders in the Church on the dangers to which their people were exposed. With the emergence of large corporations, the mass production made possible by new inventions, and the development of the railroads linking all parts of the country, industrial competition reached national proportions. For the once independent craftsman this change had dire consequences, because, as each new machine further simplified the processes of production, he found his place taken by an increasing number of unskilled or semi-skilled workers — men, women, and children. By the mid-eighties an ever-increasing supply of this unskilled labor was coming from Southern and Eastern Europe in what was known as the "new immigration." Used to a lower standard of living than the native American, these people fitted well into the scheme of things by making possible mass production of a high quality, at a low labor cost.[27] The laborer then, became a mere cog in the industrial machine dominated by financial magnates interested only in business efficiency and profits.

Caught in this vortex, the individual laborer was helpless before the evils to which he was subjected — low wages, long hours, dangerous working conditions — all aggravated by the ups and downs of the business cycle.[28] Only by matching organization with organ-

11

ization could he hope to improve his lot. Labor organizations, begun on a local scale, battling against the restraints of the old conspiracy laws, the power of industrial magnates, the hostility of public opinion, and unfavorable court decisions, by 1860 were successful in forming national unions in twenty-six trades.[29] As employers combined against them, however, the need of a national program for labor as a whole became apparent.

The first successful attempt to bring American labor together in a common program was made at Philadelphia, in 1869, when Uriah S. Stephens and eight associates organized the Knights of Labor. Secret and highly ritualistic, this organization united the skilled and unskilled workers, employer, and professional groups in a program of "education, legislation, and mutual beneficence."[30] About a decade later appeared the American Federation of Labor, which, under the leadership of Samuel Gompers, accepted the capitalistic system, but, on the principle of "trade unionism pure and simple," fought for the rights of its members "here and now." By means of the strike, picketing, and the boycott, trade unionists tried to offset the effects of the lockout and the black list.

Oftentimes the battle was violent and bloody when the employer's or the state's militia was called in to break up union resistance. Aggravating the tendency to violence, and increasing public prejudice, were the presence in these labor organizations of socialists and anarchists. Coming into this country in the early fifties as refugees from the European revolutions, these radicals received little attention at first from Americans. The panic of 1873, however, created the conditions that brought these subversive elements into the open in three main groups — the anarchistic International Working People's Association, affiliated with the "Black International" of Europe; the International Workmen's Association, or "Red International"; and the Socialist Labor Party.[31] Of the three, the Socialist Labor Party, under the leadership of the autocratic Daniel de Leon, was the most effective. Using a policy of "boring from within" and dual unionism, in his Socialistic Trade and Labor Alliance, he tried to take over the labor movement.[32]

From these problems, the Church could not afford to remain

aloof. Many Catholics joined these labor unions and were exposed thereby to all sorts of dangerous influences. Terence V. Powderly, the influential Grand Master of the Knights of Labor, was a Catholic, and many members were Irish Catholics. Yet the Knights of Labor was a secret organization and some of its leading members, like Albert B. Parsons and Peter J. McGuire, were prominent also in the anarchist and socialist movements.[33] The violence attendant on labor's struggle for justice led churchmen to confuse *bona fide* labor unions and their legitimate practices with the revolutionary elements and the reactionary employer groups that discredited their practices.

In 1880, for example, the Right Reverend John L. Spalding, Bishop of Peoria, viewed the Molly Maguire assassinations as warnings of the dangers of labor agitation and concluded:

> Even if the evil should go no further than strikes and trades-unions, this will be enough to undermine the moral character of our people and to wean them from the Church.[34]

Other ecclesiastical leaders shared his view.[35] Fortunately, however, the enlightened members of the hierarchy hesitated to press the adoption of a definitive policy regarding labor unions, but left to the individual ecclesiastics the applications of the general principles relative to secret societies.[36]

When Cardinal Eleazer-Alexandre Taschereau of Quebec raised the question of the condemnation of the Knights of Labor, the consequences of such a course were apparent to farsighted men like Archbishops Gibbons and Ireland and Bishop John J. Keane. Gibbons' famous memorial addressed to Cardinal Giovanni Simeoni, Prefect of the Propaganda, sought to counteract the reports Taschereau had made at Rome.[37]

Describing carefully the "grave and threatening social evils" and "public injustices" rampant in the United States, Gibbons insisted that "the organization of all interested persons" was not only a "means altogether natural and just" but "almost the only means to invite public attention, to give force to the most legitimate resistance, to add weight to the most just demands."[38] On the other hand, the newly made Cardinal did not deny the existence of "athe-

13

ists, communists and anarchists" in the labor unions of America, but he professed confidence that American Catholics would meet these trials of faith with "good sense and firmness"; nor did he consider the organization of Catholics into separate unions "either possible or necessary."[39] Finally, Gibbons maintained that

> since it is acknowledged by all that the great questions of the future are . . . the social questions — the questions which concern the improvement of the condition of the great popular masses, and especially the working people — it is evident that the Church should always be found on the side of humanity — of justice towards the multitudes who compose the body of the human family.[40]

Rome's withholding condemnation of the Knights of Labor in the United States as a result of Cardinal Gibbons' action was victory of a sort for those ecclesiastics who favored the cause of trade unionism. Catholic workingmen had at least tacit permission to enter these organizations and join with non-Catholics and even revolutionaries in furthering the cause of labor. Gibbons was correct in insisting that the influence of the Knights of Labor was waning in favor of the newly-founded American Federation of Labor. It would become the business of the Catholic members in this organization to use their influence to keep the A. F. of L. Christian in its policies and decisions.[41] To guide Catholic trade unionists to that end was to be the dominating purpose of Father Dietz's priestly career.

In the meantime individuals in the Church advocated remedies for the social injustices of their day, defended trade unionism, and even went so far as to venture the opinion that only through the intervention of the state could industrial wrongs be righted.[42] For this group the appearance of Leo XIII's great encyclical, *Rerum Novarum,* in May, 1891, was an encouragement and a vindication.

The encyclical recognized the evils in modern industry that had left the workingman "isolated and defenseless," suffering under a "yoke little better than slavery itself," and offered an outline for a remedial program.[43] Apart from its atheistic tenets, Socialism as a remedy merited papal denunciation because it was impracticable

14

and unjust. The "inviolability of private property" which Socialism rejected for the "community of goods," must be, the Pope declared, "the first and fundamental principle" of any effective program of reform, allowing always for the claims of justice and charity.[44]

For the "practical solution" of the social question, Leo XIII looked to three sources — the Church, the state, and organizations, especially workmen's associations.

> Religion teaches the laboring man [he wrote] . . . to carry out honestly and well all equitable agreements freely made, never to injure capital . . . never to employ violence in representing his own cause, nor to engage in riot and disorder.[45]

On the other hand, religion teaches the employer

> that it is shameful and inhuman to treat men like chattels . . . to make one's profit out of the need of another, [or] to defraud any one of wages that are his due.[46]

But knowing human nature well, and realizing that men ignore the demands of religion, Leo XIII did not leave all to the voluntary cooperation of employer and employees. Furthermore, other contingencies might prevent the solution of difficulties by cooperation alone. In such an eventuality, the role of the state was made plain:

> Whenever the general interest of any particular class suffers, or is threatened with evils which can in no other way be met, the public authority must step in to meet them.[47]

But, Leo warned,

> the law must not undertake more, nor go further, than is required for the remedy of the evil or the removal of the danger.[48]

The encyclical especially recommended certain "public remedial measures" such as the provision for Sunday rest and the regulation of hours, wages, and conditions of work. It insisted that, since a man's labor was "necessary" and "personal," his wages must be sufficient to support himself and his family in "reasonable and frugal comfort," regardless of any agreement to the contrary into which he might have entered.[49] The number of hours a person could reasonably be expected to work depended upon "the nature

15

of the work, on circumstances of time and place, and on the health and strength of the workman."[50]

Significant for the times was the enthusiastic endorsement of workingmen's associations. To form such associations was the natural right of man, the encyclical declared, and therefore the state, whose duty was to safeguard natural rights, must protect these associations.[51] But Leo warned against organizations that were "managed on principles far from compatible with Christianity and the public well-being."[52] He left the sincere Catholic only one alternative — the formation of separate Catholic unions.

Having indicated the principles and means by which the great problems of the workingman could be solved, the encyclical concluded with the mandate to each one to "put his hand to the work which falls to his own share . . . at once and immediately, lest the evil which is already so great may by delay become absolutely beyond remedy."[53] The role of the clergy emerged clearly: "Every minister of Holy Religion must throw into the conflict all the energy of his mind, and all the strength of his endurance."[54]

A few individuals and organizations obeyed this mandate of Pope Leo XIII in the decade following its utterance, but an organized effort, sponsored by the hierarchy and enlisting the aid of laymen, had to await a later time. That the Church in America was slow in doing much about the social problem is partially explained by her absorption in other important matters. The problem of organizing parishes, building schools, and caring for those unfortunates who had always been considered the peculiar charges of the Catholic Church — the orphans, the poor, and the aged — engaged much of the attention and energy of the leaders of the Church.[55] No doubt, also, the complexity of the social problem, requiring for its solution a knowledge of economic and social processes which the average priest did not have, held back those otherwise qualified to lead.[56] But more significant as a deterrent to a common program of social reform were the differences of opinion that had divided Catholics over such questions as the Knights of Labor, the McGlynn case, Cahenslyism, the school question, and the general role of Catholics in American life.[57] Only

16

time would eradicate the effects of these controversies and permit the development of Catholic solidarity of thought and action.

In the meantime individuals endeavored to show the need of a Catholic program. Giving point to their importunings were the growth in influence of Socialism of the Debs type in the American Federation of Labor and the condition of labor under the mass offensive of employers after 1897.[58]

Some stressed the importance of the role of the priest in the guidance of Catholics in trade unions lest these men "drift away from the Church and become the prey of designing demagogues."[59] In preparation for this work, he should not merely read the encyclical but should study it until he had thoroughly assimilated its principles. In addition, a knowledge of the social sciences seemed essential for a scientific approach to the social problem.[60] A few priests acted as labor mediators in time of strikes. Noteworthy among these was the Reverend John J. Curran of Wilkes-Barre, Pa., affectionately known as the "miners' friend." In the great anthracite coal strike of 1902, Father Curran, supported by his Bishop, the Right Reverend Michael J. Hoban of Scranton, endeavored to bring together in conference the officials of the coal companies, the Morgan interests, and John Mitchell, labor's representative.[61] Well known, also, is the work of Bishop Spalding on the commission set up by President Roosevelt to arbitrate the strike.

Responding to the leadership of priests and bishops, Catholic laymen participated in this early social movement. At the second lay congress — the Columbian Catholic Congress — which met in Chicago during the World's Fair in 1893, they gave serious consideration to the recent encyclical and the problems of capital and labor peculiar to the United States. A significant resolution urged clergy and laity to "create, or use existing societies 'for the diffusion of sound literature and the education of their minds on economic subjects.'"[62]

Forerunner of societies of Catholic trade unionists was the Reform Association of Buffalo, organized in 1901 by the Reverend Herman Maeckel, S.J., pastor of St. Anne's parish.[63] The Right Reverend James E. Quigley, the progressive Bishop of Buffalo, im-

pressed upon its members their responsibility to the trade union
movement. At a mass meeting of three thousand workers of the
city, the Bishop told them:

> With the approbation of your Church . . . you have or-
> ganized your labor unions and it rests with you, Catholic
> Workingmen of Buffalo, to see that these unions shall not
> become hotbeds . . . of irreligion, atheism, and anarchy.[64]

A resolution adopted at this meeting called for frequent conferences
in the various parishes to make known to every Catholic the stand
of the Church on Socialism and particularly the rights and duties
of both capital and labor, as set forth in *Rerum Novarum*.[65]

One society giving thought to the social problem was the German Catholic Central Verein. With the inspiring tradition of the
work of men like Father Adolph Kolping and Bishop William
Emmanuel von Ketteler, it was natural that its members responded
readily to the challenge of American social conditions. Immediate
recognition was given *Rerum Novarum* at the Catholic Day
(*Katholikentag*) held in Buffalo in 1891. A resolution adopted by
its members thanked the Holy Father for his encyclical and pledged
all their effort

> to the application of the principles and instructions which are
> laid down in the Encyclical and also to help others, in the
> widest circles possible, to the acceptance and execution of
> them, in the firmest conviction that only by adherence to
> those principles can the solution be found to this highly im-
> portant question of our time.[66]

Subsequent conventions of the Central Verein continued this interest, which reached its peak in 1907 with plans for a Bureau of
Social Propaganda.[67]

Members of the Central Verein and others believed that the
Catholic minority in American society could be more articulate if
its members united in one Catholic organization. Taking the initiative in this direction, the Knights of St. John, called representatives of several national organizations to preliminary meetings at
Philadelphia, September 16, 1900, at New York, and at Long
Branch, New Jersey, in August, 1901.[68] The Right Reverend

18

James A. McFaul, Bishop of Trenton, attending this last meeting, gave great encouragement to the assembled delegates. A constitution tentatively adopted declared one of the objects of the organization, the American Federation of Catholic Societies, to be "the study of conditions in our social life."[69] At the first convention in Cincinnati, in 1901, three hundred delegates attended, claiming to represent six hundred thousand Catholics. One of the resolutions adopted by this convention recommended to all the study of *Rerum Novarum*.[70] Interest in the social problem continued as a part of each convention. At Detroit in 1904, the members endorsed the formation of trade unions as a means of bettering the material conditions of the workingman, but exhorted Catholics to form special associations which would provide for "religious and moral wants and instruct them properly on the social question, and a practical solution thereof."[71]

These two societies, the Central Verein and the American Federation of Catholic Societies, provided fitting channels through which Father Dietz carried out much of his social program. By 1904 both were well conditioned to receive his ideas. By that time, too, we may conclude, a Catholic social conscience was awakening. The American hierarchy, clergy, laity, and press had striven to make rank and file Catholics cognizant of social injustices. At least the foundations were laid. Upon them, ultimately, would be erected a Catholic social movement on national lines. Practically every type of endeavor that would characterize such a movement had been agitated by someone, somewhere, since 1891. These beginnings gained momentum in the first decade and a half of the twentieth century, and foremost among the leaders was Peter Ernest Dietz.

Father Dietz had adequate equipment by nature and experience to carry forward the cause of social reform. The times were ripe for a man with his personal qualities. Zealous and enthusiastic, he could rouse others from their lethargy and convince them with his forceful logic. Multiplicity of burdens or unfavorable criticism never checked his drive to do things, and the very impatience at delayed action that marked the years of preparation for the priesthood urged him into projects that would have made the more conservative plan and wait. Dr. Kerby, on one occasion, frankly evaluated Dietz thus:

> You are a man gifted with very noble and unselfish instincts. You have an exceptional lot of personal power and restless energy. You are too impatient of social processes in life and possibly your ideals have a little too strong hold on your judgment.[72]

Important for a "trail blazer" such as Dietz was his recognition of the necessity of ecclesiastical approbation. His manner of approach to his superiors was devoid of any great deference, for he was no respecter of persons, but he never acted without his superior's permission, believing, as he did, that ecclesiastical orders manifested God's Will for him.

In many respects Father Dietz was a paradox. Lacking many of the social graces, abrupt and often harsh in manner, he made loyal friends among all types of people — bishops, priests, trade unionists, students at his school, and parishioners. The "sad melancholy" that plagued him as a very young man seemed to bear in later life the "dire fruits" which he predicted. Recurring attacks of neuralgia and other nervous disorders aggravated his natural tendency to irritability. His *Diary* contains frequent references to the ungrateful way he repaid the kindness of others, particularly his mother and sisters. Those who survived his brusqueness, accusations, suspicions, and harsh criticism, found that he was honest in his dealings and that his sympathies once aroused were deep and generous.

For all his impulsiveness and drive, Father Dietz was something of an introvert. Some say he inclined toward the mystical in his great admiration of the writings of Blessed Anna Catherine Emmerich, the German mystic. In this inner life, no doubt, is the secret of his power over others that made them overlook or accept his personal peculiarities. Many who heard him preach a sermon or deliver an address listened spellbound, yet agreed that he was no orator and had no commanding pulpit or stage presence. The idealism in his program for the Militia of Christ that made him want to raise it above a mere "economic machine" reflected the "fire of enthusiasm" that had almost consumed him as a young seminarian at St. Gabriel's. Father Dietz's high sense of dedication found expression in his life's motto — *Fiat Voluntas Tua* — not so much in the spirit of resignation, he explained, as in the spirit of enterprise to "restore all things in Christ."

It is difficult, therefore, to imagine Father Dietz settling down to the obscurity of a small town parish. His very vocation to the priesthood was admittedly linked inseparably with his desire to do something about the "workingman's difficulties and possibilities." Time and circumstances revealed to Father Dietz, where precedent could not, the way to reconcile these seemingly conflicting goals.

Chapter Two

The Catholic
Crusade Against
Socialism

D URING HIS STUDENT DAYS, Peter E. Dietz had displayed a lively interest in social questions. From the day of his ordination, December 17, 1904, he apparently considered social service a vitally important part of his priestly duties. Soon after beginning parish work in 1905, at Elyria, Ohio, he revealed his basic ideas concerning the labor movement and the Church's relation to it. In a speech on Labor Day, 1906, he urged workers to form unions with a view to controlling their labor just as the trusts were controlling the consumer markets. Since many persons doubted the desirability of trade unions, the newly-ordained priest counselled workers to be "prudent and honest and just and self-controlled."[1] With the Socialists in mind, Dietz warned his listeners above all to "beware of agitators and idle theorists who continually appeal to the future because they have no share in the present."[2] As they formed unions, workers should, he stressed, cooperate with the Church, the employer, and the unorganized, for the peaceful settlement of all economic and social problems.

In April, 1906, Father Dietz addressed the priests of Lorain County, Ohio, on the role of the priest in modern society. Dramatically he queried:

> upon the battlefield and amid bodily plagues the priest is a familiar sight — why should he not be equally familiar amid the spiritual death dealers and social plagues that have nailed suffering humanity to the cross of wealth and organized industrial injustice?[3]

22

By doing something for the workingman, priests could defeat Socialism "which as a protest against existing conditions is justified indeed."[4] The program he recommended included the following: societies of all kinds and the federation of societies; Catholic loan associations; building associations; accident insurances; Catholic influence upon trades councils; a definite, systematic, regular, uniform policy in the Catholic press; more literature and lecture courses for the enlightenment of the working people, not only on industrial problems, but upon all problems before the American public, especially political ones. "Local endeavors have not been wanting in various instances," he noted; "maybe what was inefficient single-handed would be successful by cooperation here among the clergy of this county."[5] Before adjourning, the priests agreed to assist the laymen of the county in forming a federation which would affiliate with the American Federation of Catholic Societies. Father Dietz supervised the organization of this Lorain County federation, and worked out a plan for the study of questions of interest to American Catholics, especially those of labor and Socialism.

The young priest's thinking and activity were obviously directed against Socialism and the discontent and strife which nourished it. The time had indeed come for the Church and other opponents of the Socialist cause to present an alternative program. By 1905 the "honeymoon" years of peaceful negotiation between capitalists and workers had ended and bitter conflict had once more gained the ascendancy. Employers had again taken the war-path against organized labor. Alarmed at the remarkable increase in trade-union membership since 1897, the National Association of Manufacturers, formed in 1895 to promote foreign trade and high tariff protectionism, turned militantly anti-labor early in the new century. Speaking in behalf of its "open shop" drive, the president of the Association, David M. Parry, informed its members assembled in convention at New Orleans in 1903 that "the principles and demands of organized labor are absolutely untenable to those believing in the individualistic social order. . . . The greatest danger lies in the recognition of the union."[6] Such groups as the American Anti-

23

Boycott Association and the Citizens' Industrial Association also strove to swing public opinion against labor.[7]

The close tie-up uniting industry, finance, and government weakened the enforcement of existing labor laws and thwarted the enactment of sadly-needed additional social legislation. The courts, on their part, upheld "yellow-dog" contracts and black lists, and in effect renewed the old conspiracy laws by applying the Sherman Act to unions as combinations in restraint of trade.[8] Under these conditions, little headway could be made against injustices in hours of work, wages, and working conditions.

But wage-earners and their friends among reformers not of the working class felt keenly their plight and bestirred themselves to remove the obstacles blocking social improvement. For the most part, they supported the mildly reformist Progressive program associated with the names of Theodore Roosevelt and Woodrow Wilson; but a growing number helped swell the rising tide of Socialism which after 1900 found expression in the Socialist Party of America whose architect was Eugene V. Debs of Pullman strike fame. Committed to "pure socialism, and no compromise," the new party hoped to overthrow the capitalistic system and establish a cooperative commonwealth through united political action in national, state, and local fields. Under the leadership of Debs, who was a presidential candidate each election year save one, from 1900 to 1920, the party polled an increasing number of votes. The 1912 election, the banner year, netted the Socialists 897,011 votes.[9] Also by that year, Victor L. Berger was representing the Milwaukee district in Congress, while many state and municipal offices had Socialist incumbents. Certain demands of the party platform appealed to voters, especially the planks for the public ownership of the great natural monopolies and trusts, the progressive reduction of hours of labor, an increase of wages, and employers' liability.[10] Since the party worked for Socialism on the installment plan, many persons wrongly identified its program with social reform. Enthusiastic for their cause, and working on the principle, "Never be satisfied with a convert, you must win an apostle," the Socialists recruited a large following among those seeking a way out of their

24

economic distress.[11]

The party revealed its political platform through a well-integrated program of educational propaganda. Socialist papers in English and foreign languages, appearing by the hundreds after 1904, appealed to numerous people in all classes.[12]

Socialist organizations and schools tried to reach the various age groups and interests. Thus the Intercollegiate Socialist Society worked to unite college people with the cause. Its official organ, *The Intercollegiate Socialist Review,* kept members informed on the work of the organization and on other points of interest while lecturers and organizers were constantly on the road. At least one Catholic paper was aware of the Society's existence. *The Central Blatt and Social Justice* carried Frederick P. Kenkel's article calling attention to the *New York Evening Post's* report of flourishing chapters in seventeen colleges and universities in 1910, as well as two alumni chapters in New York and Washington, D. C.[13] The officers of that year included names that were bright lights in Socialist history: J. G. Phelps-Stokes of Yale, president; Morris Hillquit of the New York Law School, treasurer, and Algernon Lee of Minnesota, secretary. Wrote Kenkel:

> It shows on the one hand how active and successful Socialists are in their proselyting effort, and on the other bids us stop to think of what is to become of these same institutions and of our public schools after the men assume charge of them who are now being impregnated with the teachings of Stokes, Hillquit, and Spargo. Such seed must of necessity bear poisonous fruit in years to come.[14]

By 1916 the chapters had increased to one hundred.[15]

Another channel of adult propaganda, the Christian Socialist Fellowship, aimed to show the "necessity of Socialism to a complete realization of the teachings of Jesus."[16] Its organ, *The Christian Socialist,* published by the Reverend Ellis Carr, was one of the most frequently quoted of the Socialist publications. Special editions directed to the various religious groups tried to offset the contention that Socialism opposed Christianity. An eight page "Catholic Edition" appeared on January 15, 1909, filled with quotations from

25

the writings of the early Church Fathers, St. Augustine, St. Ambrose, St. Chrysostom, and from contemporary Catholic leaders, to show that the Catholic Church had always favored the things for which Socialism stood. Even *Rerum Novarum* was "analyzed" to prove that the Pope was not really hostile to Socialism.[17] Such captions as "Socialism Insists upon Private Property," "Father Dowling Speaks Out for Socialism," must have made a strong appeal to bewildered Catholics.

Not even children escaped Socialist propaganda. Socialist Sunday Schools established in nearly every important city taught the child to "realize the class struggle and his own part in it." Catechisms and the magazine *The Little Socialist* served as textbooks. One edition of *The Young Socialist* denounced the Boy Scouts as an organization controlled by the capitalists for use against the workers when the revolution came. Then New York City would be "Comradeville" and May 1 the best holiday of all.[18]

Many leaders for this work studied in the Rand School of Social Science in New York City. Endowed by Mrs. Carrie Rand of Iowa, the school opened in 1906. By 1911 it was offering a six months' course of intensive study in a wide range of subjects based on such textbooks as Frederick Engel's *Origin of the Family*, Karl Marx's *Value, Price, Profit*, and Karl Kautsky's *Social Revolution*.[19]

Though not without results, the Socialist educational propaganda failed of its purpose to mobilize all discontented Americans behind the Socialist program. At the heyday of its strength in 1912, the Socialist party claimed only 113,371 paid members.[20] Since this figure did not include the undoubtedly numerous "fellow travelers," it was not a true index of the party's strength. The Socialist party failed to win the support of all Socialists. Thus those Socialist workers who favored "direct action" rather than political agitation formed in 1905 the Industrial Workers of the World (the I.W.W.) in order to counteract the Socialist party as well as the conservative trade unions. More successful was the party's "boring from within" strategy in the American Federation of Labor. Father Dietz reported in 1909 that well over ten per cent of the membership was Socialist.[21] In 1912 the Socialist candidate, Max Hayes, opponent

26

of Gompers for president of the American Federation of Labor, polled one-third of the votes.

The resurgent strength and popularity of Socialism in the labor movement endangered the faith of the many Catholics who made up about fifty per cent of the total trade-union membership.[22] These Catholics absorbed the Socialist propaganda rife in nearly every union; they read Socialist newspapers, including the attractive *Appeal to Reason,* furnished gratis in certain unions. This propaganda seemed all the more convincing when Catholic workers saw priests, notably Father Thomas McGrady of Kentucky and Father Thomas J. Hagerty of Chicago, lend ardent support to the Socialist cause. McGrady lectured early in the present century at the Boston School of Political Economy, a Socialist project of Mrs. Martha Moore Avery and David Goldstein until they abandoned the movement in 1923.[23] Hagerty helped organize the I.W.W., his graphic representation of that organization's structure being named by Samuel Gompers "Father Hagerty's Wheel of Fortune."

Hagerty, McGrady, and other Catholics of like mind[24] accepted the statement in the Socialist platform of 1908: "The Socialist Party is primarily an economic and political movement. It is not concerned with religious belief." The Irish Socialist Federation, organized by James Connolly, avowed that "Socialism is purely and absolutely an economic theory dealing exclusively with economic factors."[25] This attitude characterized also the Catholic Socialist Society of Chicago formed in 1909, which announced that it advocated no special brand of Socialism but stood for the same principles as the recognized Socialist bodies, and sought to spread these principles among Catholics.[26]

But most Catholics condemned the Socialist system *in toto*, at least during the first decade of the new century, opposing its economic program only less strongly than its materialistic and anti-religious philosophy. This negative approach did not impress Catholic workingmen; it gave point in fact to the Socialist contention that the Church was indifferent to their material welfare. In view of this fact, the more thoughtful Catholic leaders concluded with Father Dietz that Socialism was a justifiable protest against existing social conditions and contained much positive good entirely in harmony with Christian ethics.[27] The Reverend John A. Ryan, professor of ethics in the St. Paul Seminary, whose book, *A Living Wage* (New York, 1906), related Leo XIII's economic teachings to the American scene, insisted by 1909 that Catholics were morally free to embrace Socialism's economic program. Essential economic Socialism, he pointed out, permitted as much private property as the moral law required.[28] He was sure it would be better to concentrate on the "philosophical, religious and revolutionary," rather than on the economic tenets of Socialism lest the workingman "come to look upon the Church as indifferent to human rights and careful only about the rights of property."[29] As a practical guide Ryan offered a plan through legislation that could protect the laborer against unjust exploitation and the public from extortionate prices. Among other things, he asked for the legitimising of peaceful picketing, persuasion, and even secondary boycotting, which he declared not "essentially immoral."[30] Significantly, he called attention to the fact that judicial decisions against these methods were based on the old Common Law of conspiracy which the British Parliament had abolished in 1906.[31]

In this spirit of accepting the good features of Socialism, Father Dietz had meanwhile broadened his efforts in behalf of the Church's social mission, stressing less the ideological than the practical and organizational aspects. A fitting agency through which to work, he believed, was the American Federation of Catholic Societies. He first attended a national convention of this body in 1906 and was pleased with its resolutions urging a study of social questions and the formation of workingmen's associations.[32] But when he subsequently proposed that the Federation take steps actually to carry this program into effect, he was, as he complained later, promptly rebuffed by Anthony Matre, the national secretary of the organization.[33] Dietz then turned to the German Catholic Central Verein, where he found, as he said, "some sort of understanding" of the things in which he was interested.[34]

In 1908 he became a member of the legislative committee of the Verein's Ohio branch (the Ohio *Staatsverband*). The following year he attended the convention of the Ohio State Federation of Labor, with whose legislative committee he met for the purpose of urging it to give up its sponsorship of two undesirable school bills.[35] The upshot of the conference was that the Ohio labor committee agreed to drop its support of the "Free Text-book" and "Compulsory Education" bills in exchange for the Verein committee's support of bills for "Employer's Liability" and an "8-Hour Day for Women Workers."[36] In 1910 this *Staatsverband* committee went to Columbus to confer with the Ohio Commissioner of Labor, C. H. Wirmel, and Governor Judson Harmon on labor problems and ways and means of promoting legislation. The Governor heard the committee's program and encouraged its efforts as aids to the cause of good citizenship.[37] The minutes of these various meetings, forwarded to the local societies of Ohio, became a basis for discussion. The committee urged local societies to "write to their Congressmen" in behalf of its program.[38]

How to promote reform legislation was the theme of Dietz's talk before the *Staatsverband* at its annual convention in 1909 at Hamilton, Ohio. To show the great need of labor legislation, he graphically pictured the conditions in the industrial areas of the country. The convention adopted a resolution urging the member societies "to secure such legislation as will advance the interests of the great mass of Catholic workingmen in reference to their social, intellectual, and wage-earning qualities."[39] In addition, this gathering amended the Constitution to make room for a Social Institute at future annual conventions. The program included three lectures on social topics — one at the Sunday evening mass-meeting; the other two for delegates only.[40]

More important than his activity in the Verein's Ohio branch was Dietz's influence in the national body. At its convention of 1907 in Dubuque, Iowa, the Central Verein mobilized for social action. It appointed a Committee for Social Propaganda with Nicholas Gonner as chairman. The recommendations of this committee were read and adopted at the next annual convention at Cleveland.[41] Present at this convention, Father Dietz was made a member of the Resolutions Committee. He was instrumental in

29

bringing about a meeting at Chicago in February, 1909, between the Executive Committee of the Central Verein, its Committee on Social Propaganda, and a Cleveland group to which Dietz belonged.[42] The purpose of the meeting was "to take into consideration the further recommendations of the Cleveland committee."[43] This committee had recommended, among other things, that the journal, *Central Blatt,* first published in April, 1908, by Rudolph Krueger, be taken over by the new Committee for Social Propaganda.[44] Although Father Dietz wished an all-English paper, the bi-lingual form prevailed, the German section to be edited by Father Augustine Breig and the English section by Father Dietz.[45] From this time on, the paper was known as *Central Blatt and Social Justice.* At this meeting also Frederick P. Kenkel was chosen director of the Committee, with headquarters in St. Louis.[46]

The program of "social enlightenment" mapped out by the Committee for Social Propaganda included the establishment of social institutes, lectures, and publishing of pamphlets, and even a social science school, the Ketteler House, to be erected near Loyola University in Chicago. At the Cleveland convention nearly two thousand dollars had been subscribed for the purpose, and subsequent years saw additional contributions to the project. At Ketteler House, training for leadership would have been available to priests and laymen, who, thoroughly instructed in Catholic social principles, could participate in public life and spread Catholic influence.[47]

Besides urging social education, the Committee for Social Propaganda agreed with Father Dietz concerning the importance of organized labor in any social reform program. More than a year before, in March, 1908, Dietz had written:

> If Socialism succeeds in America it will be because labor-unionism failed. . . . Therefore, the Catholic has a most important and responsible share in the industrial readjustment of society. By his intelligent, Christian membership he will be the only solid guarantee that the labor-unions will not become socialistic but the keystone of a social reform that will remove the most distressing features of the social problems as they confront us today.[48]

Father Dietz restated his idea many times during his year (from April, 1909 to April, 1910) as editor of the English section of *Central Blatt and Social Justice*. With force and brilliance he encouraged and exhorted Catholics to greater effort. The best in the social programs of Germany and England, past and current, he brought to the attention of his readers. In a section called "Tilt and Tournament," he fought social error, whether it stemmed from Individualism or from Socialism. "The Open Court of Justice" answered the questions of correspondents. The thought and activity of personalities like Joseph Goerres, Karl Lueger, John Mitchell, Martha Moore Avery, and Eleanora Marx made up the material for the section called "Men and Women." Occasionally Dietz published a "Bibliography for Social Science Clubs" based on the list of books offered by the International Catholic Truth Society.[49] A Catholic social program based on education and trade unionism had at all times his unswerving support.

Eager, as always, for quick results, he presented an interesting plan in behalf of the program. "We have had preamble enough," he wrote, "we must have a Constitution now. Effective propaganda will follow only in the path of effective organization."[50] He suggested that the presidents come together in an Executive Council which with a General Executive Secretary would form a Central Administrative Council or Central Bureau, with special offices in a strategic location. He would set up similar bureaus on state and local levels. The work of the Central Bureau would be distributed among five departments: Organization; Press and Lyceum; Records; Agriculture, Industry, and Sanitation; Legislation. These departments should form and direct a Catholic Press Association, Catholic organizations of trade-unionists, employers, farmers, and doctors, and Catholic bar associations.

Eventually, "in the prosperous course of events," the Bureau would establish a printing press and a School of Social Science. The latter would offer to high school graduates courses in political science, economics, sociology, logic, oratory, and journalism. This trained group would be "at home in the world of public affairs; they would make public opinion and accept leadership as a matter

31

of course."[51] In addition the school would arrange sociological courses of a less formal character from a week to a month's duration. Finally, the plan would build "into an organic system a nation wide propaganda much on the lyceum plan combined with the methods of the mission fathers and the diocesan apostolate."[52]

On his own initiative, Dietz put a small part of his plan into practice when he organized the first Social Institute at Oberlin in September, 1909. The twenty-three delegates who attended this first venture represented practically every walk of life — priest, laborer, merchant, and student. Two Oberlin College professors, Dr. Carl F. Geiser, of the Political Science Department, and Dr. Albert B. Wolfe, of the Economics and Sociology Department, gave the lectures. The former discussed the American Constitution and the history and problems of political parties, the Prohibition, the Populist, and the Socialist parties as well as the two major ones. Dr. Wolfe handled the trade union movement, giving its history, philosophy, and problems. Members of the Institute visited the steel plant of the National Tube Company in Lorain, Ohio, which employed 8,000 men.[53] The lively discussion and the demand for a second Institute led Father Dietz to believe the venture a success:

> We are far from entertaining delusions that a week's discussion of this kind will make of the participants political economists and sociologists. . . . We do believe that the impulse and direction received will act as an incentive to further and deeper study, and as a general leaven in their own proper sphere. In all the work we have struck the key-note of harmony; harmony between the pastor and his people; between capital and labor; between organized and un-organized.[54]

The day after this Institute closed, the national convention of the Central Verein opened at Indianapolis. At the customary mass-meeting, Father Dietz substituted for Dr. Charles P. Neill, United States Commissioner of Labor, who was unable to attend. In his address Father Dietz praised the work of the Central Verein, "a modern element of Christian civilization," in its effort to solve the social question. He praised trade-unions, also, but warned against Socialism. "Shall we stand by and let Socialism pass in the path to destruction and say it is merely rash and ill-advised?"[55] The

resolution adopted at this historic convention endorsed social education and trade unionism, urged the organization of Catholic Workingmen's Welfare Associations in the spirit of Leo XIII's encyclical,
and favored cooperation with all organizations working for remedial
labor legislation, such as the National Civic Federation, the American Federation of Labor, and the American Association for Labor
Legislation. Subsequently, the state conventions of the Central
Verein adopted similar resolutions.[56]

In no small part the work of Dietz, the Central Verein's constructive program met a real need and for this reason exercised a
wide influence. If carried out, its educational policy should, within
a decade, predicted John A. Ryan, provide men "able to justify
Catholic opposition to both the abuses of capitalism and the excesses
of Socialism" and with the "ability and the courage to defend
plans of positive social reform."[57]   He also lauded the Verein's
recognition of organized labor, for

> men who talk of uplifting the laboring classes through Catho-
> lic principles, while denouncing or discouraging the labor
> union movement, show themselves ignorant of the industrial
> history and the actual industrial conditions in America.[58]

Ryan also approved the Verein's liberal policy of refusing to sponsor the organization of separate Catholic trade unions. By becoming more active in the established unions Catholic workingmen
could "oppose more effectively Socialism, unwise racialism, and
every other tendency or method that is hostile to genuine reform."[59]

In an effort to get its excellent program before the Catholics of
the country, the Central Verein promoted study clubs, institutes,
and summer schools, in some of which Father Dietz was tirelessly
active. In January, 1910, at Belleville, Illinois, he and Peter W.
Collins, secretary-treasurer of the Electrical Workers of America,
conducted a social course under the direction of Monsignor J. J.
Schlarmann, chancellor of the diocese and later bishop of Peoria.[60]
Dietz stressed Catholic responsibility for the solution of the labor
problem, and Collins lectured on government and Socialism.[61]

This idea of short courses in the social sciences, initiated by
Dietz, continued in a series of social institutes sponsored by the

33

Central Verein during the years 1910 to 1917 in connection with the Western Catholic Chautauqua at Spring Bank, Wisconsin. Here a wide variety of social topics was handled by informed leaders, among them, the laymen Peter W. Collins and Frank O'Hara, professor of economics in the Catholic University, and the priests, John A. Ryan, William J. Kerby, William Engelen, S.J., professor of moral philosophy at St. John's College, Toledo, S. P. Hoffman of Effingham, Illinois, and Frederick Siedenberg, S.J., of Chicago, these latter two having recently returned from studies of social questions in Germany.[62] As for Father Dietz, he had no official connection with this summer school work at Spring Bank, or with the extensive lecture tours of David Goldstein and Peter W. Collins, under the auspices of the Verein's Central Bureau during 1911-1913.[63] The truth is Dietz left the Central Verein in 1910 after only a year as editor, speaker, and organizer. He did not see eye to eye with Frederick P. Kenkel, the director of the Verein's Central Bureau for the promotion of Social Education. Kenkel wanted to limit the work of the Central Bureau in the beginning to study alone, whereas Dietz wanted to combine study with action thus widening the scope of the Verein's influence so that the best in the German character could be brought to bear on the American social problem. At the same time he wanted to save the Verein from the deleterious effects of self-isolation.[64] Dietz's methods in carrying out this aim were not acceptable to Kenkel. As was later explained, the "rapid fire action desired by Father Dietz did not agree with the more conservative attitude of the leaders of the Central Verein."[65]

The deposed editor, in search of a channel for aggressive social action, turned again to the American Federation of Catholic Societies. This time he was not rebuffed, but was welcomed and listened to. By 1910 this organization in its fight against Socialism began to promote a positive social program. In statements and resolutions approved by successive conventions after that date, the Federation declared for the living wage, and to this end endorsed trade-unionism and the campaign for additional protective labor legislation.[66] At its annual convention of 1911, in Columbus, Ohio,

Dietz suggested in the course of a speech that the Federation create a standing "Committee on Social Reform." Having familiarized himself with the labor committees and social service commissions recently established by the leading Protestant denominations,[67] Dietz believed that the time had come for Catholics to set up a similar body. In response to his plea, the American Federation of Catholic Societies organized a Social Service Commission, and instructed it "to devise ways and means for the further amelioration of conditions among the working people for the preservation and propagation of the faith."[68] The original members, five in number, were the Right Reverend Peter J. Muldoon, bishop of Rockford, chairman; the Very Reverend John W. Cavanaugh, C.S.C., president of the University of Notre Dame; James E. Hagerty, professor of economics at Ohio State University; Charles J. Denechaud, a lawyer of New Orleans; and Father Dietz, who was made secretary of the Commission. "We are ready," stated Bishop Muldoon,

> with our condemnation of this and that dangerous tendency of the hour, but unless we go out into the open and do something practical for the solution of our pressing problems our condemnations will react upon us. We want to establish a department or departments of Federation activity that will work all the year through. In Federation we have the machinery. Our object is to start the machinery going.[89]

On Father Dietz principally devolved the task of getting "the machinery going." The Federation's official organ, *The Bulletin,* published since December, 1908, allotted pages to the Social Service Commission and its work. Made editor of this social service section, Dietz summarized Catholic and secular news bearing on social questions. As the Commission's secretary, he sent a weekly press service to Catholic and labor papers, wrote pamphlets and countless letters, lectured, planned annual conventions of the Social Service Commission, attended meetings and cooperated with organizations doing related work, sparing no effort to make the Commission effective. During the life of the Commission, from 1911 to 1918, Father Dietz served as its power-house of action.[70]

Dietz's organizational work in connection with the Central

35

Verein and the American Federation of Catholic Societies may well have suggested the promotion of other Catholic social groups. His friend and adviser, the Reverend William J. Kerby, took the lead in the organization in 1910 of the National Conference of Catholic Charities. Designed primarily to coordinate Catholic charitable effort, the Conference also stressed the preventive and social aspects of charity. "Relief that stops short of prevention," Kerby wrote, "appears to be but a small part of the duty of charity."[71] He referred also to the "industrial mission of charity," part of which was to "humanize the industrial processes by helping industrial leaders to understand the humanities of industry and to respect them."[72] In an address on "The Reform Problems which the Church should meet," at the first national convention of the Conference in Washington, D. C., in 1910, Monsignor William J. White, of Brooklyn, deplored the fact that Catholics were so slow in launching a Catholic social movement.

> It is time for us to awake to the fact that if we wish to keep our workingmen practical Catholics, we must give them some tangible proof that the Church is alive to the struggle they are making to better their material conditions.[73]

The first great need, the Monsignor pointed out, was study. Pamphlets in popular style on questions like the relation of capital and labor, Socialism, the functions of the state, the importance of the family, would find a "wide field." For the second need, action, Monsignor White recommended the establishment of a Catholic social reform magazine and Catholic social reform clubs in industrial areas.[74]

More agitational in character, the Common Cause Society began in Boston in 1912, under the inspiration of William J. Mullaney of Charlestown. Fifteen young men, accustomed to visit radical meetings held on Boston Common and in other parts of the city, formed the nucleus of the organization that within a short time numbered hundreds. Fearing the insidious effects of Socialism on American life, the Society determined to do something, in the words of its preamble:

> to defend our national inheritance, and advance the cause of

equity within the sphere of economics upon the basis laid down by Pope Leo XIII in his encyclicals on the social problems of our times, especially to bring forth by argument and given facts the falsity of Socialist principles and their treasonable use of the ballot.[75]

Since the Socialists held their meetings on Pemberton Square, Boston, on Saturday nights between nine and ten, the Common Cause Society obtained permission to hold its meetings there the same night from ten to eleven.[76] Before audiences of a thousand and more, Charles Fay, George McKinnon, or David Goldstein answered attacks on the Church made at the Socialists' meeting, and presented the Catholic position on all the questions of the day. The society met also on Boston Common each Sunday afternoon, and in 1913 launched an in-door forum during the winter months. The Society went on record at the Massachusetts State House as advocating various social reform bills.[77] A monthly magazine, *The Common Cause,* and a weekly newspaper, *The Live Issue,* published by the Social Reform Press of New York City, promoted the purposes of the Society. That its efforts were effective was indicated by the report of the state Secretary of the Socialist Party, complaining that because of the Society's work many Socialist locals were making no impression on the voters and some locals were even dying out.[78]

Less spectacular than the Common Cause Society were the American Eunomic League (Well-lawed league) and the League for Social Order, both formed in New York City in 1913. Made up of Catholic college and professional people, the American Eunomic League studied to "effect a return to clear thinking and applied Christianity in the everyday problems of life, whether personal, legal or economic."[79] With Richard Dana Skinner as president, the League published a four-page magazine, *The Eunomic Review,* for the discussion of social questions. The members of the League were urged to "assume their proper place as energetic leaders in all sound movments toward a better public morality and more judicious, effective laws."[80]

The League for Social Order, with Mary Stebbins as president and Cardinal Gibbons as honorary vice-president, strove to advance "social order and security in accordance with principles of justice and patriotism."[81] The organization denounced Socialism as a "grave national danger" to the unity and stability of the family which was the paramount consideration in any plan of social reform. A series of lectures by William M. O'Donnell of the New York bar inaugurated the League's work.[82]

If, as seems likely, the origin and work of these leagues and similar bodies owed something to Father Dietz, his own plans after 1914 to promote social education in a systematic way were certainly influenced, as will be shown, by some of the Catholic seminaries and institutions of higher learning.[83] As early as 1900 John A. Ryan began teaching social science in the St. Paul seminary,[84] a pioneering effort not repeated until 1911 when Father Charles Bruehl introduced optional courses in economics and sociology at St. Francis Seminary near Milwaukee. This study of the social sciences "wishes" to make seminarians "realize," he said,

> that abuse, irony, and ridicule are very ineffectual weapons against the powerful propaganda of Socialism. It gives them the necessary orientation in the bewildering mass of social problems and furnishes the standards by which wholesome social reform may be distinguished from utopian, visionary, and destructive schemes. It instills into them a sense of social responsibility, a cautious and enlightened conservatism and a prudent progressiveness.[85]

Laymen as well as priests needed systematic social instruction. To provide it, the New York Laymen's League for Retreats set up in 1911 a "School for Social Studies" in connection with the Fordham Law School. As in all agitation for social action, the question of Socialism played a major part in the school's first course of twenty-four lectures, divided into three main departments. The Reverend T. J. Shealy, S.J., spiritual director of the school, gave twelve lectures on the thesis: Socialism in its Principles is Irreligious and Immoral; Dr. Ryan showed that "Socialism's Appeal to the Workingman is Delusive and Dangerous"; while Thomas Woodlock, president of the League, proved that Socialism's proposals were impracticable and impossible. These men received no compensation for their lectures; the students paid no fees; there was to be no admission charge for the lectures the students would give to clubs, especially for those they gave to workingmen. They were to contribute their services gratis to spread knowledge of the social questions of the day.[86] The second course, which considered a constructive social reform program, employed a more positive approach.[87] By 1917 the School for Social Studies had become the Fordham University School of Philanthropy and Social Service.

In 1912 Father Frederick Siedenberg, S.J., established a Lecture Bureau at Loyola University in Chicago. Its opening program included thirty addresses of a popular nature covering practically the entire industrial, economic, and social fields.[88] Because of the interest in these lectures (over one hundred were given the first year) two systematic courses were offered from October, 1913, to April, 1914. In addition to the lectures given by Siedenberg, about fifty special lecturers were brought in. Encouraged by the attendance, the University decided to continue this work in a larger and more permanent way by establishing a School of Sociology.[89]

Meanwhile Father Dietz and other priests, not satisfied with study and discussion alone, but aware of the need for Catholic leadership in public affairs, lent their support to reform legislation and tried to secure justice for the workingman in the capacity of labor mediators. Addressing the members of the American Association for Labor Legislation, in 1908, Dietz pleaded for a "practical programmatic, well-defined campaign" for laws that would improve the lot of the workingman.[90] He recommended, especially, laws abolishing child labor, establishing maximum hours, providing social insurance, and protecting workingmen in such hazardous occupations as the manufacture of white lead and phosphorus matches, stonecutting, and glass-blowing. Such an enlightened program, Dietz believed, would dispel the idea that the "government is the servant of the corporations and the moneyed interests of the country," and, by removing the causes of discontent, strike a vital blow at Socialism.[91] Father Dietz had further opportunity to express his views along this line when Governor Harmon of Ohio commissioned

39

him and four others to represent the state at a convention in Washington, in January, 1910. Six hundred delegates representing commercial, agricultural, manufacturing, labor, financial, and professional groups discussed the question of uniform state legislation on such diverse matters as conservation of natural resources, corporations, divorce, child labor, accident compensation, and factory and mine inspection.[92]

Known for his interest in reform and his opposition to Socialism, Father Dietz was selected by the Lorain County Progressive League as a candidate for the Ohio Constitutional Convention. Going on record as favoring woman suffrage, tax reform, the sale of intoxicating liquor, and initiative, referendum, and recall, Dietz solicited the votes of

> fairminded and patriotic citizens, who with him, believe in the sanctity of the home, the reasonableness of the trade union, the stability and sovereignty of the state, and the redemptive power of religion.[93]

Father John A. Ryan and Father Edwin V. O'Hara of Portland, Oregon, likewise appreciated the role of the state in social reform. From 1910 to 1915 Ryan devoted his attention to reform laws in Minnesota, particularly as chairman of the State Child Labor Committee. An ardent supporter of the minimum wage, he wrote the Minnesota law passed in 1913.[94]

Father O'Hara won distinction for his work as chairman of the Industrial Welfare Commission to which he was appointed by Oregon's Governor Oswald West in 1913. Despite the opposition of the Portland Employers' Association, O'Hara succeeded in having a minimum wage law for women upheld as constitutional by the United States Supreme Court in *Stettler vs. O'Hara*.[95]

When reform legislation and peaceful negotiations were wanting or ineffectual, and strikes ensued, priests often played a significant role as mediators between employer and employed. The famous Lawrence (Massachusetts) textile strike of 1912, complicated by the tactics of the I.W.W., offered an excellent opportunity for such mediation. Credit for the success of the strike must be attributed, in a large measure, to the work of the Reverend James T. O'Reilly,

O.S.A., of St. Mary's Church, Lawrence, the Reverend Mariano Melanese, O.S.A., pastor of the Italian Holy Cross parish, and the Right Reverend Michael J. Splaine.[96] At the request of Governor Eugene N. Foss, Cardinal William O'Connell appointed Monsignor Splaine, his chancellor and secretary, to investigate the strike. Splaine interviewed the mill owners, the local priests, and the strikers, and eventually succeeded in terminating the strike. Because of the critical situation in Lawrence, Cardinal O'Connell chose relations between employer and employed as the theme of his pastoral letter for Advent, 1912. Attributing the cause of the strike to the attempt of the parties to treat their relations on a material basis alone, O'Connell recalled the words of Leo XIII emphasizing the need of the Christian approach. He exhorted the Holy Name Societies to become centers of study of "truly Christian sociological principles" and urged his priests to instruct both rich and poor in their duties and obligations.[97] Dietz considered the pastoral a "classic" and received permission from the Cardinal to have it printed in pamphlet form for distribution as part of the literature of the Social Service Commission.[98]

The total effort of societies and individuals to combat Socialism with social reform was notable in the decade after 1904. In 1916, taking stock of the progress made, Father Dietz made point of the fact that there was still no "American Catholic Social movement in any national sense of the term." Wrote Dietz:

> There are sectional efforts and local works. Some have a more religious and charitable color as those of the St. Vincent de Paul Society; some a more deliberative character, like those of the National Conference of Catholic Charities; others have a more militant and popular program, as those of the Central Verein and the American Federation of Catholic Societies. All these movements have a place and a mission. When and where and under what constellation they will form the focus of a truly national movement, no man can foretell. That it were desirable, no man will deny . . .[96]

He encouraged those interested to continue their analyzing and studying, influencing public opinion from the platform or through the Catholic press. But little progress could be made, he believed, "until all Catholics alike, whether rich or poor, employer or worker, learn to square their private interests with the known and approved doctrine of the Catholic right ordering of society."[100] Something of the efforts of Father Dietz in cooperation with others to further the acceptance of this "Doctrine" of the "right ordering of society" has been noted. It remains to examine in detail those particular means he used to advance the Catholic social movement: his Militia of Christ for Social Service, the Social Service Commission, and his American Academy of Christian Democracy.

Chapter Three

The Militia
of Christ for Social
Service

As ONE OF the few churchmen who spoke freely in behalf of labor, Father Dietz's name will always be associated with the labor movement. Convinced that any sound program for social reform must take cognizance of trade unionism, Dietz stressed the mutual benefit to church and labor from cooperation. Despite the presence of Socialists and other radicals in the American trade unions he urged Catholics to join the unions of their respective trades, to be active in them, and to exert influence to keep the labor movement Christian. Mindful of Leo XIII's insistence that Catholic workers organize their own trade unions rather than associate with the radical elements, Dietz yet agreed with Cardinal Gibbons and others that separate Catholic unions were not feasible in the United States. To keep the spirit of *Rerum Novarum* and to harmonize it with American ways, Dietz organized among the Catholics in the American Federation of Labor his Militia of Christ for Social Service.

Precedent for such an organization existed in parish societies like that established in Buffalo in 1901, by the Reverend Herman Maeckel, S.J.,[1] and the Workingmen's Welfare Associations (*Arbeiterwohl*) set up in St. Louis in 1909. In approving the latter organization, Archbishop Glennon voiced an opinion similar to that of Father Dietz:

> There is not only a sufficient, but a very urgent reason why Catholic workmen should unite, not in opposition to the labor unions as they exist, but to the end that they will be able to discuss and interpret their rights and duties as laboring men from the standpoint of Catholic ethics.[2]

The occasion that brought the Militia of Christ for Social Service into being presented itself when Father Dietz attended his first convention of the American Federation of Labor at Toronto in 1909. The impressive address of the Reverend Charles Stelzle, official representative of the newly founded Federal Council of Churches of Christ in America, made only too apparent to Dietz the absence of an official spokesman for the Catholic Church.[3] Conversing later with some of the leading Catholic trade unionists at the convention, Dietz learned that they were not a little ashamed of the fact that Protestantism was officially on record in support of the American Federation of Labor, while their own church remained aloof.[4]

That these Catholic trade unionists needed guidance became more apparent to Father Dietz as he listened to the speeches of local officers and visiting delegates during a reception at the Knights of Columbus clubhouse in Toronto. These men pointed out that the moral issues frequently involved in labor problems made education and Catholic solidarity imperative. Under the influence of Father Dietz they set up the temporary organization which eventually became the Militia of Christ for Social Service.

Peter J. McArdle of Pittsburgh, president of the Amalgamated Association of Iron, Steel and Tin Workers, was chosen temporary president; Thomas J. Duffy of East Liverpool, Ohio, president of the National Brotherhood of Operative Potters, was elected temporary secretary. All agreed that by the next convention at St. Louis plans should be ready for a permanent organization. Attendance in a body at Sunday Mass in St. Michael's Cathedral greatly heightened the *esprit de corps* at Toronto. Father Dietz made this "Labor Mass" a feature of every A. F. of L. convention that he attended from 1909 to 1922.[5]

The labor convention at St. Louis in November, 1910, was a memorable one for Father Dietz. Archbishop Glennon had given permission for his proposed organization,[6] and Dietz was there as fraternal delegate from the American Federation of Catholic Societies. Introduced by Samuel Gompers, he addressed the members of the convention, assuring them that the American Federation of

Catholic Societies, representing over 3,000,000 men of all nationalities "holds out to the trade-union movement the hand of fellowship and support," believing that the American Federation of Labor "offers a safe, real, constructive, sane, and Christian solution of many of our social problems."[7]

The climax of the convention for Dietz and the Catholic delegates was the meeting, in the Knights of Columbus clubhouse, which made permanent the Militia of Christ for Social Service. The next day, November 21, Foundation Day,[8] the newly elected officers met with Archbishop Glennon to receive his blessing on their program. Enthusiasm highlighted Glennon's letter to Father Dietz:

> My dear Father:
> I have before me the programme yourself and the gentlemen of the committee handed me yesterday. I cordially give my approval to the same. I regard the time opportune for its inauguration and I pledge you my continuous interest and cordial support.
> You may inscribe my name as an applicant for membership in the society, and accept now and at all times my best wishes.
> Sincerely yours
> John J. Glennon, Archbishop of St. Louis[9]

Most of the officers of the new organization were labor leaders, though membership in the society was not restricted to trade unionists. Peter McArdle and Thomas Duffy were confirmed in their offices of president and secretary. The three vice-presidents were John S. Whalen, of Rochester, New York, former Secretary of the State of New York, Peter W. Collins, and John Mangan of Chicago, editor of the *Steamfitters' Journal*. Father Dietz was executive secretary. The Directorate of twelve included among its members such prominent leaders as John Mitchell, second vice-president of the A. F. of L., James O'Connell, president of the International Association of Machinists, and Frank Duffy, international secretary of the United Brotherhood of Carpenters and Joiners.[10]

The constitution, adopted in final form in 1912, provided for a closely knit organization rising from local chapters to the national

45

Directorate and Common Council. Twelve charter members were required for a local chapter, based, not on parish lines, as in previous associations for Catholic workingmen, but on the political divisions of the country.[11] Three local chapters constituted a state chapter, whose officers, president, vice-president, and chaplain, made up the Common Council. The National Directorate, chosen for a term of three years, included only laymen.[12] Between annual conventions, held at the same time and place as the convention of the A. F. of L., the executive secretary, who acted in the name of the Directorate, held full executive power.[13] Executive membership in the Militia of Christ was limited to practical Catholics who accepted the "principle of unionism." This principle, it was explained

> regards industrial conciliation as preferable to industrial warfare; realizing that while the capitalists have on a lower plane a common interest against the laborers, and the laborers a common interest against the capitalist, from a higher point of view, the interests of capital, of labor and of the public are not in conflict but essentially one and the same. In effect it does not abolish the conflict of material interests, but ameliorates the conditions of conflict to insure fair play and to protect the non-combatants.[14]

Associate membership, open to non-Catholics, had no other requisite than subscribing to *Social Service,* the official organ of the Militia.

While the structure of the organization was suited to trade union activities, the program of the Militia of Christ as Father Dietz envisioned it was much wider in scope, embracing a comprehensive plan for social reform through three kinds of service: personal service, social service, and press service. Admittedly "tentative in nature and rather ideal" the program was to take on reality with time and circumstances.[15] Meanwhile the "Rules of Conduct" printed on the membership card made plain the type of service Dietz expected from each member.[18]

To give reality to the program was the responsibility of all Catholics. Students in colleges, universities, and seminaries were to prepare themselves through the study of the social sciences to become the natural leaders of the future. Vacation time was ideal,

Dietz suggested, for trying out some practical social investigation.[17] One of the channels he used for student participation, partly to offset the influence of the Intercollegiate Socialist Fellowship, was the Catholic Students Association of America. Organized at Purdue in 1908 to promote the welfare of Catholics in secular universities, it had affiliated twenty-two Newman and other Catholic clubs on university campuses by 1912. Raymond Achatz, president of the Association when the Militia of Christ was organized, became one of its first members.[18] He recommended that the member clubs of the Association sponsor a series of lectures at their respective schools, and that a copy of *Social Service* be placed in every college library.[19]

A far-sighted and comprehensive program for the clergy included parish lecture courses, sermons on social topics, retreats for trade-unionists and professional men, social conferences among priests, and a Catholic celebration of Labor Day. As for the adult laity, it was urged to participate in social lyceum work, university extension courses, social surveys, and generally to cultivate fraternal relations with all existing societies with similar aims.[20]

Unity of purpose and action could be attained through an annual convention evaluating the year's achievements and planning for the coming year. Eventually, Dietz believed, class prejudices and selfish interests would give place to a great Catholic social movement on national lines — a movement no longer class-conscious but "Christ-conscious."[21] In the official organ, *Social Service,* (the first number appeared in May, 1911), Father Dietz outlined correct principles of social reform, and made practical suggestions for realizing the goals of reform.

Such a pretentious program required the cooperation of all if a fraction of the expected results were to materialize. The important work of advertising the new movement began at once. Through the Catholic press and circular letters, the hierarchy, priests, and lay leaders became aware of it.

The Apostolic Delegate, His Excellency, the Most Reverend Diomede Falconio, added his endorsement to that of Archbishop Glennon:

> I am happy to add my commendation to that of Arch-

47

bishop Glennon of St. Louis in regard to the work undertaken by the "Militia of Christ." The Society has done well in taking its basic principles from the great encyclicals of the Popes, and it cannot but be productive of good, so long as it adheres to the fundamental tenets of right and justice therein laid down.[22]

Dietz addressed a letter to the bishops of the country, inviting them to become members, asking for suggestions, and requesting the names of priests and laymen of the diocese having the disposition and the ability to be of executive service. Bishops from all parts of the country responded with varying degrees of enthusiasm. Archbishop James H. Blenk of New Orleans, one of the most enthusiastic, wrote:

> The interests and purposes in the movement . . . give concrete expression to views I have been cherishing with the hope and firm determination of carrying them into the practical field of action in my diocese.
>
> The vast scope of interests and wide range of work outlined in the programme you have sent me, impresses me most favorably. To my mind your undertaking will be a successful attempt to answer along national lines national needs and demands. I am heart and soul with you in this timely and splendid endeavor and will deem it a duty as well as an honor to cooperate with you to the full extent of my modest powers.[23]

From the west coast Bishop Thomas Grace of Sacramento, California, declared the program "worthy of every commendation."[24] Bishop Joseph J. Fox of Green Bay, Wisconsin, was impressed by the names of the Directorate, believed they augured success from the start. He approved the "great work" as "most timely" and wished it "every blessing from on high."[25] Bishop Patrick J. Donahue of Wheeling, West Virginia, asked that the literature be sent to all the priests of his diocese.[26] Even from Manila, P. I., Archbishop Jeremiah J. Harty wrote:

> The work is practical and urgent, especially in this country. I have been preaching social work among the laboring classes, and will welcome the Militia of Christ in the great field of this diocese.[27]

The Right Reverend John W. Shanahan of Harrisburg, Pennsylvania, expressed the only dissenting and totally unsympathetic opinion when he scribbled these few remarks on the letter Father Dietz had sent him:

Name—stupid

Badge—absurd; the designer of it knows absolutely nothing about heraldry—Your programme is confusing.[28]

Conspicuously absent from these comments on the Militia of Christ are the opinions of the more famous members of the hierarchy. Cardinal Gibbons gave tacit approval in his effort to affiliate the Militia with the Catholic University, and Bishop Denis O'Connell later approved Dietz's school of social service, but there is no evidence of a direct or indirect nature that Archbishops Ireland and Keane, or Bishop Spalding made any reference to the organization. On the other hand, there is no indication that Dietz solicited their opinion.

Father Dietz's fellow priests, especially those who had been thinking along the same lines on social questions, wrote encouraging letters. Foremost among them, was Father John A. Ryan, who thought the organization embodied "a splendid idea and great possibilities for good" since it covered "a special field not occupied by any other agency, or person, or movement." He doubted the likelihood of its rapid growth because of the "inertia" of the Catholic trade unionist and the "discouragement from above."[29] Dietz suggested that Ryan become editor of *Social Service,* the magazine designed by Dietz in behalf of the Militia. But Archbishop Ireland would not grant the permission, since he wanted Ryan to devote all of his time to the Seminary.[30] Ryan did contribute to the magazine however.[31]

Father Herman Maeckel, S.J., of Canisius College, Buffalo, a contributor to *Social Service,* congratulated Father Dietz on "reading so well the signs of the times."[32] Monsignor William J. White, of the Brooklyn Catholic Charities, thought the Militia of Christ had been organized "at the psychological moment" and had no suggestions to offer to so "comprehensive a plan."[33]

But the Reverend William Engelen, S.J., did not think the movement was timely. He felt that the Catholic trade unionist would be alienated by the fighting spirit evident in the very title of the organization, since he was not ready either "theoretically or practically" to give battle. Engelen also criticized the structure of the Militia, because it did not rest on a parish foundation it might alienate the "union man" from his pastor. He did not doubt, however, that the movement was "born of true love for the laboring classes."[34] Father Joseph Husslein, S.J., editor of *America,* mentioned the Militia on several occasions in his editorials and personally expressed his great interest in and hope for the movement.[35] Besides these mentioned, over twenty-five priests indicated their sympathy with the program mapped out by Father Dietz.

Though clerical cooperation was important, it was quite as necessary to have the new movement accepted by the Catholic laity outside the labor movement. Among the influential laymen impressed by the importance of the undertaking was Dr. Charles P. Neill, the Commissioner of Labor, who wrote:

> I looked over your prospectus and am thoroughly in sympathy with your aims. It is rather an ambitious movement, but if you can secure the men and means necessary to carry it on, it cannot but be productive of tremendous good.[36]

Fearful of unduly extensive early attempts, he suggested that the new organization start with activities easily executed at small cost and, with these successfully launched, expand its program step by step.[37]

Attorney Gerald Connelly of Newport, Kentucky, agreed with Neill on the comprehensiveness of the Militia's program and believed it would "produce the lecturers and literature" to meet one of the "crying needs of our people," namely "political program and training in the Catholic social principles as outlined by the Encyclical on Labor of Pope Leo."[38]

Others like Walter George Smith of Philadelphia, president of the American Federation of Catholic Societies, and Charles J. Bonaparte of Baltimore, statesman and civic leader, extended only a qualified endorsement. While they agreed with the Militia's program in general terms, they hesitated to accept the principle of trade-unionism, a requisite for membership. Both were alarmed at the militant trend in the A. F. of L. and pointed to the action of the United Mine Workers which had forced John Mitchell to choose between membership in their organization and in the National Civic Federation.[39] "Was this action on the part of the United Mine Workers consistent with the 'principle of trade unionism'?" questioned Bonaparte.

In other words, does that principle permit trade unions to

forbid their members to belong to a body with the aims of the Civic Federation? If it does, is the principle in question altogether consistent with the purposes of your own organization? If it does not, is not the principle in question disregarded by the most powerful of the trade unions?[40]

Smith favored organization in principle, but deplored the "tyrannical and lawless methods of the Western Federation of Miners and some other misguided organizations led by those who proclaim themselves the friends of labor."[41] He conceded that the Militia of Christ aimed to combat these influences, but hesitated to identify himself with a movement that seemed "more special to the Federation of Labor than to the general cause which its Constitution covers."[42] Presently, however, Smith actively supported both the Militia of Christ and the American Federation of Labor.[43] The membership blanks indicate that many lawyers, bankers, clerks, real estate and insurance men associated themselves with the purposes of the Militia of Christ.

It was not surprising that many Catholic labor leaders welcomed the movement. Four members of the Executive Council of the American Federation of Labor were members of the Directorate of the Militia of Christ—John Mitchell, James O'Connell, Denis Hayes, and John Alpine. Of these the most prominent was Mitchell. While he was in Oberlin, in 1911, to give a lecture at Oberlin College, Mitchell had an opportunity to discuss with Father Dietz the Militia's theory and plan of action.[44] Soon after, he wrote Dietz:

> I have no hesitancy—not even a mental reservation—in saying that you have presented a program of constructive social service that is sound and progressive; a program that is calculated to meet the requirements of our time and our people . . .
> I believe that the Catholic people should be in the vanguard in the movement for constructive social and industrial reform, and whether there be any justification for the charge there is a widespread impression that our Church is just a little over-conservative in matters of this kind; therefore, it seems to me that our people should adopt and pursue a systematic program for social betterment; that we should identify ourselves with the movement to promote legislation, that is, constructive legislation, for the protection of that great part of the people

in our country who are least able to protect themselves.

The Militia of Christ for Social Service presents an avenue through which good work can be done for our less fortunate fellow beings, and at the same time credit can be reflected upon the Church itself.[45]

Later, however, he criticized the proposed constitution and by-laws for their failure to "declare specifically . . . for certain definite principles and reforms" such as minimum wages, limitation of hours, and collective bargaining. So keenly did Mitchell feel the necessity of this, that he hesitated to "participate officially in the organization."[46] But until his death in 1919, Mitchell was Father Dietz's friend and advisor.

The other officers and directors were not so articulate as John Mitchell. James O'Connell, Denis Hayes, John Golden, and T. V. O'Connor were inclined to accept the program and constitution in its totality.[47] Some twenty letters from rank and file union men and officers expressed satisfaction with the program and a willingness to cooperate.[48] No doubt F. J. McNulty, president of the International Brotherhood of Electrical Workers, represented a certain class of Catholic trade-unionists when he wrote that he enjoyed *Social Service* as a Catholic but that as a trade-unionist he did not care "to become identified with any sectarian movement that might reach within the organized 'Labor Movement'."[49]

This fear that the Militia of Christ would split the labor movement undoubtedly held many back from active cooperation. The Socialists in particular played upon this fear in their attacks upon the organization. Victor L. Berger, Socialist editor and Congressman, maintained that the Militia of Christ was

> frankly designed to separate organized labor on religious lines and bring existing unions under the domination of the Roman Catholic hierarchy. . . . One can understand how the Reverend Peter Dietz can engage in such an enterprise, but how John Mitchell, Peter McArdle and other Irish-Catholic labor leaders who have subscribed to the Constitution of the order of the Militia of Christ can look their fellow-workers of Protestant and non-Catholic belief in the eye without feeling the shame of Judas, is a mystery which may be revealed when the workers that they are seeking to betray into the hands of their

enemies come to realize the full extent of their perfidy.[50]

James Oneal had this to say in the *Coming Nation*:

> The "Militia of Christ." What a sinister meaning has the second word in the tragic history of labor struggles. . . . The workers who have sacrificed for years to build up their unions have to break down prejudices of race, nationality and creeds. Now a sinister influence is organized as an 'inner circle' in the unions to promote a 'propaganda' of hatred and suspicion along religious lines.[51]

In non-Socialist ranks, opinion was on the whole favorable to the new organization. But, as time was to show, many who approved the movement were unwilling to sacrifice time, energy, and money to put it into operation. Father Dietz, on whom the organizing devolved, soon realized that the duties of the pastorate at Oberlin left him little time for work in behalf of the Militia of Christ. His Bishop, the Right Reverend John P. Farelly, while not forbidding him to engage in the work, still wished him to devote all of his labors to parish effort.[52] This attitude irritated Dietz, but Archbishop Glennon was philosophical about it:

> If you are delayed in your efforts to organize and develop a society, it means only that the foundations are being more safely laid and are given some time to settle.[53]

Not one to brook delay, Dietz decided that he ought to resign from his pastorate and give full time to the Militia. He questioned the wisdom of remaining in Oberlin, or even in the Cleveland diocese. His bishop had never publicly approved of the Militia of Christ, and, while Archbishop Glennon's support was impressive, some felt that the approbation of Father Dietz's own bishop was essential. He sought the advice of Dr. Ryan, who suggested that he ask for a leave of absence for a year or two and make the experiment in Chicago under Archbishop Quigley, a prelate who was "fully awake to the need of Catholic activity in the social field."[54] If Archbishop Quigley were not willing, perhaps St. Louis or Milwaukee would do just as well.[55]

Apparently Dietz did not follow these suggestions, deciding instead to center his activities, if possible, in the Catholic University at

Washington. Archbishop Glennon agreed that the University would be the ideal place, and reassured Dietz that the giving up of his parish was "not a very serious matter."[56] At the suggestion of Cardinal Gibbons, Glennon presented the proposal to the Board of Directors of the University.[57] The Board was not favorably impressed, the rector, Monsignor Thomas J. Shahan, explaining to Dietz:

> As Rector of the University, I am unable to hold out any assurance that now or in the future you may in any way whatever be identified with the University in your capacity as head of the Militia of Christ. . . . I have spoken to Dr. Kerby about you and your work. He made known to me his doubts concerning the practical outcome of your plans, but he paid the highest tribute to your character and unselfishness.[58]

The failure of this plan discouraged Dietz, but again Archbishop Glennon tried to hearten him:

> Your affiliating with other societies, organizations, or institutions may have some value in the sense that it will be a protection to you in the movement, but it will not be able to put life in the movement, nor become the primary reason for its success. . . . That depends upon you and your directors, and the soul of it must be within, and not outside the body of it.[59]

In the meantime a movement was on foot to affiliate the Militia of Christ with the Catholic Church Extension Society. Father Francis C. Kelley, president of the Society, wanted to open a Department of Labor and Social Service and approached Dr. Kerby on the matter. The latter wrote Father Dietz:

> I suggested you to him as probably just the kind of secretary that the work would need. He knows something of you and your work. . . . He has a fund from which he can pay your trip expenses and he will gladly do so.[60]

The plan developed far enough to have a prospectus drawn up. Dietz was to be the director of the new department, and to go out among the organized laborers of the country and bring them together on a "Militia basis."[61] For some reason the plan did not go through, perhaps because the Social Service Commission had been created at the Columbus Convention in 1911 and Father Dietz, as secretary, had new responsibilities.

Release from parish work now became imperative. On July 7, 1911, Father Dietz wrote Bishop Farelly, resigning from his pastorate at Oberlin, and asking for a year's leave of absence. Farelly accepted his resignation, but, regarding the leave, wrote:

> Permission to absent yourself from the diocese for one year can be granted only under one condition, that as long as you remain a subject of the Diocese of Cleveland, you will of course hold yourself ready for recall in case of need.[62]

Surely this did not encourage Father Dietz to involve himself deeply in the new work. He sought the advice of the Apostolic Delegate as to his obligation to submit to recall. His Excellency replied:

> Since you have received a formal leave of absence for a year, it would seem that you can properly commence to devote yourself as intended to the work of the Militia of Christ. Should the Bishop at any future time during said year recall you for service in the diocese, you could then set forth any reasons which you might feel yourself to have for continuing in the work of the society.[63]

A few months later, however, he took steps to leave the diocese altogether. Father Dietz's friend, Bishop J. M. Koudelka, invited him to the Milwaukee Archdiocese where he was adopted by Archbishop Messmer.[64] The official transfer was dated February 9, 1912.[65]

The status of the Militia of Christ under the changed circumstances was settled in March at the meeting of the Executive Board of the American Federation of Catholic Societies. There it was agreed that half of the *Bulletin* would be devoted to the work of the Social Service Commission under the editorship of Father Dietz. The Militia of Christ for Social Service became a member of the Federation like the other Catholic societies, and the organ of the Militia, *Social Service,* of which three numbers had been issued (May, August, November) was merged with the *Bulletin.*[66] The Militia, henceforth, would devote itself primarily to labor problems.

By that time the Militia had been in existence over a year, and the membership had increased from some one hundred and sixty charter members, to over seven hundred. Most of the original subscriptions came in response to the first letters announcing the new organization.

Active charter members brought in others, but the two thousand members which Father Dietz deemed necessary "to start right and strong" never materialized. Although not easily disheartened, he was disappointed. He wrote to John Mitchell:

> I have gone through the first year without being in debt. For all my pains I have an ideal consolation only and not a promising outlook. The earliest hopes of the 'Militia of Christ' are not fulfilled yet I am equally sure that the movement has justified itself.[67]

He complained of a lack of cooperation:

> Mr. Mitchell, those who are in the Directorate of the Militia of Christ have done little beyond lending their names. I have been left alone without men and without means. The seven hundred subscriptions, the literary contributions, the sporadic words of encouragement—all these things helped and were most gratefully received—but they did not fan the spark to the point of ignition. The hope of existence was kept alive—that's all.[68]

John Mitchell could not be included in these accusations. He reported his efforts to Father Dietz in September, 1911:

> I have not had time to look over the second number of *Social Service* . . . I did, however, go downtown to see some of my friends there and suggested to them the advantage of assisting in the work you have undertaken to do. I regret to say, however, that the response to my suggestions were not encouraging. It seems that everybody in New York who has money is afraid that the country is going to the 'bow-wows.' I suppose this is due to the 'slump' in the stock market, as to many rich men in New York, of course, the stock market is the larger part of America. I am going to make some further inquiry and if anything favorable develops, I shall communicate that fact to you.[69]

But most of the labor leaders were too involved in union affairs to have time to organize the Militia. Again Father Dietz saw the necessity of a school to train a corps of workers who would give themselves entirely to the work. He suggested to Mitchell that they begin a school of social service on the plan of the Rand School of Social Science in New York.[70]

In the meantime one man was in the field working for the

Militia of Christ. He was Peter W. Collins, its second vice-president, and, from 1905-1912, International Secretary of the Brotherhood of Electrical Workers. In 1908 he had been appointed a member of the Industrial Commission of Illinois, the first of its kind in the country, and was responsible for several bills improving the industrial conditions of the workers in Illinois.[71] In March, 1911, Collins began a special lecture tour under the auspices of the Militia of Christ. Some of his lectures attacked Socialism, exposing its hostility to the labor movement, marriage, and religion. Others dealt with social problems and social reform. Wherever he went he talked about the Militia of Christ, left subscription blanks with the Council of the Knights of Columbus, urging them to interest their members in the organization.[72] His experience taught him the need of an alert Catholic resistance to Socialism, and had a great deal to do with his resignation from the International Brotherhood of Electrical Workers. He asked the advice of Father Dietz:

> Will I give up this job and go into the battle *now* and fight Socialism and the enemies of the movement or will I stay and be hampered by McNulty who will put every obstacle in my way . . .[73] Some of these yellow men who call themselves Catholic injure the name of our people by being classed as of us. . . . My heart and soul are in the movement for real *Catholic Social Action and the Militia of Christ.*[74]

Collins resigned in April, 1912, to give his full time to Catholic social action. During 1912 he lectured for the Militia, but with the beginning of 1913, Father Dietz was forced to admit: "I have not been able to supply Collins with sufficient lectures—so he went to the Central Verein."[75]

Collins' place was taken by William Francis Keates of Cannelton, Indiana, who went into the field in the spring of 1913 to expedite the formation of local and state chapters. Keates was a native of England and a convert. When he came to the attention of Father Dietz, he had been in the United States fifteen years, and was known as a ceramist and clay expert. Apalled at the activity of the Socialist Party and the ignorance and apathy of Catholics in fighting it, Keates became a student of Socialism and wanted to give all of his time, energy and abilities toward "fighting this slimey octopus."[76] His first itinerary included those towns where charter members lived, beginning with Cincinnati. But Keates did not prove satisfactory. He was slow in carrying the work of organization forward, was more of a dreamer than a practical man of affairs, and most important, he did not know the labor movement.[77] After he had spent some time in Cincinnati and Evansville, Indiana, Dietz decided to try him as an organizer for the American Federation of Catholic Societies, but in March, 1914, he dispensed with his services.[78]

Despite the lack of "men and means," a few chapters were established. In those places where the initial enthusiasm was highest, Father Dietz himself had been the organizer. He set up the first chapter at New Orleans, when he came to address the Louisiana State Federation of Catholic Societies at its convention in April, 1912. In his lecture Dietz stressed the fact that:

> Social service is not only a religious duty, but is also a duty of national and patriotic importance. Peace is the foundation of prosperity in the nation, therefore to promote, to create, to extend industrial peace is a work of national and patriotic importance . . .[79]

Thirty leaders of labor responded to his challenge and organized a chapter of the Militia of Christ. The beginning was auspicious, for within a week over sixty members had joined the chapter. Archbishop Blenk supported the venture enthusiastically and named Father Edward Rombouts of Welsh, Louisiana, the first chaplain.[80] Shortly after the chapter organized, its president, Peter Clark, received a letter from W. J. Smith, secretary of the Socialist Party, which stated:

> We beg to call your attention to the fact that while the Militia of Christ, to the best of our knowledge is a Catholic organization, there are also many Catholics in the Socialist party, . . . and if the Militia of Christ can show where these Socialist Catholics are in error in their fealty to Socialism you will have done a great service to the Church in whose interest you are working.[81]

The Militia met this challenge by inviting the Socialists to a meeting of the chapter, where they could hand in questions on any points they wanted discussed. The chaplain, Father Rombouts, answered the questions very ably at the next meeting. Father F. X. Gassler also addressed the meetings, pointing out the fallacies of Socialism.[82] But internal difficulties soon weakened the organization. The secretary, Daniel Downing, Inspector of the Immigration Department of New Orleans, complained of the ineptness of the president; his ignorance of Parliamentary Law made the meetings a shambles, when he refused to put motions to a vote because he did not approve of the views of the people presenting them, and he "harangued the members with random talk."[83] Father Rombouts wanted to make some changes in the organization; he did not like the name; would abolish all feast days except Labor Day and the first Sunday in May, the last to commemorate *Rerum Novarum* and to offset the red May Day.[84] Dietz was not particularly concerned over these changes. As he wrote to Archbishop Blenk:

> In the matter of the Militia of Christ of New Orleans, I did not try to impose myself too strongly, because Mr. Denechaud was on the spot and I have always kept him well informed about my ideas in this work.[85] Besides, there are a number of undetermined fundamentals that will have to be settled, if the works of this nature are to multiply and become effective. . . . Father Rombouts has misgivings about the title: 'Militia of Christ,' but I have always loved it for many reasons, but particularly for the reason that I did not want the work to develop into a mere 'economic' machine. I wanted before everything else to keep before the members that they are fighting for Christianity and nothing pleased me more than your Grace's letter in the beginning when among other things you told me that the 'name was most happily chosen.'[86]

Shortly after this letter arrived, the name of the New Orleans chapter was changed to the "Catholic Social Guild of Louisiana."[87] Its program remained similar to that of the Militia, "the studying, propagating, defending and applying to actual conditions the principles laid down in the social encyclicals of Leo XIII and Pius X."[88] Denechaud informed Father Dietz: "Since this work has gone off on a tangent, we, of the Federation, have withdrawn from it, as we do not feel it will accomplish any practical results."[89] At the Baltimore Conference of the Social Service Commission in 1914, Father Gassler, reporting for the Guild, admitted it had done little, but was planning a series of lectures for the following winter.[90]

The other chapters followed much the same pattern, beginning with enthusiasm and then slowing down to sluggish inactivity. Father Dietz organized a chapter in St. Louis when Archbishop Glennon invited him to address the Archdiocesan Conference on Charities and Social Service, May 8, 1912. James Pendergast, secretary of the Building Trades Council of St. Louis, was elected president.[91] Father Patrick P. Crane was the enthusiastic chaplain. But scarcely a year later, Dietz inquired of him:

> What has become of the Militia of Christ of St. Louis? Where I am able to go into the work in person, as at Chicago and Milwaukee, I find that I can get the finest kind of an avenue . . . Don't you think St. Louis could push along a bit?[92]

The Chicago chapter, organized in December, 1912, had Philip J. Walsh of the International Union of Steam Engineers, for its first president. He wrote later to Father Dietz:

> We are living in a hotbed of Socialism here and they are conducting an educational campaign among our boys and it will be my delight when we have our men in every factory in Chicago, to beat them to it.[93]

Claiming that the Militia of Christ was trying to get control of the labor movement to turn it over to the Church, the Chicago Socialists had countered with a Menace Club whose name was taken from the widely read anti-Catholic newspaper.[94]

A conflict with Socialists brought the Militia of Christ into the limelight in Milwaukee, before a chapter was formed, when the convention of the International Molders' Union of North America met in that city in September, 1912. A resolution introduced by Delegate D. E. Lanigan of Vancouver, B. C., ordered that no member of the I.M.U. could be a member of the Militia of Christ or of the National Civic Federation.[95] Rejected by the Committee on Resolutions, the proposal was carried to the convention floor where a spirited argument took place. Through the efforts of Militia members the resolution was defeated by a substantial majority.[96] In reporting the incident the *Milwaukee Journal* noted that "all the trade unions are exhibiting interest in this religious organization since the fracas which enlivened the Molders' Convention."[97] A few days later Dietz spoke to the delegates at the Convention of the International Association of Operative Plasterers, urging the men to keep the trade union movement neutral because the importation of anti-Christian issues would mean its disruption.[98]

A few months later, in February, 1913, Father Dietz and "eleven picked men" organized the Milwaukee chapter.[99] To give the men time to become familiar with the purposes of the movement, elections were delayed for a month. Dietz's circular letter announcing the meeting for permanent organization made it clear that the Militia of Christ would not divide the labor movement as its enemies claimed, but would rather strengthen it and

> the strengthening of the Catholic trade union sentiment will do much for the preservation of legitimate trade union ideals; it will enlist the great influence of Catholic public opinion in the cause of labor; it will elevate the conditions of industrial peace while it stands opposed to the false doctrine of class antagonism, which regards all employers alike as enemies of labor; it will cultivate the possibilities of conciliation, conferences, trade agreements, to the fullest extent, consistent with honor and the proper dignity of labor.[100]

The new president, Philip Almanrade, appointed two committees; one to take up the question of Sunday labor with the street railway company; the other to investigate complaints regarding the treatment of working girls in Milwaukee.[101] The *Catholic Citizen* reported the regular meetings and activities of the chapter to June, 1914. Some of these meetings were of a religious nature, like the service held in the old Cathedral in May, 1914, to commemorate the anniversary of *Rerum Novarum*. About five hundred attended the Mass and heard Father Dietz preach on the relation of Christianity to the labor movement.[102] In July Father Dietz left for Europe.

In Cincinnati Joseph Meyung of the Journeyman Barbers' International wanted to start a chapter. He tried to cooperate with Keates but with little success. Meyung, however, did secure Archbishop Henry Moeller's consent. Moeller wrote:

> The object for which the 'Militia of Christ' was organized, namely—'The defense of the Christian Order of Society' is indeed a very laudable one and is deserving of much help and encouragement.
>
> I hereby authorize the institution of a Chapter of said organization here in Cincinnati and will be very glad if all the pastors will lend their best efforts to cooperate with you in this great work.[103]

Although fourteen trade unionists attended the organizational meeting in November, 1913, there is no evidence that a chapter was actually formed.

Father Dietz organized a chapter in Knoxville, Tennessee, when he went there to deliver a sermon at the Knights of Columbus initiation. The chapter elected R. S. Allison president.

Indianapolis seemed a likely place for a chapter, since many trade union organizations were centered there. Dietz solicited the help of Louis Budenz, an active member of the Catholic social movement in that city.[104] Too busy at that particular time, Budenz promised to take the matter up later.[105] "I really believe," he wrote, "that it is a very efficient way of putting into practice our Catholic idea of Solidarism. In all my talks I will mention the matter."[106] Later he wrote of a meeting of young trade unionists at which he planned to lay the foundations for a chapter:

> I prefer to start with the young men, as they are less stubborn and more responsive to leadership and to the acceptance of Catholic ideals. . . . Those whom I have approached on the subject are enthusiastic about it, but prefer to work quietly at present. I, too, think that this plan is best here.[107]

When Budenz left for St. Louis to take up his work with the Central Verein, he sent Dietz the names of three of his friends who might carry on the work of organization in Indianapolis. Though Father Dietz followed up the suggestion, apparently nothing came of it.[108]

Peter Collins was impressed with the possibilities of a chapter in

Boston, when he lectured there in January, 1913. Accordingly Father Dietz asked Cardinal O'Connell's opinion of such a venture. Explaining the movement Dietz wrote:

> There are some prejudices against the work and the task is a very delicate one. Men are not accustomed to the idea behind it and as a result the education process is slow. . . . The *ratio existendi* is this: there is no bridge between the Church in America and the labor movement. The pulpit and the press speak to the individual only and existing Catholic societies are an imperfect medium. It is not possible to *take hold* of the labor movement in these ways. At a critical moment it would be very difficult for the Church to influence a given situation. The Militia of Christ would have a disciplined array of responsible Catholic Trade-unionists, prepared to act in concert at a moment's notice.[109]

The Cardinal suggested they postpone the decision until Father Dietz came to Boston to address the Archdiocesan Convention of the American Federation of Catholic Societies. Father Patrick Supple, who had invited Dietz also promised to arrange a lecture before the Boston Central Labor Union, "the most powerful organization in New England."[110] It seemed such a promising arrangement, but actually nothing was accomplished toward organizing a chapter since the plan to address the labor union miscarried, and the Cardinal was not in Boston when Father Dietz arrived.[111]

These failures on the local scene never seemed to disturb Dietz unduly. He realized his handicaps on every side. Lack of funds limited the amount of help he could afford, as well as the quantities of literature that should have been sent gratis all over the country. The vast correspondence such an organization called for would have kept a number of secretaries busy. Without persistent prodding by the executive secretary there was little chance of overcoming the inertia of which Father John A. Ryan had spoken. Only the Milwaukee chapter really functioned, and that we may believe was due to the drive and enthusiasm of Father Dietz. Though many had hailed the advent of the movement, admired its program, and prayed for its success, none came forward to finance it. The membership blanks available show only an occasional dollar or two "for the Cause" in excess of the one dollar membership fee. Yet Father Dietz was not discouraged, as his circular letter to the members in May, 1914, indicated:

> The work of the Militia of Christ is more difficult than many other Catholic works, because it makes a trade-union appeal for which many people have no sympathy or proper understanding. In spite of this, steady progress has been made.[112]

This circular letter announced that the Milwaukee chapter had passed a resolution to submit the question of a change of name to a referendum of the members. The name suggested was "American Conference of Catholic Trade Unionists." Dietz had at last yielded to the pressure of those who did not like the name, Militia of Christ. John Mitchell, Denis Hayes, and Archbishop Messmer, in particular, had questioned the suitability of the name. Messmer thought it was "too pious" for its purpose and would convey to many trade-unionists the idea of a "pious sodality or confraternity." He also thought it might offer the enemy a convenient weapon for ridicule or fear.[113] The June edition of the *Newsletter* announced the adoption of the Milwaukee chapter's resolution, but Father Dietz rarely used the new name.

The work of the Militia in its chapters represents only one phase of its history. More illustrative of its purpose and possibilities is the work done under the personal leadership of Father Dietz. Alone, or supported by one or more of the leading Catholic trade-unionists, Dietz worked consistently and persistently to make Catholic influence felt in the labor world. Something of the complexity of his task he confided to Archbishop Glennon:

> Theoretically it is very fine to discuss the Catholic position or philosophy on labor matters, to talk about neutral, or Christian or Catholic trade-unions, but when you face concrete situations in this country and concrete labor leaders with their own peculiar development, it is imprudent to attempt to break things over the knee. Therefore in contending with such movements, one must yield to the stream and try to direct the current.[114]

One of the "concrete situations" Dietz met frequently was the failure of Catholics to make practical their devotion to trade-union-ism by employing union labor. For instance, John Dougherty, sec-retary-treasurer of the International Brotherhood of Bookbinders, called attention to the fact that Dr. J. J. Walsh had his books printed by the Werner Company of Akron, which had been warring for five years with the Allied Printing Trades, over an eight-hour day.[115]

More frequent complaints came from the Building Trades. Catholic trade unionists were embarrassed and puzzled at Catholics giving a whiphandle to the Socialists by erecting churches and other buildings with non-union labor.[116] Dietz wrote to Father O. M. McGee of Springfield, Massachusetts, protesting this practice, after he read in a Worcester labor journal that six churches had been built in the vicinity in the past two years, with non-union labor.[117] He was bet-ter able to act in Milwaukee where several buildings were being erect-ed under Catholic auspices. Among these was a clubhouse for the Knights of Columbus. When in an interview he found the architect set against "unionizing the job,"[118] Dietz arranged a conference with the Building Committee of the Knights of Columbus. A number of the men on the Committee admitted that the conference had been an education, and promised, if things were approximately equal, to give the work to union men by preference.[119] But the clubhouse was not erected by union labor. In retaliation the Building Trades Council of Milwaukee passed a resolution barring from the American Federa-tion of Labor Conventions fraternal delegates representing religious societies, since these societies were not willing to "assist and cooper-ate in the establishment of trade union conditions, for the workers in the various industries, and especially in those over which they had full power to act."[120] The preamble referred specifically to the Knights of Columbus building and made point of the fact that even conferences with the Building Committee, Archbishop Messmer, and Father Dietz had not altered the situation.[121] Dietz sent a copy of the resolution to the Knights of Columbus with the comment:

> There is no point to sending lecturers to fight Socialism by mere word of mouth and then fall down in the application of Christian principles to actual conditions of the industrial struggle.[122]

Although Father Dietz was a staunch defender of trade-unionism, he was not blind to the flaws in trade-union policy. On one occasion Father Francis Van Nistelroy of Kimberley, Wisconsin, asked his advice on the best procedure regarding the unskilled laborers of the Kimberley and Clark Paper Mills. The Company had announced a wage cut of twelve cents a day, bringing wages of the unskilled down to $1.75 per day. Dietz replied:

> To tell the men off-hand to go on strike would hardly be prudent for they would have no funds to fall back upon . . . and . . . would lack the orderly organization which alone can conduct a strike and in which the proper leadership has been previously developed. . . . This proves the necessity of industrial organizations (unions) to take in not only the craftsmen but also the unskilled. This form is often denounced as socialistic but you plainly see how in some industries it is necessary on the point that 'an injury to one is an injury to all.'[123]

Father Dietz was particularly concerned over the role of the Church in the copper strike in Upper Michigan which began in July of 1913 and involved some 15,000 strikers. Since they were largely from Southern and Eastern Europe—Croatians, Italians, and Hungarians—he felt keenly their need for proper guidance. Accordingly, he made a survey of the field in late November. His way was prepared by a letter from John H. Walker of the United Mine Workers, president of the Illinois Federation of Labor, to Charles Mahoney of Calumet:

> The bearer Father Dietz and I have talked over the entire situation in the strike situation, particularly the religious aspect of it and I feel that if you will give him your hearty cooperation he will be helpful in straightening at least that phase of it up, if indeed he does not accomplish more. I have advised President Moyer and Brother Cannon and both of them are in accord with this sentiment.[124]

While in Calumet Father Dietz, in an attempt to learn both sides of the situation, interviewed the strike leaders, a representative of the Company, clergymen, miners, and Judge O'Brien of the Circuit Court of Houghton County, who was friendly to the strikers.[125] He also interviewed the Right Reverend Frederick Eis, Bishop of

Marquette, Michigan, to induce him to act, but the Bishop refused to have any part in it.[126] Armed with the information he had secured, Dietz devoted two *Newsletters* to the strike. He criticized the Calumet and Hecla Company for refusing to meet with the representatives of the strikers and thus failing to recognize the Western Federation of Miners.[127] Concerning the union, he wrote:

> It must be remembered that the W.F.M. is a western organization. The conditions in the West have been rougher in every way than in the East. They are still. But with the elimination of 'Big Bill Haywood' and the taking back of the W. F. M. into the A. F. of L., a new and more conservative era began.[128]

As a proof of this conservatism he cited the fact that the officials of the W. F. M. had asked the assistance of the officials of the United Mine Workers at the beginning of the strike. It was the "stubborn resistance of the corporations" that forced the use of "more primitive weapons." One of these "weapons" was the permission given Carlo Tresca, organizer of the I. W. W., to handle the Italian end of the situation. This alienated the Italian priests from support of the strikers.[129]

John Hogan of *The Gateway,* Detroit, took exception to some of the contentions of Dietz regarding the strike. He contrasted the record of the W. F. M. with the benevolent policy of the Calumet and Hecla Company in providing churches, schools, libraries, and low rent cottages for its workers.[130] Father Dietz agreed that

> the Company has done certain benevolent things, but benevolence cannot come before justice, in a homely way, men would rather own their own tin bath tub than use the Company's public bathhouse, and this simile can be applied all along the line.[131]

He believed the "admixture of Socialism" in the Western Federation of Miners was a lesser evil, since the A. F. of L. was coping with it and "the Catholic Church could cope with it more effectively still, if it were so minded and ready."[132] Dietz expressed to Cardinal O'Connell his opinion of the stand of the Church on the strike:

> The Copper strike in Upper Michigan . . . would have been settled months ago, if the Catholics in the district had been

prepared and guided by a Catholic policy. As it is the Church has practically ignored the situation and permitted all the other forces to make all the issues. I believe the Church could have assumed, if she wanted to, the intellectual and moral leadership to the benefit of all contending parties.[133]

The conviction that the Catholic Church had a significant and responsible role to play in the labor world motivated the career of Father Dietz as labor priest. He believed his Militia of Christ provided a channel for that leadership. Through the various chapters in New Orleans, Chicago, Milwaukee, and other smaller cities, he hoped to develop a feeling of solidarity among the Catholic trade unionists of the country. As first Catholic fraternal delegate to the conventions of the American Federation of Labor, Father Dietz exerted a strong personal influence on many Catholic leaders in trade unionism, which gave them the courage to stand firm against the assaults of hostile factions. A case in point is Peter McArdle's refusal to resign from the Militia of Christ, when a resolution calling for his resignation was pending in the convention of the Iron, Steel and Tin Workers at Canton, Ohio, in 1911.[134] In individual cases similar to this and in the scanty evidence of the work of the various chapters of which there is record, there is a consistency of policy consonant with the convictions of their founder, that Socialism, the insidious enemy of trade-unionism, must be defeated at all cost.

Ever alert to radical influences, Father Dietz maintained his faith in trade-unionism and used every means available to convert others to a like support of the cause of the workingman.

Chapter Four

Urging
a Catholic Labor
International

FATHER DIETZ HAD read the times correctly when he organized his Militia of Christ for Social Service in 1909. The Christian Socialist battle for control of the labor movement was under way along the entire labor front, in Europe and Canada as well as in the United States. It was an old challenge, met by European Catholics with the organization of Catholic trade unions. Leo XIII's encyclical, *Rerum Novarum*, applauded and greatly stimulated this policy. The result was inevitable—antagonism and rivalry between the Socialist and Catholic trade-unions.

The situation was particularly acute in Germany where three types of labor unions had been organized—the Christian (Catholic and Protestant), the liberal, and the free (really Socialist). Controversy over Catholics associating with Protestants in the Christian unions called forth Pope Pius X's encyclical *Singulari Quadam,* in which he permitted Catholics to join Christian unions but left no doubt that he preferred separate Catholic ones. In recognizing the Christian unions, however, the Pope sharpened the resistance of the Socialists.

This European conflict was reflected in the trade-union movement in the United States. Socialism reached its peak of strength in 1912. Almost every convention of the A. F. of L. had to deal with resolutions introduced by Socialists condemning clerical interference in the labor movement, applauding the "free" unions of Germany, or attempting to give a new twist to the "neutral" A. F. of L.

That Father Dietz was aware of the situation his Militia of Christ bore witness. His experience in trying to organize this clearing house

69

for Catholic trade-union thought and make it function effectively had taught him the great need for an official "Catholic policy" toward the labor movement. Such a policy formulated by the American hierarchy should delineate the specific application of *Rerum Novarum* and *Singulari Quadam* to conditions in the United States. An official pronouncement of this kind would clear the air, dispel much opposition to trade-unionism, and make possible a consistent and nationally acceptable plan of action.

With this in mind, Dietz approached some of the Catholic labor leaders at the Rochester convention of the A. F. of L. in 1912. These men seconded the idea and helped Dietz draw up the following testimonial which James O'Connell, Dr. Kerby, and Father Dietz presented to Cardinal Gibbons on December 26, 1912.[1]

> Your Eminence:
> We, the undersigned, affiliated with the Militia of Christ, and interested directly in the conservation and progress of trade-union ideals, feel certain that much harm can be prevented and much good accomplished by the publication and promulgation of an official document on the part of the hierarchy of the United States, that will make clear once and for all the Catholic position in the organized labor movement of this country.
>
> Pope Leo XIII, in his letter on the labor question has laid down in unmistakeable language the universal teaching of the Church, yet in the local application, especially as pertaining to the problems of labor organizations, there has been a variety of interpretations on the Continent, and in this country we are confronted with a situation equally if not more difficult. We therefore petition your Eminence most humbly and respectfully for an official document in these premises.
>
> Among the reasons that prompt us are the following: 1. The unsettled state of the Catholic mind and of many priests on the relation of Pope Leo's Encyclical to the organized labor movement in this country, the American Federation of Labor. This neutrality especially on the part of many of the clergy is a positive obstacle to progress and ready weapon for the enemy. 2. Catholic laymen in the ranks and as leaders of labor, are oftentimes discouraged because of the lack of moral support by the Church in their struggle for the betterment of human conditions. 3. The enlightened attitude of the secular

press in particular, added to other causes contributes not a little to the demoralization of the Catholic laity both within and without the movement of organized labor and calls for positive declaration and guidance. 4. On the other hand, we feel positive that from the intellectual and moral treasury of Christian Doctrine there may be brought forth both norms of trade-unionism, but [sic] also its complex problems as affecting legislation and the courts as well as society in general. In our Catholic confidence we feel that here is a splendid opportunity for the Catholic Church in our time and country.

If, in your good judgment, it appears opportune to prepare such an official document, we stand ready to assist in the preliminaries by way of counsel or conference, or in whatever way that suggests itself to your Eminence.

In conclusion, we again express our conviction that such a document dealing concretely especially with the problems of labor organizations in this country, when read from the pulpits of our churches, and promulgated in our Catholic press and societies will be a veritable God-send to the Catholic laity.[2]

Father Dietz thought it a hopeful sign that all of the prominent Catholic labor leaders, save two, signed it.[3] "If they will do this," he wrote Archbishop Glennon, "they will do other things as they develop their Catholic solidarity."[4]

The Cardinal received the committee graciously, promised to consider the matter with the Archbishops at their next annual meeting, and asked Dietz to write him in detail the specific things that should be included in a Bishops' Pastoral.[5] The comprehensive list of topics Dietz suggested included the union shop, collective bargaining, the restriction of output, the speeding up process, the limitation of apprentices, the strike, the boycott, the injunction, the black-list, the lock-out, picketing, the militia, arbitration, trade agreements, and conferences.[6] He thought the Pastoral should remind trade-unionists of their duties as well as of their rights. Among these duties Dietz included consideration for the public, the extension of the benefits of organized labor (sickness, death, and old age benefits) to the unskilled worker, resistance to Socialism and all radical tendencies, and a positive manifestation of faith. By regular attendance at union meetings, by serving

71

on committees and using the ballot, the trade-unionist could combat Socialism and use his influence to establish industrial peace, "so that a good Catholic will be not only a good father and a good citizen, but also a good trade unionist."[7] Such a Pastoral would have a "healthy" effect not only upon Catholics, but also upon national public opinion generally. It would be of particular value to seminarians and priests. As an alternative to the Pastoral, in the event that the "postulated document were deemed inopportune," Dietz suggested that the bishops call a Conference "composed of a limited number of prominent lawyers, canonists, sociologists, labor leaders, employers of labor and judges . . . presided over by a delegated member of the hierarchy."[8]

To ensure a "bloc" in favor of the Pastoral at the next Archbishops' meeting, Dietz asked the support of Archbishop Blenk, Archbishop Glennon, and his Eminence John Cardinal Farley.[9] Glennon was not optimistic about the Pastoral. He was sure the bishops would not approve the A. F. of L. "as such."[10] Neither did Dietz expect their approval but he thought some statement by the American hierarchy, such as the Holy See had made to the German bishops on the proper conduct of Catholics in interdenominational trade unions, was necessary "in order to hold the Catholic Trade Unionist more closely to the Church."[11] But Glennon held out against any definite pronouncements that would probably be largely adverse to labor. "The best is for those in highly responsible positions to state 'principles,' " he insisted, "and to leave to people like you and myself the privilege of applying them as best we may."[12]

Dr. Kerby believed that in view of the investigation being made by the Commission on Industrial Relations, appointed by President Wilson in 1913, the hierarchy should act slowly. "The hierarchy would have to make a national document," he explained. "It must be practical, not merely speculative. It will hardly venture to do so without national knowledge of facts. The federal investigation promises the information needed."[13]

At the annual meeting of the Archbishops in 1913, Cardinal O'-Connell was charged with naming a sub-committee to report on conditions relating to the matter of the Pastoral. Unable to secure information as to whether the report was made, Father Dietz finally concluded the matter had been dropped.[14]

In the meantime, he bent every effort toward the calling of a Catholic Industrial Conference. His first plan was to bring the Catholic labor leaders together, with Cardinal O'Connell as chairman, during the meeting of the Social Service Commission at Baltimore in 1914, and let them "have it out in public discussion rather than in private criticism."[15] The great parade and mass meeting would impress these men with a feeling of Catholic solidarity and "make the Church stronger with the workers than any other outside influence."[16] Then the next year the Catholic employers could be brought together and obliged "to acknowledge that the Church has something to say to them too."[17] He stressed labor's need of the Church many times noting that

> all the various Catholic Charities have some one or some organization behind them and are looked after more or less, but this is the one field almost wholly neglected and the one upon which the future democracy will be almost entirely built.[18]

In a few years, he warned, unless something were done soon the "anarchy of secularism," more insidious even than Socialism, would have a strong hold on those "innumerable Catholic workers" who were real 'Modernists' without knowing it, in that they believed that religion and labor problems are like two different pigeon holes in a desk.[19] Reading the labor papers, Father Dietz could see the "evidence piling up" and could also "see how the Church could *really do something here* to set men right." To be condemned to "inaction and the nothingness of individualism" was hard and discouraging, he complained.[20]

When the proposed plan for a conference of Catholic labor leaders at the Baltimore convention of the American Federation of Catholic Societies did not materialize, Dietz approached Cardinal O'Connell on the matter of a conference that would bring together the Catholic personnel already proposed to Cardinal Gibbons, representatives of the A. F. of L., and the members of the Commission on Industrial relations. Following a conference with O'Connell in April, 1914, Dietz consulted with Dr. Neill, Frank Walsh, chairman of the Commission, Frank Morrison, and Samuel Gompers.[21] Neill was skeptical about anything done by the Church in labor matters, lest it would not be well done or sufficiently fair to government and labor circles. After further conversation, he became more conciliatory.[22] Walsh, a Catholic, was surprised that the "Church had an eye to the Labor movement."[23] Dietz visited some of the sessions of the Commission and was impressed with its possibilities, but he told Chairman Walsh that he believed "a great danger to the real efficacy of the final results would be a 'secularistic' report to Congress, leaving out largely the ethical aspects into which industrial relations in the final analysis resolve themselves."[24] Before the interview ended, Walsh was ready to submit the question of an industrial conference to the steering committee.[25]

Fearing the divisive effect of religious dissension on the American Federation of Labor, Gompers and Morrison wanted to ignore the growing conflict between Catholics and Socialists in the labor movement. But Father Dietz insisted that it was impossible to avoid the issue, for, when the Church took a positive stand on the industrial question, as it would sooner or later, the American Labor movement would have to "square itself" with the Church in some fashion or other. Both labor leaders agreed, that, if a conference were held, the A. F. of L. should have official or unofficial representation.[26]

Early in 1915, when the Commission on Industrial Relations neared the end of its work, Father Dietz again broached the subject of a conference to Cardinal O'Connell. In such a conference, Dietz believed, Catholic influence could be exerted on the members of the Commission to ensure that none of the "ethical aspects" of industrial relations would be omitted from the Commission's final report to Congress.[27] This was an opportunity the Church dare not ignore. He warned the Cardinal:

> What a pity it would be to be compelled finally to yield the A. F. of L. to the enemy when by proper forethought and action the enemy can be kept on the offensive.[28]

If a special group of priests went as fraternal delegates to the central labor bodies, as many Protestant ministers were already doing, and became acquainted with the local men and movements, they could exert a powerful influence particularly over the Catholic trade-unionist.[29] After a time, some of the Dietz proposals were accepted: in 1920 the bishops issued a social Pastoral and, beginning in 1923, sponsored Catholic Industrial Conferences through the National Catholic Welfare Conference.

As fraternal delegate of the American Federation of Catholic Societies to the A. F. of L. conventions, Dietz did what he could to prevent the labor movement from tying up with any radical groups. From 1909 to 1922 he went to every convention except the one at San Francisco in 1915. That year his friend Archbishop Edward J. Hanna of San Francisco attended in his place. Father Dietz did not often address the conventions, leaving the formal speaking as a rule to his associate delegate.[30] He was content to exert his influence through contact with individual trade-unionists. When he did address them it was in forceful style, stressing labor's need of religion and the guidance of the Church. That he drew reactions from Socialists was evident in at least two cases.

At the Rochester convention in 1912, after listening to the fraternal delegates from England and Canada, "so frankly and outspokenly socialistic," Dietz claimed the same freedom when it was his turn to speak, directly challenging the neutral character of the labor movement:

> The first point I want to make is this: That mere economic strength is not a determining factor in industrial progress . . . it must be built on the foundation of justice to God, . . . to yourselves, . . . to your fellow man. . . . God has planted that seed [justice] in every soul and He has established religion to foster that seed. The [second] point is this . . . religion is not a private matter. . . . It is necessary that religion penetrate into the . . . union and into the factory, into the market place and into the parliaments of the nations. . . . Suppose you could carry out the slogan of some that tell you 'Workers of the world unite. You have nothing to lose but your chains and you have a world to win.' Suppose you could cast off that which you regard as a chain, the Christian heritage of the past . . . and then go forward and win a world. . . . Christ will be there ahead of you and . . . will address to you that same old question, 'What does it profit a man even if he does win the world, but suffers the loss of his own soul?'[31]

Repercussions from this address found expression in a resolution introduced into the convention:

> That all religious or anti-religious discussions as such shall be prohibited at all future conventions of the A. F. of L.[32]

When the Committee on Resolutions failed to approve this proposal, its friends demanded a roll call. The Committee was upheld and the resolution defeated.[33]

The next year at the Seattle Convention of the American Federation of Labor the European labor situation came before the assembly. George Perkins, president of the Cigarmaker's Union, reported on his study of labor conditions throughout western Europe. He described the division of the movement among Catholics, Protestant, and Socialists, particularly in Germany. Following the report, the Socialists introduced a resolution:

> Whereas, the German trades unions bitterly complain against the so-called Christian and Catholic unions, which are used as strike-breakers and have created discord and delayed the progress of the labor movement in Europe more than anything else has done; and
>
> Whereas, We have seen clergymen of this country taking sides with capital against labor, as was shown by the action of a Catholic bishop in West Virginia against the striking miners, and by the actions of Protestant preachers joining the militia in Michigan against the miners and other cases that are known to the trade-unionists; and
>
> Whereas, The so-called Christian and Catholic unions are a detriment to the labor movement, therefore be it
>
> Resolved, That we condemn any movement Christian or Catholic, which is harmful to the labor movement, and we warn our members not to encourage any such movements, nor give assistance to organizing such unions.[34]

The editor of *The Miner's Magazine,* organ of the Western Federation of Miners, exposed the part Dietz played in the defeat of this resolution when he warned his readers about "an element present at Seattle that should be seriously considered by all members of the organized labor movement." The leader was "one of the busiest men in the hotel lobbies . . . one Father Peter E. Dietz of the Militia of Christ, who in conference with Catholic delegates became indignant when they showed their approval of the resolution."[35] Dietz denied any conference, but admitted lobbying as a part of his "business in learning to understand and appreciate the labor movement," and quite his privilege.[36] Later Dietz learned that the "Big Six"—No. 6 of the Typographical Union in New York—had adopted a resolution similar to that of the Milwaukee Building Trades Council.[37]

> That we favor the exclusion of the fraternal delegate of Church organizations from all future conventions of the A. F. of L., and that we request all other affiliated trades unions to take similar action to the end that the American labor movement shall not be retarded through the minds of its individual members being fettered by insidiary appeals to religious prejudices.[38]

On the international scene, difficulties arose in Canada between the Catholic unions and the A. F. of L. The source of the trouble lay in the historic past. Predominantly French and Roman Catholic, the people of Quebec had maintained a highly integrated culture, resisting most English and American influences. When Western Canada was opened to settlement, the industrialism of the St. Lawrence region developed rapidly. The Knights of Labor were successful in organizing in Quebec in 1881. Their subsequent condemnation by Cardinal Eleazer Alexandre Taschereau, Archbishop of Quebec, and the appearance of *Rerum Novarum*, fostered the development of separate Catholic trade unions.[39] The first of these was organized in Quebec in 1901; others followed shortly in Montreal, Chicoutimi, and Three Rivers. By 1912 they totalled 6,325 members.[40] Besides these, ninety-nine other unions existed in Canada, eighty-two of them affiliated with the A. F. of L. The latter represented over 93,000 workers.[41] The continued growth of the Catholic unions was stimulated by various incidents, chief among them the attempt of Socialists to control the labor movement. Socialists were especially strong in western Canada around Winnipeg, where the I. W. W. and the Western Federation of Miners had penetrated in 1906.[42] They were attempting their "boring from within" policy in the unions affiliated with the A. F. of L. Consequently the ecclesiastics of eastern Canada believed a situation existed similar to that described in *Rerum Novarum,* which called for the organization of separate Catholic unions. Furthermore, the A. F. of L. was looked upon as a foreign organization to which was contributed money better kept in Canada. Also in French Canada the use of the word "international" had an opprobrious connotation associated with the red flag, Socialism and anarchy.

Strengthening the argument for separate Catholic unions was the appearance in 1912 of Pope Pius X's letter to the German bishops, *Singulari Quadam Caritate.* The letter, intended to settle the controversy over Catholic or interconfessional unions in Germany, gained acceptance in Quebec, especially the part which stated:

> Wherever possible, Catholic unions must be formed, founded, encouraged and supported. In such cases Christian unions must not be established. Catholic unions are possible in exclusively Catholic regions and wherever they serve the needs of the members.[43]

The Seattle Convention of the A. F. of L. confirmed the continuing suspicion of Canada's hierarchy that the American Federation of Labor was a Socialist-dominated body.

These views regarding the A. F. of L. were summarized in a pamphlet, *La Fédération Américaine du Travail,* written shortly after the Seattle Convention by Arthur Saint-Pierre of the *Secretariat de L'École Sociale Populaire.* The author recognized that the Federation had done much to ameliorate the material conditions of the workers, but quoted *Rerum Novarum* to show that such amelioration was not enough, since the principal object that ought to motivate all economic societies is the moral and religious perfection of the members.[44] The A. F. of L. was attempting, the author contended, to separate two essentially inseparable questions—the social question and the religious question.[45] Worst of all, the A. F. of L. was permitting the "germ of socialism" to develop freely within it. Cited as examples of these contentions were the resolutions at the Seattle Convention, the Federation's advocacy of uniform state-selected textboks for the schools, and its alleged endorsement of the brochure *Philosophy of Trades Unions* which was grossly materialistic and anti-clerical.[48] Therefore, the author concluded:

Judged from the moral and religious point of view it does not merit, in any wise, the sympathy and encouragement of the Catholic workers.[47]

This opposition to the American Federation of Labor Dietz tried to break down in order to secure in the labor movement that unity which was necessary for real progress. Two years before the pamphlet appeared, Frank Duffy, of the Brotherhod of Carpenters and Joiners, had written duplicate letters to Cardinal Gibbons and Father Dietz acquainting them with the Canadian situation. Reports indicated that certain bishops in eastern Canada were advising Catholics not to join A. F. of L. unions, representing their leaders in the States as Freemasons and Socialists.[48] In some cases ecclesiastics commanded from the altar that workers give up their affiliation with the A. F. of L. and join the Catholic labor movement.[49] Duffy wrote:

> I thought it only right that you should be acquainted with these facts, and thought you might be able to do something to counteract them, if in no other way than by . . . pointing out . . . what they [unions] have accomplished in a legitimate way for their members and what they propose to do in a legitimate way in the future.[50]

Cardinal Gibbons replied in part:

> In this country the trade unions have when under proper control, done a great deal towards the uplifting of the skilled workmen. However, in this matter I can speak only in reference to the United States, not knowing the conditions existing in Canada.[51]

Duffy read Gibbons' letter at a mass meeting at Three Rivers, Quebec, in the fall of 1913. He explained the meaning of the word "International" as used by the A. F. of L. and assured the group that his organization was opposed to Socialism and all similar radicalism. While at Three Rivers he tried to see the priests of the district, but they refused to meet him.[52]

Daniel Tobin also asked Dietz if he could "give editorial comment" to the Canadian situation, or correspond with the Cardinals about it. He expressed his confidence in Father Dietz:

> I am sure that your work in behalf of Labor and your en-

deavor to educate Catholics outside of the Labor movement as to the necessity of their cooperating with bona fide trade unions in this country, is a work that will, in time, be beneficial towards removing this prejudice existing now against trade unions in certain districts throughout the world, where some of the priests of the Catholic Church seem not to understand the object of the trade union.[53]

Dietz took up the matter with Cardinal O'Connell and suggested that a conference between representatives of the A. F. of L. and the French Canadian bishops might bring about a better understanding.[54] His first hope was to effect something through a *rapprochement* between the Militia of Christ and the *L'École Sociale Populaire*. But Arthur Saint-Pierre assured Father Dietz that their ideas were different on the matter of organizing Catholic workers—that Canada was executing faithfully the directions of Pius X.[55] Saint-Pierre did, however, send Dietz the names of bishops to whom he should write regarding a conference and the names of the officers of the various Catholic unions.[56]

Dietz wrote also to the Reverend V. Germain of Quebec, Associate Editor of *L'Action Catholique*, official organ of *l'action Sociale Catholique*, suggesting that those at the head of the Catholic labor movement in Canada officially invite the Executive Council of the A. F. of L. to a conference, pointing out that five members of the Council were Catholics.[57]

World War I interrupted further planning, but in 1920, labor was again on the defensive—this time against the open shop campaign of the National Association of Manufacturers. The A. F. of L. was scheduled to meet in Montreal that year, and Dietz, seeing the possibility of trouble, wrote to Samuel Gompers:

> When the A. F. of L. meets in Montreal this year, a local controversy may arise on the 'Christian Trade Union issue.' Bad blood may be stirred and the end far worse than the beginning.
>
> In this matter I may be of some service; I think I could prepare the ground and exert conciliatory influence and secure a peaceful antecedent conference for both parties.
>
> If you see any value in this suggestion and give it your

approval, I will in all matters of prudence be guided entirely by you.[58]

Gompers did not answer this letter, but neither John Voll nor Daniel Tobin thought Father Dietz should become involved in the situation again. Tobin recalled earlier unsuccessful attempts, on the part of Dietz, O'Connell, and Gibbons.[59] However, when Father Dietz went to Montreal to the convention, he carried a letter of recommendation from Archbishop Henry Moeller of Cincinnati, to the Archbishop of Montreal, the Most Reverend Paul Bruchesi. It read in part:

> He wishes to confer with your Grace regarding the purpose of his visit in order not to take any step which might not meet with your hearty approval.
>
> The Reverend Peter Dietz has attended quite a number of Labor Conventions. He is familiar with the various phases of this intricate question and highly respected by many of the prominent Labor Union Leaders. He always endeavors as far as possible to induce the unions to adjust their grievances in accordance with justice and the solid principles laid down by Leo XIII in his famous encyclical.[60]

Dietz was successful in arranging an interview with the Archbishop of Montreal and a committee of the A. F. of L. But, since Quebec was the headquarters of the National Catholic Unions, nothing authoritative for all of Canada could be achieved. Dietz decided to go to Quebec to interview Archbishop Paul Eugene Roy. Bruchesi gave him a letter of introduction to Monsieur l'Abbe Fortin, Chaplain of the National Catholic Unions.[61] The trip was not successful; the Cardinal was in New York, the Archbishop was out confirming, and Father Fortin was in Ottawa.[62] He did visit the headquarters of the National Catholic Unions, however, and was astounded to find a three story building housing various propaganda offices and a complete printing establishment. Despite all of this apparent progress, Dietz felt that the movement was a "misguided one."[63] Since the interview with Archbishop Roy was impossible, Dietz decided to send to the Directors of the N. C. U. a letter to be read at the "Social Week" (*Semaine Sociale*) in Montreal in late June, asking for a conference, near the end of July, 1920, between representatives of the Catholic unions and "five select A. F. of L. men."[64] This letter was never acknowledged and Dietz complained to Archbishop Bruchesi. The latter's Chancellor reported that the Archbishop knew nothing about the letter and regretted the lack of courtesy on the part of the Directors. But he encouraged Father Dietz by adding:

> You know our Archbishop's stand on these questions, and let me tell you, Father, His Grace has only words of praise for you and your Catholic trade-unionists for the manner in which you treated these matters while in Montreal at your Convention.[65]

When the visit to Quebec, as well as the attempted conference with N. C. U. representatives failed to bear fruit, Father Dietz wrote directly to Archbishop Roy, at the suggestion of the Most Reverend Alfred Sinnott, Archbishop of Winnipeg, whom he had met in Washington. Dietz enclosed a copy of the letter he had sent to the *Semaine Sociale,* and told the Archbishop that three representatives of the A. F. of L. had already been chosen to take part in a conference with the Quebec unions.[66] Dietz assured the Archbishop:

> I can vouch for the conciliatory spirit animating our side of the controversy and believe that the Conference will result in permanent good; for, even in the event of a continual disagreement in principle, it will yet be fruitful in correcting some misunderstandings and in establishing perhaps a measure of common ground to the advantage of all of us.[67]

Archbishop Sinnott also named the Most Reverend Oliver E. Matthieu, Archbishop of Regina, Saskatchewan, as an influential go-between with Roy and advised putting the matter before Archbishop Neil McNeil of Toronto as well.[68]

At a conference in Indianapolis Father Dietz and the committee of three decided to wait one month for a response from Roy, and then proceed to Toronto for a conference with McNeil.[69] The letter from Archbishop Roy, written October 11, agreed to a conference on two conditions,

> if, on the one hand the representatives of the American Federation of Labor would participate without discussing the fact of the existence of the National Federation of Catholic Workers of Canada, and if, on the other hand they would make known

what questions they would wish to discuss in the course of the conference.[70]

The letter further explained to Father Dietz that the *Semaine Sociale* and the National Federation of Catholic Workers were two entirely independent organizations which might account, in part, for his failure to receive an answer to his letter. On the basis of the above, Dietz asked Roy for a conference on May 20, 1921, somewhere near Buffalo.[71] But delays on both sides prevented the carrying out of the plan.[72]

About the time the above conference was to have taken place, Father Dietz visited Archbishop McNeil in Toronto and was most cordially received. The latter promised to do two things: he would get out a pamphlet in English giving the facts of the whole situation, and he would try to bring about, in October, a general meeting of the bishops of Canada, with a view to formulating a uniform policy for all Canada in matters pertaining to labor. The Archbishop wanted Dietz to write the pamphlet but the latter believed it would antagonize the opposition unnecessarily. Dietz did agree, however, to write a letter for the Introduction.[73]

During the A. F. of L. convention in Denver a few months later, Tobin, Woll, Duffy, Gompers, and Father Dietz discussed the best way to collect the necessary data for the pamphlet.[74] Later Gompers sent a circular letter to unions with Canadian connections asking for comparative data as between the Federation affiliates and the Catholic unions on wage scales, hours of labor, dues paid, policy regarding "open shop," number of French Canadians in each, and the general effect on the membership of the local unions. He forwarded the results to Archbishop McNeil.[75]

By the fall of 1921 Father Dietz concluded that any hope of unity of action in Canada was useless, since the patriotic and religious factors loomed so large in the province of Quebec. He called Archbishop McNeil's attention to the editorial policy of two papers which he had read carefully for a year. *Devoir* took a political view of the matter, emphasizing the danger to French-Canadian nationalism in being subject to the imperative demands of non-Canadians from beyond the border; *Action Catholique* played up the religious angle, making members of the A. F. of L. a "Godless crowd" incapable of honor, justice, respect for contracts, and the like.[76]

Archbishop McNeil did not favor a conference because he did not believe a sufficiently large representation would come from Montreal or Quebec and, in a lengthy interview with Matthew Woll, he expressed his belief that the only way to influence the attitude of the Church in Montreal and Quebec was to appeal to the Pope.[77] This was not done and the Catholic unions of the Province of Quebec continued to grow in strength, though always remaining numerically few. The efforts of Father Dietz were not entirely lost, however, for ecclesiastics like Archbishops Bruchesi, Sinnott, and McNeil were more sympathetic toward the A. F. of L. as a result of his work in Canada.

During these same years, Father Dietz was interested in the European labor situation, where attempts were being made to federate Catholic workers on an international basis. The movement was an extension on an international scale of the Socialist-Christian struggle taking place in the countries of western Europe. The Catholic social movement began in Europe before the movement in the United States. Names like that of Bishop Wilhelm Von Ketteler, Henry Cardinal Manning, Count Albert de Mun, and Baron von Vogelsang were well known even before *Rerum Novarum* appeared. The establishment of Catholic trade unions was an important part of this social movement.[78]

Aside from the social conditions attendant on industrialism, little similarity existed between conditions of Catholics in Europe and in America. Socialism, atheism, and political oppression necessitated defensive organization, not only among Catholics, but among Protestants as well. As a result, Catholic, Christian, and Socialist-dominated trade unions existed side by side in most of the countries of continental Europe.

Reference has been made to the difficulties in Germany between the Christian and Catholic trade-unions, that called forth Pope Pius X's letter to the German bishops in 1912. The Christian Trade Unions, composed of Catholics and Protestants, began in Germany in 1894 with headquarters at Cologne. From the first they were recognized and supported by the Catholic Workers' Unions (*Arbeiter-vereine*) of south and west Germany, but opposed by the Catholic unions of the east, particularly around Berlin. The Berlin unions objected to them on religious grounds—membership in them would endanger the faith of Catholics.[79] This controversy heatedly involving clergy and laity, so weakened the Christian cause against Socialism that the Holy Father intervened. Although the Pope in his encyclical recognized the Christian or "mixed unions," he ordered Catholics to form their own trade-unions wherever their numbers warranted it.

Also important was the People's Union for Catholic Germany (*Volksverein*) with headquarters at Muenchen-Gladbach. Its Central Bureau distributed much social literature in the form of newspapers, pamphlets, and leaflets. The members of the Volksverein (650,000 in 1910) were an effective bulwark for the Center Party.[80] The Catholic Social Guild of England, begun in 1909, corresponded to the Volksverein in Germany. It supplied the literature for the study clubs of the National Conference of Catholic Trade Unionists, organized about the same time as the Militia of Christ. The sponsor of these Catholic trade-unionists of England was the far-sighted Dr. Louis Charles Casartelli, Bishop of Salford, to whose diocese many of the workingmen of Lancashire belonged.[81]

Through these organizations of Germany, England, and the United States, various leaders, including Father Dietz, planned to organize a Catholic International. Its specific purpose was to counteract the International Federation of Trade Unions whose organization was completed in 1913, with Karl Legien, secretary of the so-called "free" but really Socialist trade unions of Germany, as president. The antecedents of this Federation went back to 1901 to a meeting at Copenhagen of the secretaries of the trade-unions of various European countries. Legien undertook the duties of International Secretary with headquarters at Berlin, though a permanent organization was not established until the Zurich conference in 1913.[82] The A. F. of L. had affiliated with the movement in 1910 and suggested the name International Federation of Trade Unions, adopted in 1913.[83]

The opposition of Karl Legien to Christian and Catholic trade-unions manifested itself in various ways. Invited to the United States in 1912, he toured the industrial centers from Boston to Denver, speaking in behalf of the A. F. of L. He found time also to lecture under the auspices of the Socialist Party, though, at the request of A. F. of L. officials, he did his lecturing for the A. F. of L. first.[84]

From his office in Berlin, Legien edited the *International Newsletter*, in which he used every opportunity to voice his anti-Catholic views. Occasional issues registered "gross cases in which the accomplices of the employers and opponents of modern trades-union movement under the protecting titles of "Christian" and "national" are involved."[85] Two of these "gross cases" were the action of the English Conference of Catholic Trade Unionists regarding an international conference, and the acquiescence in such a conference by the Militia of Christ—"a Catholic and very aggressive combination of trade-unionists in the U. S. A." Regarding the Militia of Christ, Legien said he would be interested to learn "how they reconcile the secessionist efforts . . . with their trade-union principles."[86]

Legien referred in the first case to the following resolution passed by the English Catholic Trade Unionists at the Catholic Congress at Plymouth:

> Resolved, That this Conference declares for the formation of an International Catholic organization, and instructs its standing committee to approach any organization of Catholic Trade Unionists in any part of the world, with the object of securing cooperation for the inclusion therein of an international organization of Catholic Trade Unionists.[87]

Thomas Burns, secretary of the N.C.T.U., sent to Father Dietz the agenda of the Plymouth Conference, writing:

> It seems to me that if you would work for the carrying of a similar resolution in your movement it would hasten the approach of the idea. . . . If you and I regard each other as the respective points of contact for Catholic trade unionism in both countries we might do some good.[88]

In accordance with Burns' suggestion, the Militia of Christ forwarded the following resolution:

> Be it resolved that we extend our sympathy to the English Conference of Catholic Trade Unionists assembled at Plymouth,

we recognize the need of inter-relations for Catholic trade unions, and stand ready to assist in the formation of an international organization and the exchange of fraternal delegates.[89]

Burns corresponded with the organizations of a like nature in each country and planned a conference to be held at Lourdes the next year (1914) during the Eucharistic Congress.[90] The English labor leader wanted only Catholic trade unionists represented in the conference and the proposed International. The Catholic organization would cooperate and assist the Christian Trade Unions, however, through the latter's Catholic members.[91]

For some time Dietz had been corresponding and exchanging literature with Dr. Theodore Brauer, general secretary of the Union of Christian Workers of Germany, and Dr. William Brauns, director of the Central Bureau of the Volksverein at Muenchen-Gladbach. Dr. I. Giesberts, noted member of the Volksverein, had translated material on the Militia of Christ.[92] Father Dietz wished to establish closer relations between the Militia of Christ and the Christian Workers' Union of Germany in order that German emigrants might be prepared beforehand to participate in the American labor movement.[93] Through the increased strength given thereby to the Christian movement, greater influence could be exerted also against the Socialist forces in the international labor organization.[94] Dietz ultimately hoped to align the A. F. of L. with the Christian labor group to offset the Legien group. He therefore believed it imperative that he attend the proposed conference of Catholic workers, and both Burns and Brauer invited him to come.[95] Finances presented a problem for, as secretary of the Social Service Commission, he received only one hundred dollars a month, most of which went to his assistant, Alfred Kliefoth. But a contribution of one hundred dollars from Cardinal O'Connell helped solve this problem.[96]

Prior to the general meeting at Lourdes there were to be preliminary conventions in the different countries: in England at Cardiff, in Germany at Muenster, in Belgium at Antwerp and Ghent, and in France at Lourdes. When he sailed from New York on the *Kronprinzessin Cecilie,* July 4, 1914, Dietz planned to visit all of these meetings.[97]

Unfortunately no detailed record exists of what transpired on this European trip. Only the little information found in letters written in retrospect and a partial report in the *Bulletin* are available. From them one can gather that Father Dietz received a wholehearted and impressive reception from the European Catholic leaders of labor. The Cardiff meeting on July 11, part of a general Catholic Congress, consisted of about forty delegates. Father Dietz was the only priest, save on one occasion when Cardinal Bourne and Cardinal Gasquet visited the meeting. Dietz occupied a seat on the platform, an honor, Burns told him, never given an English priest.[98] In his address to the assembled delegates, he stressed the point that Socialism did not predominate in the American labor movement, and that as fraternal delegate to six conventions, he was in a position to know. Speeches of the fraternal delegates from the British Trade and Labor Congress to the American Federation of Labor, revealed that Socialism did predominate in the English labor movement. Dietz urged them in the future to send delegates who were more representative of real trade-unionism.[99] In his interview with Cardinal Bourne, arranged by Burns, Dietz was impressed with the unaffected strength of the Cardinal, with his thorough understanding of the labor movement in England, and with his hearty sympathy with the progress of the National Conference of Catholic Trade Unionists.[100]

While at Cardiff, Dietz learned that the plans for the international meeting at Lourdes had stalemated, the German and Austrian Catholics objecting to Lourdes because of the distance.[101] Determined to act as go-between to try to effect a compromise, Dietz left England. Interviews with the various labor leaders in Antwerp, Muenchen-Gladbach, and Muenster resulted in an agreement to meet at Geneva, August 8, 1914. England, France, Germany, Austria, Switzerland, Italy, Belgium, Holland, Spain, and the United States promised to send Catholic trade-union delegates.[102]

Just a week before the meeting was to take place, however, the war broke out. Father Dietz was at Lourdes at the time, and was able to exchange enough money to take him to Spain, where he was forced to remain until the United States Government chartered the ship *Infante Isabel* in September.[103]

Thwarted in his first attempt at a world federation of Catholic trade-unionists, Father Dietz immediately began planning for a post-war conference. Knowing well what the war would do in stirring up national suspicions and hatreds, Dietz turned to the one source which he believed could restore the former amicable relations—the Holy See. On Pentecost, 1915, he wrote to Pope Benedict XV, outlining pre-war events, and presenting his plan for the future:

> It is plain, how Christian Charity has a first claim upon the hearts of all Christians, and how after the war the submerged Charity of the nations ought to be immediately raised to the surface and enthroned in the hearts of men.
>
> It would be a striking demonstration to the world if the example of brotherly forgiveness and generosity could be made at the same time to have a direct bearing upon the peace negotiations of the belligerent powers, in order that the agreement of human brotherhood may properly balance the claims of nationalism.
>
> It is also evident, how the problems of modern trade-unionism, with well-developed international tendencies, being the subsoil of democratic futures, will merit special consideration from the Catholic point of view.
>
> I, therefore, humbly petition your Holiness on this day of Pentecost, to call a conference of the officers of all national Catholic federations of the world, to meet at the time and place of the prospective peace negotiations, under the presidency of a delegate a latere from the Holy See.
>
> I am confident that the resumption of the aims of Christian democracy and the future development thereof can be enlivened and quickened in no better way than by the divine power of the living Church, which overcomes frailty, prejudice and animosity deep-seated in human nature.
>
> Prudence, furthermore, would seem to require the necessary consents and adhesions to such a program at the present time, before victory or defeat shall have compromised sentiment or given rise to a resentment in the more unfortunate sections, that may well prove insuperable.[104]

Although the Holy Father did not act on his suggestion, Father

Dietz continued his interest in a Catholic International Conference. As soon as the war was over he reestablished contact with Thomas Burns of England and Dr. Brauer of Germany. To the former he, wrote:

> When you get ready to work on the International again, please ask me to handle it from this end for there is no one of the clergy in this country familiar with the psychology of American labor, since I have been constantly associated with it.[105]

While plans were going forward for a meeting of the Catholic and Christian trade-unionists, the International Federation of Trade Unions met at Amsterdam, July 28 to August 2, 1919. Samuel Gompers and Daniel Tobin represented the A. F. of L. at the meeting. At Amsterdam the old International was dissolved and a new one organized, the International Federation of Trade Unionists, with headquarters at Amsterdam. On several occasions during the conference Gompers and Tobin clashed with Legien and his fellow Socialists. The United States delegation stood alone against a resolution to commit the International Federation of Trade Unionists to an all-out effort toward complete trade-unionism as the "necessary basis for the realization of the socialization of the means of production."[106] Legien scored "any delegate who would vote against the proposals of the committee" as one "in the pay of the capitalistic class."[107] Gompers repudiated "with intense emphasis the imputation" cast upon the A. F. of L. and denounced the attack of Legien as a "mean, contemptible lie."[108] Despite the seeming strength of the Socialists, Karl Legien was defeated for the office of first vice-president, though the Socialist Jan Oudegeest, president of the Dutch Trade Union Center, was elected treasurer. Gompers' nominee, W. A. Appleton of England, was elected president.[109]

Father Dietz was not at all pleased with the outcome of the Amsterdam meeting. By the resolution, supported by Tobin and Gompers, to admit only one trade-union center from a country, he maintained they had excluded all possibility of the Christian Trade Unions becoming members of the I. F. T. U., thereby giving recognition to the anti-Christian unions. "We did this," Tobin explained, "so that the Socialist Party, the I.W.W. and the one big union of our country could not demand recognition from the I.T.U. congress."[110] In a letter to Matthew Woll, secretary of the Committee on International Labor Relations, Dietz made clear his ideas on the International situation:

> If the American Labor movement does not want to isolate itself and get into a wrong rut, it must find and give expresion to an attitude which Christians in Europe can respect in conscience and in public.[111]

To Woll's request for further explanation, Father Dietz replied:

> The Christian trade-union movement in Europe is growing very rapidly. It is conceivable that at some future time . . . the Christian trade-unions . . . will wrest supremacy from the red trade-unions. . . . If the American labor movement at that time should still be committted to its present European arrangements, would it be isolated or not.
>
> The Christian trade-unions of Europe include Protestant as well as Catholic; in fact no one is excluded except Marxian socialists. These Trade Unions historically originate in the vile and brutal policies, attitudes and practices of European socialists. . . . There was only one thing that self-respecting non-socialists could do and that was to organize in self-defense and safeguard what was sacred to them. . . . By every noble human standard save that of expediency, the Christian trade-union movement of Europe has a claim and an appeal to right-thinking movements elsewhere.[112]

For meeting that appeal he suggested proportional representation at international congresses on a trade-union basis, granting as many delegates "pro rata of membership as are now *exclusively* recognized for the neutral (in truthful reality) Socialist trade-unions."[113] There was not parity, he claimed, between the Christian trade-unions and the I.W.W., for the former were "bona fide unions" whereas the I.W.W. was not. As a matter of fact, the Christian trade-unions resembled American Unions more than their antagonists did in that they recognized the rights of capital in principle, while the Socialists did not, and "only on the strength of the principles adhered to by the Christian trade-union movements of Europe can Europe be rebuilt at all."[114] Father Dietz saw that the next great struggle is not going to be so much between capital and labor as between Christian and anti-Christian views of capital and labor.[115]

He described the A. F. of L.'s policy of not permitting religious issues or discussion to enter into its counsels or influence its decisions as "an unhistorical position, and a false position, and a position that cannot be maintained with success. . . . In Europe by shying needlessly at the name of Christ, the A. F. of L. becomes in fact anti-Christian (by default)."[116]

Father Dietz's prediction that the Christian trade union movement would grow, soon proved to be correct. The international meeting of Catholic and Christian trade unionists took place at the Hague on June 16, 1920. Father Dietz was invited to attend and participate. He wrote Bishop Muldoon, now chairman of the Social Action Department of the National Catholic Welfare Council, of his "keen interest" in this meeting, the culmination of efforts begun in 1914 of which he had been "one of the prime movers."[117] Unable to attend because he had no money, Dietz asked Muldoon to send him in the name of the Committee on Social Action, in return for a report of a "character fit for publication in pamphlet form."[118] For some unknown reason he asked that the idea be kept confidential, and in no way brought to the Committee on Social Action.[119] Bishop Muldoon's reply was of the briefest:

> The request you make I cannot grant without referring to the Committee, and as such action is contrary to your wishes, there is nothing to be done.[120]

Both Thomas Burns and Dr. Brauer sent reports of the meeting and of their several conversations about Dietz and his correspondence.[121] Ninety-eight delegates from the Christian and Catholic Trade Unions of Germany, Italy, Holland, Belgium, France, Hungary, Germany, Austria, Spain, Switzerland, Czechoslovakia, and Luxembourg, representing over 3,000,000 members organized the International Federation of Christian Trade Unions. Brauer was chosen vice-president and editor of the Federation's organ, the *International Review*.[122]

Not long after the adjournment of the Amsterdam meeting, the officials of the A. F. of L. questioned the wisdom of continued affiliation with the I. F. T. U. They were alarmed at a manifesto written by Oudegeest in French and given to the press over the signatures of the members of the Bureau, without their knowledge and consent. The manifesto was a veritable call to arms of "Comrades" all over the world to unite against the "reaction" with the common aim of the socialization of the means of production, "not in the sense of government exploitation—, but . . . with joint-management deputies of Labor and consumers."[123] At the Montreal convention the A. F. of L. decided not to recognize the I. F. T. U., since the "political and revolutionary tone" of the organization was not in line with A. F. of L. philosophy.[124]

This turn of events encouraged Dietz to do all he could to prevent future affiliation with the Amsterdam International by effecting a *rapprochement* between the A. F. of L. and the Christian International. Encouraged by the reaction of the Executive Council when he broached this idea to the members at their meeting in Cincinnati in 1921, Dietz thought of bringing Dr. Brauer or someone from the Secretariat to the United States to explain the whole Christian Trade Union movement to the Executive Council and to the A. F. of L. in convention.[125] Brauer agreed to come if his expenses were paid.[126] Father Dietz, totally lacking in financial resources himself, contacted Mr. Kenkel, asking that the Central Bureau sponsor Brauer.[127] The Bureau did not care to cooperate and Dietz reluctantly wrote Dr. Brauer to that effect, expressing the hope, however, that at some future time they could again attempt a meeting.[128] But a year later (1922), when he was forced to close his school in Cincinnati, Dietz withdrew from active participation in the labor movement.

Father Dietz's fears and hopes regarding world labor were later vindicated. In 1945, despite the opposition of the A. F. of L., the International Federation of Trade Unions merged with the newly-organized Communist-dominated World Federation of Trade Unions. When the W. F. T. U. proved to be just another agent for Communism, the C. I. O. and the British Trade Union Congress withdrew from the organization to lend their support to a new movement that was taking shape.[129] This movement culminated in a Free World Labour Conference in London in November, 1949, at which the International Confederation of Free Trade Unions became a reality.

Meanwhile the International Federation of Christian Trade Unions continued to carry out its objectives, holding congresses regularly until World War II interrupted them. After the war the I. F. C. T. U. revived with its program unchanged and celebrated its silver jubilee in 1946 at Amsterdam, the organization's headquarters.[130]

When the Preparatory Committee met at Geneva in June, 1949, to plan the London Conference the question of the I. F. C. T. U. arose. After deliberation the Committee decided to invite the Christian unions "only if no objections were raised by the national trade union centre with whom international contacts are normally maintained."[131] As a consequence only the *Confédération Francaise des Travailleurs Chrétiens* attended, since the trade-union centers of other countries objected to the Christian unions being invited. This procedure was challenged at the opening sessions in London and a reconsideration of the question led to the adoption of a resolution to invite all Christian trade unions

> on the understanding that before the next Congress in two years' time they, along with all other affiliated bodies, accept and give effect to the principle of affiliation to one trade union international.[132]

The General Council of the I. F. C. T. U. meeting in Brussels in April, 1950, finally decided to continue as an independent organization.[133] Offers to cooperate with the I. C. F. T. U. were "flatly refused."[134]

Father Dietz would have applauded the decision of the Christian International and would have appreciated the sympathetic attitude toward the Christian trade unions expressed by members of the A. F. of L. and the C. I. O. at the London Conference. Leaders in both organizations could see in 1950 what the A. F. of L. could not see in 1920, that the Christian trade-unions of Europe as bulwarks against radical influences represented trade-unionism according

94

to the American pattern more truly than did some of the unions admitted without question to the London Conference.

Those who opposed Father Dietz through fear of dual unionism failed to understand that his basic aim was not to split the labor forces by setting up separate Catholic trade-unions but to unite them on a solid foundation of Christian principles. Dietz opposed the separate Catholic trade-unions as they existed in Canada and although he cooperated with the Christian trade unions of Europe he had no intention of setting up a similar pattern in the United States. In his agitation for a Labor Pastoral and Catholic Industrial Conferences, as well as in his personal efforts through his Militia of Christ to influence conventions of the American Federation of Labor, Dietz tried to identify the Catholic Church with the labor movement. The Pastoral, he believed, would clarify and unify divergent Catholic opinion and provide a directive for the support of organized labor.

Chapter Five

Piloting
the Social Service
Commission

AFTER 1910, the American Federation of Catholic Societies provided an ideal medium through which Father Dietz could actualize
his social theories.[1] The Federation, designed primarily for laymen,
had grown from 600,000 members in 1902 to 3,000,000 by 1912,
representing practically every state in the union, as well as Alaska,
Hawaii, Porto Rico, and the Philippines. The nationalities represented had likewise expanded from the original German and Irish
elements to include Italians, Poles, Bohemians and Slovakians.[2] Over
one hundred Councils of the Knights of Columbus had affiliated.

The officers of the Federation, a president, six vice-presidents, a
secretary, a treasurer, a marshal, and a color-bearer, were assisted
by an Executive Board of nine, chosen by the delegates at the annual conventions.[3] This Board, in turn, selected members of the
hierarchy to form an Advisory Board.

The *Bulletin,* official organ of the Federation, published bi-
monthly under the supervision of Anthony Matre, the national secretary, reflected in its early numbers the problems that absorbed the
attention of the members at each convention. Such problems as divorce, intemperance, the immorality of the stage, white slavery, and
the school question, including the question of free textbooks and the
problem of religious women teaching in public schools, found place
on the agenda. Although each convention since 1904 had endorsed
trade-unionism and exhorted its members to study the encyclicals,
the first reference to labor problems or to general economic conditions appeared in the *Bulletin* for July-August, 1909, in the report
of an address by Father Dietz before the Ohio Staatsverband of the

Central Verein.[4]

Father Dietz resumed his association with the Federation when Anthony Matre invited him to report on his Militia of Christ at the Federation's convention at Columbus, Ohio, in 1911. Dietz seized the opportunity to urge the creation of a standing "Committee on Social Reform." In response to his suggestion, the delegates resolved to set up a Social Service Commission. Largely on the advice of Dietz, the secretary of the Commission, the following members were appointed: the Right Reverend Peter J. Muldoon, Bishop of Rockford, chairman, the Reverend John W. Cavanaugh, president of the University of Notre Dame, James Hagerty, professor of Economics at Ohio State University, and Charles I. Denechaud of New Orleans.[5]

Planning of the Commission's program fell largely to Father Dietz, as the following letter from Matre indicated:

> As soon as you have your program outlined let me see a copy of the same before you submit same to the entire committee, and I can about tell you how far our societies are ripe for the matter you will propose in said program. After the program has been accepted by your committee, it should receive the endorsement of the Executive and Advisory Boards and then the work could systematically begin.[6]

Few of the members had any suggestions to offer regarding the work of the Commission. Wrote Father Cavanaugh:

> Bishop Muldoon spent a day or two with me recently and we talked of you and your movement. Neither the Bishop nor myself has a very clear idea of what our committee is to do. I had not heard a word of it until you wrote me about serving on it. I shall be very grateful if you will tell me just exactly what you are thinking of in connection with it.[7]

Professor Hagerty, on the other hand, thought the Commission ought to "thrash out" some of the important developments in "trust control and labor organization," and by learning more about Father Dietz's program "cooperate more enthusiastically" with him.[8] Hagerty was certain

> that the Church ought to take a very important stand on some

of our social and economic questions and . . . the earlier that stand is taken the better it will be.[9]

Moreover, he criticized the haphazard way the Federation conducted its conventions and presented its resolutions to the public. For that reason he hoped their Commission henceforth could guide Federation procedures.[10]

The members of the Social Service Commission met at Notre Dame in their first planning session on February 8, 1912. To the disappointment of Father Dietz, the Militia of Christ was not merged with the Commission, which decided to confine its work to study and writing. The *Bulletin,* issued every month, devoted sixteen columns to a social service section, edited by Father Dietz and replacing his magazine, *Social Service.*

Since Father Dietz had by this time transferred to Milwaukee, the headquarters of the Social Service Commission were located there. Archbishop Messmer released him from all parish duties so that he might devote full time to his office.[12] Messmer promised Dietz "all the moral help and support . . . in private and in public" within his power, but promised nothing in the way of financial help other than to offer Dietz board and lodging at the Chancery and the use of an adjoining hall for meetings.[13] All did not share the Archbishop's confidence in Dietz, however, for, when the Executive Board of the Federation met in March, 1912, to confirm the proposals made at Notre Dame, Nicholas Gonner questioned Father Dietz about his qualifications for secretary of the Commission. Dietz resented the inquiry and replied brusquely that it was a personal question. Messmer took Dietz to task for this attitude and defended Gonner's question as wholly justified. Wrote Messmer:

> You may be very well posted on Trade-Unionism. I do not doubt it for a moment and I most gladly admit your merit in what you have done this far to counteract Socialism and Infidelity in the trade-unions. But you understand as well as I do, that this is not the whole social question and that social service and reform are demanded in many other fields. . . . Now in your work as Editor of the social department of Federation *Bulletin,* you will be called upon to speak, either personally or by your contributors (for whose utterances you are

responsible), on all the questions of social service and reform. This demands an extensive knowledge, not only of the material conditions and relations of the present social life, but also of the philosophical principles, the religious and moral teachings, which are to govern the social convictions upon which every true and beneficial social service and reform must be built.[14]

Messmer assured Dietz, however, that personally he had no misgivings about his ability and based his confidence primarily on the praise others had given the work Dietz had already done.[15]

The Archbishop's confidence was not misplaced. Dietz's concept of the work of the Social Service Commission proved broad and inclusive. Basically his plan was not new—it was similar to the one he had prepared for the Central Verein in 1910,[16] and to the one he had outlined for his Militia of Christ for Social Service in 1911.[17] The Commission offered an opportunity to try it again, with better chance of success since he expected now, the support and backing he had lacked before. Gradually under his leadership the American Federation of Catholic Societies attempted to direct a unified Catholic social movement on national lines.

Realizing from the beginning that the Federation was "heavy and slow" like all large bodies, Dietz tried to build up cooperation through the state and county federations. To facilitate this he and Hagerty compiled a questionnaire based on one Dr. Kerby had prepared, which they called "An Examination of the Social Conscience." Covering the areas of education, justice and charity, public morals, the press, and organization, it was at once suitable as an agenda for local meetings, as a standard for evaluating activities, or as a guide for a report to headquarters.[18] It was this last that particularly interested Dietz, for using this data he could set up a Bureau of Statistics. Discouraged over the returns from the questionnaire (only about ten per cent responded), he recommended that a similar questionnaire be appended to that used in the yearly compilation of the *Catholic Directory*. Through cooperation with diocesan chanceries he could do this with little expense, and the returns "would furnish splendid material for a Catholic Social Year Book."[19] Eventually he hoped to provide a "general social program uniform and official" and thus avoid duplication which meant "extra expense and effort and smaller results."[20] In short, Dietz recommended "a national program and one great national campaign, one headquarters in each state and city, from which social centers or Catholic city halls all social activities would be directed."[21] With practically no secretarial help and limited financially, he set out to actualize this program.

The Commission arranged to integrate its work with that of the Federation, providing a separate Commission program with a mass meeting at night as a part of the annual Convention. The secretary read his report and made recommendations at the business meetings held jointly with the Executive Board during the convention and some time during the year.

At the business meeting in Chicago in February, 1912, the Executive Board instructed the Commission to prepare a program, its first, for the coming Federation convention at Louisville. To obtain ideas for the program Dietz sent out a circular letter which read in part:

> We feel that the best advice on the problem of the industrial relations, would come from men, who in the exercise of their public career are in constant touch with the problem, viz., employers, labor leaders, legislators, social workers, and public spirited men in the professions.
> We will feel very grateful to you for a word of advice. Kindly give a few moments to a brief statement, telling how in your opinion, the Catholic Church could best show her interest in social questions and her love for the laboring classes.[22]

The replies provided a good cross section of opinion. All agreed that the Church should take a stand on the social question, either by coming out openly for trade-unionism, or by working for legislation that would improve the lives of working people, or by providing parish priests who understood the problems of the workingman.[23] Daniel J. Tobin noted that in several sections of the country priests stood on the side of the unjust employers, especially during strikes.[24] John Golden, a union organizer, cited a case in point. Girls were on strike against deplorable conditions in a textile mill. The officials of the company, all Protestants, called in the parish priest and told him that Golden and other labor disturbers induced the girls to strike against

The First Social Institute of the Central Verein

their wills. The priest then talked to the girls, got them to promise not to go on the picket line, and later persuaded a few to return to work. Later, in an interview with Golden, the priest admitted that he did not know the first thing about labor unions.[25] Charles J. Bonaparte saw the need for a "free and incorruptible press" that would submit facts when there had been any "infringement of rights," especially when moral issues were involved. He believed, furthermore, that the Church should be the "conscience-keeper" of all Christians.[26] W. L. Parn, vice-president of the Illinois Central Railroad, wanted a "literal application of the Golden Rule" by trade-unionists and employers alike, especially in the matter of keeping agreements. The unions, Parn believed, ought to select "honest, intelligent and conservative leaders" to offset the "omnipresent first, second, or seventeenth vice-president" who lived high at the expense of the rank and file.[27] Dr. Kerby had only one suggestion to make and that was to put less emphasis and time on the statement of principles while neglecting the

> concrete definition or expression of these principles. . . . Until we can agree on what a minimum wage is, how can we say much about justice in wages? Until we can define concretely what social decency is, what sanitary housing is, no landlord will be effected by our statement of principles of social reform.[28]

The tenor of all the answers agreed with Dr. Kerby that the approach to the social problem must be positive, practical, and definite. On the basis of these replies the Commission prepared the following program for the first general conference, at Louisville in August, 1912:

Social Service . . . . Michael Fanning, President of the Preston Coal Lands Co.
The Unorganized Worker. . . . . Dr. J. E. Hagerty
Socialism vs. Trade Unionism. . . . . Peter Collins
The Catholic Employer. . . . . Nicholas Gonner
Public Opinion and Social Legislation. . . . . Peter McArdle

It was not surprising that the labor question, the chief interest and concern of Father Dietz, should have place on the first program. In a letter to Father Cavanaugh, Bishop Muldoon, the chairman, voiced something of the uncertainty about the reception of this program and the Commission's plans:

I have no idea what they will do for us or to us. I am going to see it out—even if they cut out our program and cut our allowance.[29]

At the business meeting held during the Louisville convention of the Federation, the Commission discussed the question of expanding the literary program by launching a weekly press service. Conveniently meeting at the same time and place were the members of the Catholic Press Association, and to them Bishop Muldoon put the proposition of handling such a service.[30] They agreed to handle it at the rate of one dollar a letter, provided the Commission furnished the material.[31] Since all applicants for the press service agreed to become members of the Catholic Press Association first, the plan served a twofold benefit.[32] About twenty-five Catholic papers contracted for the service, which began January 18, 1913, with the first installment of the *Newsletter*.[33] The number of subscribers soon increased to one hundred and twenty.[34]

The mast-head indicated the nature of the contents:

> Containing a brief summary of important matters, affecting labor and social service, occuring in the religious, fraternal, unionist, industrial, legislative and administrative fields, and such other information that will tend to secure the Christian order of society and to promote industrial peace and prosperity.

A study of the various volumes of the *Newsletter* from this first one to the last one on April 16, 1918, shows how well Dietz fulfilled his editorial responsibility. Though he presented all phases of the social question, the volumes are partial to the labor movement as articles on the following topics signify: A summary of labor legislation (December 5, 1913); the activities of the I. W. W. and the Socialists in general (March 26, 1914; April 7, 1913); reviews of significant books like Commons and Andrews, *Principles of Labor Legislation* (July 24, 1916), and Supreme Court decisions (September 4, 1916). Some complained with F. William Heckenkamp of the too frequent articles on unionism and the A. F. of L. "Not that I disagree with you in principle," he wrote, "but I believe the doses at times are a little too big . . . they don't all get time to soak in on the minds of a good many that we wish to reach."[35] On the whole, however, the first numbers were well received, as Claude Becker, secretary of the Catholic Press

104

Association, reported to Dietz:

> I have heard nothing but satisfactory criticism since the service was started, and noticed a great many of the papers giving the front page to it which is a good sign.[36]

Catholic editors expressed their opinions of the service. Charles Phillips of the San Francisco *Monitor* congratulated Dietz on "the excellent reading material," about which Phillips was making "editorial note" that week.[37] "Your weekly bulletins are great," wrote Charles Zenkert of the Reform Press, ". . . *The Live Issue* is going to assume a more out-and-out Catholic tone, and your weekly bulletin is just the matter we want."[38] Contrariwise, Scannell O'Neil of the *Catholic Citizen,* Milwaukee, thought a "more Catholic tone ought to be given it" so that Catholics would "find it more interesting."[39]

Although Father Dietz appreciated this encouragement he found the *Newsletter* a real burden. Coming out every week, it called for a continuous supply of material which he was sometimes hard put to find. "I haven't a system of correspondents," he wrote Heckenkamp,

> I have written all over the country asking all kinds of people to keep their eyes pealed [sic] for local events that would be of value for this letter, but in all I have not received five letters in spite of all the promises. It would not be so hard to give 'views' but the newspapermen have a dislike for views and want 'news.' . . . It gives me a lot of worry, though I suppose in time progress can be made also in the development of a news-system. If there was a fund of money, it would not be so hard.[40]

The problem of editing the *Newsletter,* however, did not lessen his zeal to add the labor press to its list of subscribers. In February, 1914, Dietz sent a circular letter offering the *Newsletter* on a new basis—twenty-five dollars for fifty-two numbers, or one dollar for each service the editor used.[41] The letter further reminded the subscribers:

> that the Catholic press has a very large share of the burden of preparing the Catholic workers of America for their mission in the secular labor movement of America, which is in these days working up to a crisis.[42]

Needing financial aid for his venture, Father Dietz turned to Father John Noll, Huntington, Indiana (later Bishop of Fort Wayne), editor of *Our Sunday Visitor,* with the following proposition:

> If you could give our Commission $1,000 for this work, I
> will agree to do this: send a weekly *Newsletter* free of all charge
> to all Catholic papers and magazines here and the leading ones
> in Europe in the various languages; to all the labor papers here
> and the principal ones in Europe. . . . This for a period of one
> year.[43]

When Noll agreed to contribute fifty dollars a month to the cause,
Father Dietz extended the news service gratis to some three hundred
labor papers. He wrote to Noll:

> It is hard for me to express how grateful I am to you for your
> generosity in responding to my appeal. . . . I trust that the
> value of the newsletter itself will be the best gratitude that I
> give.[44]

From time to time Dietz solicited from the patrons opinions of his
Newsletter to use as arguments before the Commission and the Executive Board for continuing the press service. Over thirty-five letters
attest the deep appreciation of this particular work. *The New York
Freeman's Journal and Catholic Register* found it to be what was
expected "from as able and earnest a worker in the cause of social
service as we had long known you to be."[45] Matthew J. W. Smith
of the Denver *Register* assured Dietz that, though lack of space prevented his using the letter regularly, "we highly appreciate the fact
that you have us on your mailing list. We have secured some splendid
reading matter through your generosity."[46] The editor of the *Morning Star* of New Orleans praised Father Dietz's

> clear insight into present social conditions which it is impera-
> tive for the Catholic Editor to know. The many problems
> constantly arising would be solved if we only had the trained
> social workers and the money to follow out the remedies you
> suggest.[47]

Father R. H. Tierney, S. J., of *America* wanted the service continued "as it often furnishes us material for comment."[48] The Bene-
dictine Press of Mt. Angel, Oregon, thought the service should be
extended to the daily papers. "You deserve high credit for your noble
and untiring work in behalf of the welfare of the country in general."[49]

Archbishop Glennon appreciated the timeliness of the *Newsletter* and believed that even though Dietz's suggestions were "not adopted now" it was "not improbable that they will be in the not far distant future." "Anyhow," observed Glennon, "the Catholic mind needs stimulants, and your writings are always stimulating. I wish you the greatest success."[50]

One of the most "stimulating" of these articles, "The American Kulturkampf," raised the question of a "Catholic Center Party" in America. Dietz's opening statement was a challenge:

> Our Lord, Jesus Christ made no promise to protect the Catholic Church against the punishment due to human weakness, wanting forethought, and fatalistic resignation to the powers of evil.[51]

He warned against basking blandly in the guarantees of the American Constitution, while failing to realize that

> the Constitution is not unalterably fixed and inviolably sacred. It is not proof against the ravages of time. Popular opinion, current thought and new movements poke around the foundations, and if they crumble, the crime is chargeable to those, who, in negligent leisure lounge under the protecting roof of the American liberties.[52]

Among the "running scores of American Democracy," Dietz listed "indifferentism, atheism, bigotry, capitalism, socialism and most of all secularism, voiced most eloquently by the ominous but all omnipotent silence of the secular press."[53] Proof of these influences he found in "the scheme of education . . . with its state resources and threat to reduce education to a government function"; "the national legislative movement to regulate, control, sterilize and secularize the Catholic Charities"; and divorce legislation that "has ruined unnumbered American homes and promises to vitiate every future marriage and family." Dietz blamed the "social incoherence" of Catholics for these conditions. "What have we done," he queried, "to meet these sinister influences?" Perhaps something in a

> half-hearted organized way, but we have never held out a national movement. . . . We have put our trust in the efficacy of truth but failed to make truth prevail; we have put our

107

trust in the hierarchy and the clergy and forgot that they could lead only at the head of an army; we have pinned our hopes to schools and colleges and failed to place our alumni within the Catholic movement. We expected wonders from the Catholic press and failed to support it; we have built up Catholic societies and we have neutralized their influence through petty jealousies.[54]

As a substitute for this divided and half-hearted effort, Dietz posed the question: "Is the time at hand for an American Center Party?" Certainly "the attempt to outlaw Catholic citizenship" called for a Catholic "organ or mouth piece to voice Catholic demands and to enforce them in the political arena." If not a Center party, at least a Catholic political program was imperative. Basic to such a program Dietz listed the following:

a) Loyalty to American institutions, decentralization of power, state rights.
b) Religious toleration and ecclesiastical freedom for all lawful denominations, Sunday observance, Christian marriage, education, charities, and morality.
c) Social welfare of the Commonwealth; Christian spirit as the mediation between capital and labor, as against socialist class antagonism; the rights of private property; trade unionism; agricultural syndicates; merchant associations; just taxation; a protective tariff; a minimum of legislation.[55]

Only by demanding that the major political parties incorporate these fundamentals into their platform could Catholics hope to prevent the exclusion of religious thought from the life of the nation. The true Catholic citizen

shall stand for no law contrary to divine law, provide cooperation but not union of state and church, defend the necessity of religion for the well-being of the state as a public policy, champion a progressive conservatism and open up to the American Commonwealth the fountains of true Catholic humanity.[56]

Dietz sent copies of this article to some of the bishops. Most of those who responded did not support the idea of a Catholic Center Party, but they approved of much that Dietz had said. Bishop James McFaul preferred to see the objective which Dietz sought accomplished through the American Federation of Catholic Societies properly organized over the whole United States. "Let us all work together for that," he urged. "The pushing forward of the programme you have outlined means the destruction of Federation."[57] Cardinal O'Connell liked the trend of the article, but warned: "Avoid any exaggeration—the thing is evil enough in itself. The movement is in the right direction."[58] Dietz commented on these letters to Bishop Muldoon: "The gist of the thing is that they [bishops] are calling for something which we haven't got and which we must create."[59] This weekly *Newsletter* was the most successful and satisfying of all of Father Dietz's endeavors as secretary of the Social Service Commission.

Father Dietz directed his attention to other phases of the Commission's work. At the semi-annual conference on February 12, 1913, the Commision added a pamphlet series to the journalistic offerings already under way. A circular letter (April 25, 1915) announced a collection of six pamphlets ready for distribution:

> *The Christian Manifesto* by Father Dietz
> *Report of the Social Service Commission Conference*
> *Socialist Science Bankrupt*
> *Right Relations Between Employers and Workers*
>   (Cardinal O'Connell's Pastoral Letter)
> *Why Socialism is Opposed to Trade Unionism*
> *What Shall our Catholic Societies Do?*

Eventually the Commission prepared thirteen pamphlets and amplified this supply with pamphlets from the Catholic Truth Society of London, and the Catholic Social Guild of England. Ambrose Willis of the Catholic Reading Guild of London, whom Dietz invited to address the Second General Conference of the Social Service Commission at Milwaukee on August 11, 1913, demonstrated the effective use and distribution of these.[60] Father Dietz reported that to date the secretary's office had sent out 3,264 pamphlets.[61] By June, 1914, the accumulated literature was sufficient to warrant the opening of a reading room at University Building, 111 Mason Street, Milwaukee, where "books, magazines, reports, and newspapers relating to labor and social reform" were on file. A circular letter to priests asked their cooperation in "creating sentiment" for the project and in helping to finance it.

Meanwhile Father Dietz struggled with the problem of the social service section of the *Bulletin*. He complained that Matre, under whose supervision the *Bulletin* was published, hampered him by not sending the news that came to his office from Federation centers.[62] His suggestion that Matre run for president of the Federation, and that Dietz take his place as national secretary in full charge of publications, came to nothing when Matre disavowed interest in a higher office.[63] Ultimately the Executive Board solved the difficulty by making Dietz responsible for editing the entire *Bulletin,* under the supervision of Heckenkamp.[64] The edition of March, 1914, the work of Father Dietz, appeared in a new format, larger and with the material arranged in sections set off in large black type under the following headings: Education, Social and Industrial Relations, Catholic Charities, Public Morality, and Press and Publicity. Pleased with the first issue, Heckenkamp wrote: "I predict that you will have some very favorable comments on the improved appearance and spicy comments."[65] Against the odds of no funds and few contributors, Dietz edited the *Bulletin* successfully from 1914 through the August issue of 1918.

The financial problem confronting the publication from its beginning offset its editorial success. The several plans to improve its financial status never materialized. One of these was to amalgamate the *Bulletin* with *Our Sunday Visitor*, making Federation news and the social service section parts of that paper.[66] Father Dietz suggested either a Catholic Federation co-operative press or a weekly paper to replace the *Bulletin*. He wrote Bishop Muldoon regarding the latter plan:

> In the chaotic condition in which Federation is as a national issue, this is the only way to jerk it up. But such a paper should have only one responsible editor for coherence and disposition of parts. . . . "The American Commonwealth" would be an appropriate name and better than Bulletin or something equally weak.[67]

In spite of his several responsibilities already noted, Father Dietz found time to share in the work of the Wisconsin Federation of Catholic Societies. He went as a delegate from Milwaukee to its convention at Grand Rapids, Wisconsin, in 1912, and was appointed to the newly formed committee on Charity and Social Service. As state lecturer for the Wisconsin Federation, he was continually on the road. The Knights of Columbus, a member organization of the Federation asked him to tour Wisconsin in the fall of 1912, lecturing on his self-chosen topic, "The Christian Social Manifesto."[68] M. L. Carey, state secretary of the Wisconsin Federation, called on Dietz frequently to organize County Federations or to revive defunct ones. He wrote apologetically:

> I do not feel quite right, in asking you to go out to the different places to organize, because I know that it takes up a lot of your time and you receive no compensation for it. . . . I only wish it were possible to get funds to pay all of your expenses and give you some compensation besides because I know that wherever you address a meeting on Federation, we are sure to have Federation organized.[69]

As a result of these tours over one thousand members were added to the Federation.

Father Dietz's association with the charity and social service work of the Wisconsin Federation led to his appointment by Archbishop Messmer to a committee of nine members set up to discuss plans for the unification of Milwaukee Catholic Charities.[70] The committee decided to federate the existing units in the various parishes first, and with these as nucleus to decide later on a plan of extension. The Archbishop appointed Father Dietz the Director of the proposed federation.[71] At the organizational meeting called in February, 1913, at which six societies were represented, Dietz presented a tentative constitution for discussion and revision. The group agreed to call the new organization the "Milwaukee Conference of Catholic Charities and Social Service," having for its objectives:

> To estabish a common centre for community and co-operation along parish lines; to collect and render centrally accessible all Catholic data bearing on Charity and Social work; to study Social Problems, to promote social reform and to take part in all social betterment activities.[72]

Four standing committees were to implement these objectives: finance;

relief; wages, housing, and health; and legislation.[73] Archbishop Messmer praised the Constitution and appealed to all the clergy of Milwaukee to support and encourage the new organization.[74] After investi-
gating the city's needs along charitable lines, Dietz appointed Miss
Mary Shea to visit all the pastors to acquaint them with the specific kinds of work the Charity Conference hoped to accomplish, such
as developing a registration system, working in the Juvenile Court,
caring for the wants of Catholic wards in public institutions, providing suitable homes for out-of-town working girls, and developing a system of parish visitors for relief work.[75]

Dr. Kerby, secretary of the National Conference of Catholic
Charities, enthusiastically endorsed the new constitution.[76] He asked
Father Dietz to help collect data from Wisconsin for his *National Directory* of Catholic Charities begun in 1910. Dietz sent a circular
letter to forty-eight institutions and societies doing charitable work
in the state, intending to use this data to compile a directory for
the state of Wisconsin before he sent it on to Kerby. When Dr.
Kerby was forced to suspend work on the enterprise in 1915, he
wrote Dietz:

> I recall with distinct gratitude the great help that you so kindly
> gave in sending material for that Directory. It is a duty for me
> to express this appreciation again in spite of the fact that un-
> sparing labor and insistence in the face of indifference, brought
> my work to naught and hindered your co-operation from the
> public recognition which it should have received.[77]

In carrying out the pogram of the Milwaukee Charities and
Conference, Father Dietz met the constantly recurring problem of the
need for a trained personnel able to give systematic and persevering
service. To solve this problem he attempted to organize a group on
a basis similar to the lay community he had planned as a student
at St. Gabriel's—the "Militia (or Apostolate) of the Divine Will."[78]
Unmarried Catholic laymen could live together on a cooperative
basis, and give their leisure time to social and charitable work. They
could be given the necessary training and guidance through study
groups at night. Archbishop Messmer gave Dietz permission to
try out his plan and offered the use of old St. Peter's Chapel for

112

that purpose. Soon a circular letter (May 27, 1913) announced the proposed establishment of this community. The letter stated that, "a Catholic lawyer, a trade-union official, an editor, and a juvenile court probation officer" had agreed to form the nucleus of the new community, in which there would be common prayer, but no vows or obligations save that of devoting their leisure hours to social and charity work. The establishment would be called Brownson House.[79] The identity of the above members remains obscure with the exception of D. J. Scannell O'Neill, the editor, who wrote enthusiastically about securing other members and getting started "even though we have to put up a tent on the lake front and *begin*."[80]

Three of the "prospects" invited to join are known. All of them were converts. One of these, H. Christopher Watts, a former member of the Caldey Community of South Wales, an Anglican group recently come into the Church, had written Father Dietz about securing a position when he came to America. Since Watts had been on the editorial staff of *Pax,* his former community's publication, Dietz referred his letter to O'Neill, who wrote Father Havens Richards, S. J., of *America,* about a position. At the same time O'Neill invited Watts to become a member of the lay community. He proposed that Watts serve as an instructor of junior choirs, since he had studied music and choir directing at Durham University.[81] Although Watts declined the invitation, he praised the movement as a chance for the layman, who is "somewhat at a discount," to show his worth.[82] He expained further to Father Dietz: "It will take me some time to swing round into the normal condition of a Catholic consequent on my waking up to the fake position of the so-called Catholicity of the Anglican Creed."[83] Another possible candidate had been a Protestant minister in Evanston, Illinois. O'Neill selected this gentleman to be cook (if he could cook) and "look after the menage of Brownson House."[84] Dietz invited David Goldstein to become a member. Though he deeply appreciated the invitation, Goldstein did not feel adequate for such a life, having "no virtues in even semiheroic degrees," besides being under "moral obligations" that would prevent his making so serious a decision at that time.[85] The records for this community end at this point. Whether it ever really materialized

113

in Milwaukee is doubtful, but Father Dietz cherished the idea of such an undertaking and tried it later with the girls who attended his American Academy of Christian Democracy, in the White Cross Nurse organization.[86]

An important part of Father Dietz's work in Milwaukee was the revival of the Milwaukee Federation of Catholic Societies. Archbishop Messmer expressed his pleasure at the proposed organization meeting:

> . . . I have always considered it derogatory to the name of Catholicity here, not to have a strong Catholic Federation. . . . I am most anxious that the priests of our city, pastors and assistants, without distinction of nationality, should take an active part in the re-organization of the Catholic Federation.[87]

In the constitution eventually adopted, Father Dietz worked out some of the ideas he wanted to see tried in the national Federation. One of these was the systematic division of work into five committees: education, law and legislation, social and industrial relations, morality, and publicity. The committee on education organized a study club which met every Tuesday evening in the Commission's reading room, and an eight-day Social Institute under the direction of Dr. Charles Bruehl of St. Francis Seminary, assisted by prominent laymen.[88] Such subjects as the basic principles of society, the social function of private property, modern city government, the ideals of Christian culture, and methods of social work were discussed at the meetings, which were open to all.[89] The law and legislation committee voted to send a representative to Madison to report on proposed legislation to be supported or opposed as the facts warranted. For a time this representative was Alfred Kliefoth.[90]

This capable young man, a graduate of the University of Wisconsin, where he studied under John R. Commons and Richard T. Ely, was assistant secretary to Father Dietz for a time in 1914. But soon after Dietz's return from Europe in the fall of that year, personal differences arose over what he believed was Kliefoth's ambition to take over the whole work of the Commission. Furthermore, Father Dietz considered him lacking in the true Catholic outlook, and the two parted.[91]

Meanwhile a revision of the Constitution of the American Federation of Catholic Societies increased the number of members of the Social Service Commission from five to seven.[92] Father Dietz wanted the two new members to represent labor and management and invited Dr. Neill and William Amberg, President of the Amberg Granite Company, and the Amberg File and Index Company, to become members, but both declined.[93] Denis Hayes, John Whalen, and F. William Heckenkamp were subsequently appointed, Heckenkamp replacing Charles Denechaud.[94] In 1915 Father William Bolger, C.S.C., replaced Father Cavanaugh on the Commission.[95]

Successful in securing Denis Hayes as the representative of labor on the Social Service Commission, Father Dietz wanted to bring the labor group further within the orbit of the American Federation of Catholic Societies. Opposition to labor, he believed, came largely from a lack of knowledge on the part of Catholics. Study could dispel some of this opposition, but only through their personal association with labor leaders did he feel that true understanding could be achieved. Frank Duffy, general secretary of the A. F. of L., had commented, in 1911, on the fact that the approaching convention of the American Federation of Catholic Societies in Columbus would have a great "outlay of hierarchy and priests, the governor of Ohio and the Mayor of Columbus," but he failed to find any representative of labor "called upon or mentioned in any manner to speak for the wage worker" despite the fact that the membership of the societies represented there included "at least 90 per cent of wage earners."[96] Dietz wanted to correct this very situation. The questionnaire sent out before the first conference of the Social Service Commission which solicited the opinion of labor leaders has already been noted. Subsequent programs of the Commission included labor leaders, as, for example, that of the Second Conference at Milwaukee, in 1913, when Frank Duffy addressed the assembly on "Apprenticeship and Industrial Education."[97]

Father Dietz again sought the opinion of labor leaders when the question of Catholic immigration was being considered as part of the agenda for the Toledo convention in 1915. From its beginning, the American Federation of Catholic Societies had concerned itself with the care of the immigrant. Since the bulk of the so-called "new immigration" from southern and eastern Europe was Catholic, the question was particularly vital. These immigrants were for the most part unskilled laborers and easy victims of unscrupulous employers. Because of its effect on labor standards, the A. F. of L. had long agitated for restriction of this type of immigration. From 1897 to 1917 attempts to put through Congress a law which would restrict immigrants on the basis of illiteracy failed. President Cleveland vetoed such a bill in 1897, Taft vetoed one in 1913, and Wilson vetoed one in 1915 and another in 1917. The last bill, however, was passed over his veto. A conference on immigration, therefore, was especially timely in 1915. Dietz hoped for a two-fold result from this discussion at Toledo: the consideration of plans for caring for those immigrants already admitted, and the formulation of a policy regarding future immigration.

Letters of prominent labor men indicated the desirability of such a uniform policy. Both Frank Duffy and James O'Connell noted the division of opinion among Catholics on the important question of restricted immigration. "There should be a general understanding . . . on this all important question," wrote Duffy, "otherwise we will be looked upon as not knowing what we want and will be the laughing stock of the country."[98] O'Connell, on the other hand, did not favor a conference at that time, believing the feeling among A. F. of L. officials "a little too bitter."[99] William Green, then secretary-treasurer of the United Mine Workers, considered it the "duty of every organization to deal with and to help . . . solve the immigration problem."[100] Denis Hayes feared that the Federation might adopt a policy running counter to that of the A. F. of L., but if a conference were held, he asked that O'Connell, Morrison, and himself be invited.[101]

A conference on immigration took place at the Toledo convention of the American Federation of Catholic Societies in 1915, but the Executive Board put the program arrangements in charge of Hagerty and Father Bolger.[102] The first part of the program conformed to Father Dietz's idea. Father Frederick Siedenberg, S. J., gave a general survey of immigration, stressing the need of scientific

116

social work, "especially work of a preventative kind" in "our immigrant parishes."[103] Charles Fay of Boston pointed out the difficulties and dangers faced by Catholic immigrants, and Father Francis C. Kelly discussed what the Church had done and might do for the immigrants.[104] But there was no resolution regarding a policy on restriction or non-restriction of immigration.

Shortly after the convention, Matre sent Dietz an article for the *Bulletin* in which he stated that Federation had always opposed the Burnett bill, which made the literacy test a requisite for admission into the United States. "When," asked Dietz, "did the American Federation of Catholic Societies formally determine its policy by vote?"[105] While awaiting Matre's reply, Dietz asked Father John A. Ryan's opinion as to whether the literacy test was so "un-American and un-patriotic that it must be opposed by all Catholic societies."[106] "I have been striving for several years," he wrote Ryan, "to keep Federation from committing itself to the policy of unrestriction and have been severely attacked for it repeatedly."[107] Ryan sent Dietz the notes of a lecture he had given on immigration. "You will see," he wrote, "that I am in favor of the Burnett bill. Catholics who oppose the literacy test on the assumption that it is promoted solely by racial and religious bigots simply do not know the facts."[108] Dietz used the notes for his *Newsletter* of April 3, 1916. A few days later Matre informed him that the Executive Board had gone on record in 1914 against the Burnett bill and had sent a letter to President Wilson asking him to veto the bill.[109] Dietz sent Matre's letter to Ryan with the query: "How shall I be able to meet this criticism at the coming meeting of the Executive Board?"[110] "It seems to me," Ryan replied, "if you succeed in preventing Federation from taking any positive action on the immigration question, you will have done all that can be expected in the circumstances."[111] He told Dietz that Frank Morrison had called him to say how pleased he was with the *Newsletter* on the subject. "I do not find fault with any man for opposing the bill," Ryan concluded. "What I object to is the refusal of some Catholics even to *consider* the objective and economic phases of it."[112]

One of the ways in which Father Dietz tried to foster closer association with labor was through national Catholic celebration of Labor Day. He had encouraged such a celebration as part of the Militia program of the Milwaukee Chapter, and also in a circular letter in 1914 to the "special friends of Catholic Federation." Early in 1915 he wrote Bishop Muldoon:

> I am contemplating a brief guide for a Catholic celebration of labor day. . . . The object of this guide is to bring about as far as Federation can, a universal Catholic Labor Day observance in America.[113]

The other members of the Commission—Father Cavanaugh, Heckenkamp, and Denis Hayes—also approved the idea.[114] According to Father Dietz's plan, a Labor Day committee in each city would interest the pastor, agree on a program, and publish it with a union label. The day's celebration would open with Solemn High Mass and a sermon, preferably at one church in a city, to which Catholic societies, trade-unionists, and city officials would be invited. In the event of a parade scheduled for the morning of Labor Day, necessitating the Mass at too early an hour, solemn Vespers could be substituted either on the eve of Labor Day or in the evening of the day itself. If possible, Dietz urged the "gratis distribution" of a pamphlet to the workers who attended the services, and of another appropriate one to the bishops and priests. To heighten the *esprit de corps* he suggested the singing of "God Bless the Worker." Dietz wrote the words to this song and used it first at the Labor Day service at St. John's Cathedral, Milwaukee, in 1913.[115]

The high point of Father Dietz's attempt to bring the American Federation of Catholic Societies and the American Federation of Labor into closer association centered in the Memorial presented to the Executive Board of the A. F. of L. in January, 1915. The Memorial pointed out that in the five years of "fraternal relationship" between the American Federation of Catholic Societies and the American Federation of Labor, the latter had been "fairly and consistently interpreted to the American Catholic public and to the Catholic movements in Canada and Europe." After calling attention to the various agencies through which "the Catholic Federation has been the ardent advocate of trade-unionism, subject only to the modification of Catholic thought," the document alluded to the recent criticism of the "fraternal delegateship"—a fact raising "the very proper question how it might be possible to make the relation more vital, definite and progressive."[116]

The two groups, the Memorialists asserted, were interested in the labor movement. Like the American Federation of Labor, the American Federation of Catholic Societies aimed to better the material, intellectual and moral interests of the American workingman, the difference being that the one stressed the material, the other the religious, aspects of the worker's welfare. This meant that there could be complete agreement on wage and other policies "resulting from the principle that the state should not do for associations and unions what they ought to do for themselves without state aid." On some points, notably industrial education "without discrimination against the parochial school system," the two organizations should be able to compromise their interests. But so far as the Catholic Church was concerned, no compromise was possible "on policies that would adopt fundamental tenets of Marxism, prohibition by legislation, or any other proposition socially unsound." On the assumption that the American Federation of Labor accepted these views, Dietz proposed that the two bodies set up joint committees to work out specific measures respecting strikes, industrial education, social service and related matters. Father Cavanaugh praised the memorial as an "admirable document . . . full of good faith and kindly intention."[117] Denis Hayes thought it was "excellent."[118] But at least one labor leader had "no use for it." Frank Duffy demanded of Dietz:

> What have you ever done for the American Federation of Labor? I fail to see what good you have accomplished. On the contrary through your actions in the past . . . you have caused ill feeling on account of injecting religion into the movement when no one's religion or religious beliefs were interfered with in any manner, shape or form or referred to at any time.[119]

Samuel Gompers gave the Memorial every consideration. Copies were made for each member of the Board, who had ample time to study it thoroughly. Finally, in an eight page reply, he analyzed and criticized the document. Gompers assured Father Dietz:

> All you have done, all that your Commission has done in furtherance of the great underlying principles and high ideals for which the American Federation of Labor stands, are fully appreciated.[120]

But he could not see how the American Federation of Labor could enter into the agreement suggested in the Memorial.

> The very fact as you point out that the aim of the American Federation of Catholic Societies is primarily concerned with religion, is in itself a bar to the American Federation of Labor to enter into such an agreement with a religious body as you propose.

Gompers agreed, however, that there was much

> common ground for cooperation but we submit that that cooperation can best be furthered by each body pursuing its own course, free to dissent from any matter upon which in the judgment of each body freedom of expression and action may be necessary.

He hoped, in conclusion, that the American Labor movement as represented by the A. F. of L. would be "left free from the influences, policies, and tactics which have to their great detriment divided the workers in several other countries." This was not what Dietz had hoped for, but he wrote optimistically to Frank Morrison:

> While the communication as it seems to me personally may appear a disappointment to some, I feel on the other hand that it is carried by so much good-will as to leave room for the future development of more amicable relations.
> What I am particularly pleased about is the fact that it gives us two official documents that may be studied, one in the light of the other. This is an evolution of order from chaos.[121]

Gompers' refusal to enter into a formal agreement with the American Federation of Catholic Societies had no effect on the friendly relationship existing between Dietz and the labor leaders.

Father Dietz's work in the field of social service merited recognition from leaders in non-Catholic social reform agencies, and they sought his cooperation. Ever alert to any anti-Catholic bias in their principles or methods, Dietz was quick to call their attention to it. On the local scene in Milwaukee he served on the executive committee of the Central Council of Philanthropies of Milwaukee and the cooperating committee of the Milwaukee Social Service Institute. The extension Division of the University of Wisconsin carried on the latter. The secretary, J. L. Gillen, asked Father Dietz for "a more immediate and personal interest" in the sessions of the Institute, complaining of the small attendance.[122] Dietz pointed out that, since the Institute was held during Lent, fewer Catholics would attend. He also took exception to the prejudiced tone of some of the speakers, particularly one who spoke at a meeting at which Dietz had presided.[123] The secretary apologized profusely.[124] Through his association with this Institute, Father Dietz was later (1916) named a member of the State Conference of Charities and Correction.[125]

Collaboration with the Federal Council of the Churches of Christ in America began in 1911 when Father Dietz took exception to a statement of the Reverend Charles I. Macfarland, to the effect that the "church should not entangle itself in the economic machinery of trade-unionism." Dietz sensed a reference to the Catholic Church, although Macfarland disavowed any thought of "Roman Catholicism as such" when he made the statement.[126] Macfarland asked Dietz to cooperate in a campaign for legislation providing for "one day in seven for industrial workers." A sort of self-appointed committee consisting of Macfarland, John B. Andrews, secretary of the American Association of Labor Legislation, John Fitch of the *Survey,* and Father Dietz sponsored the introduction of such bills into the legislatures of Georgia, Kentucky, Louisiana, Maryland, Massachusetts, Mississippi, New Jersey, New York, Rhode Island, South Carolina, Vermont, Virgina, Arizona, and New Mexico. Propaganda committees in each of these states, representing the Protestant and Catholic Church and labor, were to introduce the bills. The committee asked Father Dietz to appoint a priest in each state to work on these committees.[127]

Two years later Father Dietz asked the Federal Council of Churches to cooperate with him in a campaign against the *Menace.* While attending the convention of the American Association for Industrial Education, in Richmond, Virginia, where the Federal Council of Churches was also holding a convention, Dietz and some of the leading Knights of Columbus drew up the following resolution and presented it to Macfarland for adoption by the convention:

> Whereas it is understood to be one of the principal purposes of the Federal Council of the Churches of Christ in America to promote concord and good will amongst the various denominations of Christians, and,
> Whereas this meeting of the Council desires to again affirm its position in this regard, it is hereby:
> Resolved: That the Federal Council of the Churches of Christ in America in meeting assembled does not sympathize with the methods employed by a certain publication known as 'The Menace' and like publications in slandering and abusing one of the most prominent Christian Churches in America.[128]

Macfarland reported later that the resolution was part of the unfinished business of the convention.[129] While he was sure most of the ministers were not in sympathy with the *Menace,* he knew they were not in favor of excluding it from the mails.[130] Father Dietz did not forget this, and, when Harry F. Ward, secretary of the Methodist Federation for Social Service, asked his aid in revising the *Year Book* of the Church and Social Service, Dietz made comment:

> It is too difficult for Catholic pride to cooperate until the veiled and sometimes open hostility of the Federal Council of Churches of Christ toward the Catholic Church, shall have been, by the correcting influence of History, sublimated entirely into thin air.[131]

Nevertheless, he made the requested changes for the *Year Book.*[132]

Seth Low, president of the National Civic Federation, invited Father Dietz to become a member of an Advisory Council to aid in a national survey undertaken by the Industrial Economics Department of the Federation. Invited to take part were the leaders of the world of labor, agriculture, and manufacturing; representatives of the press, church, colleges, finance, law, and medicine, as well as officials of national organizations familiar with many of the specific problems covered by the inquiry.[133] There were eighty-eight members in all on the Council, including Drs. Kerby, Neill, Conde Pallen, and

Father John A. Ryan. During the course of his work with the National Civic Federation, Dietz served on a committee on Child Labor and on one on the Church's Influence on Social and Economic Progress.[134] Governor Philipp of Wisconsin appointed Dietz, a member of the National Child Labor Committee since 1912, to represent the state at the Eleventh National Conference in San Francisco in 1915. Because of "academic work" Dietz could not go, but he did attend the Asheville conference the next year.[135]

From 1914 to 1916 Father Dietz participated in the work of the National Municipal League, the National Economic League, and the American Institute of Social Service.[136] Serving with him on the National Council of the second organization were such well known men as David Starr Jordan, Louis D. Brandeis, Charles J. Bonaparte, Charles P. Neill, and Franklin K. Lane.[137]

Graham Taylor, associate editor of the *Survey* and president of the Chicago School of Civics and Philanthropy, especially appreciated the importance of Father Dietz in the field of Social Service. Taylor was helpful in acquainting Pauline Martin with the work of his school. She had come from Oberlin, Ohio, to be Father Dietz's secretary. Taylor waived tuition charges and permitted her to live at the Commons for a nominal sum.[138] Under his guidance she went with one of the workers to visit the Juvenile Protective Agency, the Juvenile Court of Cook County, and other public and private agencies. [139] Father Dietz visited Chicago Commons while Miss Martin was there and reported his reactions to Bishop Muldoon:

> I felt somewhat 'creepy' in seeing the crowds of Catholic children hanging around—some at sewing classes, others in the nursery, some in the gymnasium, etc. There is a big dispensary also on the premises; mothers came with their babes and every single one of them appeared to belong to us.[140]

When Taylor opened a new department in the *Survey,* in 1912 the "Church in Social Action," he asked Dietz to provide data on the Social Service Commission and the Militia of Christ.[141] These two, he believed, together with the National Conference of Catholic Charities, "mark a new advance in social service in the American Catholic Church."[142] Taylor was especially impressed with the Commission's program at the Louisville convention of the American Federation of Catholic Societies in 1912 and considered "significant . . . in the rapidly developing social service of the Roman Catholic Church" the resolutions passed by the Federation, which he quoted in full.[143] The resolutions made no mention of Socialism, but reiterated the reforms recommended in *Rerum Novarum*, pointing out that "the conditions which have called for the Encyclicals . . . remain to this day a menace to the Church and to society."[144] A final resolution urged that "all . . . affiliated organizations become vital centers for the extension of the program of the Social Service Commission . . . and coordinate all their various endeavors through the national office of the Social Service Commission."[145]

Believing the national secretary of the Social Service Commission to be the official spokesman for all Catholic societies, Taylor frequently turned to Father Dietz for information, as when he wanted to know the Church's program "for training of children and youth for civil and social responsibilities."[146] Taylor likewise quoted from the *Bulletin* Dietz's article on the copper miners' strike in Upper Michigan.[147] Finally, in 1915, he asked Father Dietz to become a regular correspondent for the *Survey*. He wrote:

> Your constant contact with your own Church press and personnel will enable you more readily than any one else to select and more or less edit such references to events, measures and opinions of special social significance which fall under your observation within your Church.[148]

Dietz agreed to keep the matter in mind and send notes occasionally that might prove of interest to readers of the *Survey*.[149]

These instances are sufficient to show the impression Father Dietz was making on groups of non-Catholics who were interested in social reform. His broad interpretation of his duties as secretary of the Social Service Commission—editing, lecturing, organizing, planning convention programs, and attending conventions, especially those of the A. F. of L. — made him a public figure.

In the diversity of his interests, however, Father Dietz never lost sight of his goal: an integrated program of social reform on national lines.

Chapter Six

Striving to Coordinate
Catholic Social Activity
–Victory in Defeat

IF COOPERATION WITH non-Catholic associations was an important phase of the Catholic social movement, Dietz contended, of much greater significance, he believed, was the unification of all Catholic agencies for social reform. Only through unification of effort could the member organizations of the American Federation of Catholic Societies avoid wasteful duplication. The office of the national secretary of the Social Service Commission was the logical clearing house for Federation affairs, Dietz believed. But his effort to win that recognition only partially succeeded. That non-Catholics appreciated him as one of the official spokesmen of Catholic social action has already been noted. Similar recognition came from the Reverend Charles Plater, S. J., one of the founders of the Catholic Social Guild of England, who wrote, at the suggestion of Father John A. Ryan, asking information on "the clergy in social action in America."[1] Besides inquiring about work being done on problems of temperance, housing, poverty, and the like, Father Plater asked:

> Have the bishops encouraged the clergy to take up social study and action? Do the priests discuss these things among themselves? What suggestions have you as to the extension of the social action of the clergy?[2]

Unfortunately copies of the "illuminating letter and report" that Father Dietz sent are not among his papers, but Father Plater gratefully acknowledged their value and used the information in the Guild's *Year Book* and as part of a chapter in his book, *The Priest and*

125

Social Action. Mrs. V. M. Crawford, secretary of the Guild, also asked the help of Father Dietz:

> I have put together as best I can the Chapter on the social work of the clergy in the United States for my book in the 'Westminster Series' and enclose the result. Now I know you are overwhelmed with work . . . but *please* continue to find time to look through this Chapter . . . make necessary corrections and also what additions occur to you. . . . My Chapter is very thin and scrappy and you may be able to strengthen it.[4]

The publications of the Social Guild, the Volksverein, and the European labor papers secured through Dr. Brauer were available in the Social Service reading room through exchanges with the *Bulletin*.[5]

Interest in the Church in Latin America led Father Dietz to attempt to offset by a Pan-American Federation the Pan-Protestant Conference scheduled to meet in Panama in 1915.[6] He asked Father L. Guillen, S. J., editor of the *Revista Catholica* of Las Vegas, for a list of Spanish-American papers to which he could send the press service, and for the names of prominent Catholic laymen of Central and South America who would be interested in such a Federation. Dietz wrote:

> There should be a closer union between the Catholics of this country and of Spanish-America and I believe if such a union had existed in the past and been properly developed the Mexican revolution would not have occurred, or at least it would have less virulence.[7]

Nothing further developed, apparently. Father Guillen sent the names of the papers but he was not able to furnish a list of Catholic lay leaders. Nevertheless he agreed with Dietz that there was

> a real necessity of strengthening the union between the Catholics of this country and those of Central and South America, in order to lessen the effects of the prejudices and calumnies so widely spread against them.[8]

He offered his help "in any way possible."

In this country the organization nearest in purpose to that of the Social Service Commission was the Committee on Social Propaganda of the German Catholic Central Verein. When the Social

Service Commission organized its program Bishop Muldoon approached Mr. Kenkel on the question of collaboration. The latter agreed that "harmonious cooperation along certain lines" could not but "redound to the benefit of all," and he presented the following proposition:

> 1. Both committees are to report one to the other any important step to be undertaken, so that each may be informed beforehand in case one should desire to participate in the work of the other.
> 2. As occasions arise, the chairmen of both commissions shall meet to discuss the problem and actions their committees are interested in, contemplating or executing.
> 3. If at any time it is deemed advisable for both committees to meet for an exchange of views or for the purpose of arriving at an understanding towards harmonious cooperation, such a combined session of the committees shall be held.[9]

Other members of the Social Service Commission agreed to the advisability of cooperation but, like Father Cavanaugh, would let "time and experience" determine how far it was "wise to carry this co-operation in concrete work."[10] Both Hagerty and Cavanaugh opposed anything like compulsion in the first proposition, but agreed that if the chairmen wanted to cooperate there was no reason why they should not do so.[11]

Harmonious cooperation between the Central Bureau and the Social Service Commission was not achieved to any extent. Heckenkamp reported receiving "several abusive and insulting letters" from the president of the Illinois Staatsverband because of a letter the Federation campaign committee sent to the clergy of the state asking for the names of societies in their parishes.[12] Later the Illinois Staatsverband revised its constitution, changed the name to the Catholic Union of Illinois, and admitted "mixed" societies as well as German ones.[13] Opposition and rivalry were evident, too, between the Milwaukee Federation and the Catholic Social Union of the Milwaukee *Districts-Verband*. The Catholic Social Union resented any attempt to increase Federation membership.[14] Hoping to clarify the situation, Dietz expressed his views on the relationship that he thought should exist between the Central Verein and the American

Federation of Catholic Societies:

> There is room for a German Federation, wherever there are a sufficient number of German societies to warrant it. The German Federation will want, first of all, to cultivate specific racial traits and national virtues that are undoubtedly an asset to Americanism; it will want to guide in its own way the process of German Americanization; it will want its own study clubs and speakers, its own charities and social works, its own literature and press. This is a necessary and laudable program. . . .
>
> It is apparent, however, that when it comes to the larger educational, social, legislative and civic problems, which are national and American in their very nature, it will be necessary to speak only after consultation with all other Catholic interests and then only in the name of combined Catholic influence.
>
> Far from hurting their own name and influence, German Catholics will add lustre to them and at the same time, prove themselves, to be, as is right and proper, German-Americans and not American Germans. . . .[15]

Kliefoth read this paper at a joint meeting of a committee from the Milwaukee Federation and the Catholic Social Union. Instead of resolving their differences, however, Father August Salick claimed that Father Dietz had insulted them, for C. S. U. was not a German Federation but an American Federation of Catholic Societies, and as American as the members of the regular Federation. They were therefore "equal and coordinate, not inferior and subordinate" as Dietz implied.[16] This local dispute was not successfully settled, even though Archbishop Messmer intervened.[17]

When World War I began, Dietz warned Joseph Frey, president of Central Verein, on the importance of cooperation:

> I believe in the contribution that German American Catholicism has to make to the cause of religion and patriotism in America. But I would emphasize this influence in and through non-German avenues, quite as much as race solidarity. . . .
>
> The greatest danger . . . that could come to the German American Catholics, would be that of self-isolation. . . .[18]

There was no thought of amalgamation; Dietz would not want a "single German American society to go out of existence," but he

128

maintained "that the influence and power of the Central Verein can make itself felt more effectively through the Federation, at least in all the great national problems."[19] Dietz wrote Kenkel:

> It seems to me, that your bureau and our Commission could evolve a common plan of action and perhaps have offices and even the eventual school in common.
>
> The good example of the Germans and Irish in true Catholic American harmony is necessary to have the determining influence on all other nationalities in America, whose affederation we need so badly in the affairs of the nation, and in the interests of the soul.[20]

Several years later (1921) Father Dietz offered his American Academy of Christian Democracy in Cincinnati as a site for the Ketteler School, if the Central Verein would pay the salary of Dr. Charles Bruehl, who would be responsible for the courses.[21] The Committee on Social Propaganda did not think it advisable to accept, though one member wrote that he could not "but be in sympathy with the laudable work accomplished by Father Dietz in Cincinnati."[22]

The program for the Baltimore convention in 1914 attempted to further the unification of Catholic social endeavor. Dietz took his "cue" from the Common Cause Society and the Eunomic League.[23] These societies thought there ought to be some "getting together of the varied Catholic forces." In response to a circular letter Dietz sent out, the following reported on the activities of their organization:

Father Siedenberg, S. J. for Loyola School of Social Science
August Brockland for Central Verein
Father Edward Garesche, S. J. for the Sodality
Martha Moore Avery for the Boston School of Political
 Economy
David Goldstein for the Common Cause Society
Father John de Ville for the Catholic Colonization
 Society of Chicago
John Judge for the Laymen's League for Retreats and
 Social Studies
Alfred Kliefoth for the Catholic Students' Association
 of America.[24]

In the ensuing discussion all agreed that something needed to be done to increase cooperation among their societies, at least to provide a channel by which each might know what the others were doing.[25] But such coordination still remained to be done two years later when Dietz wrote:

> One of the greatest wants in Catholic association work is accurate and authentic knowledge of itself. One branch does not know what the other is doing. . . . When delegates register for conventions it should be possible to hand them a directory of the National Federation and its affiliated branches . . .
>
> Much of Federation success is due to the enterprise and initiative of local Federationists; men who have realized the need for a certain kind of action and have not hesitated to act alone or in union with others. Something has been accomplished. It would be of interest to all like-minded men. . . . A system of reporting must be adopted through which local Federation comes to county; county to state, state to national.[26]

Assembled at Baltimore also were some thirty delegates, representing over ten fraternal insurance societies.[27] F. William Heckenkamp, president of the Western Catholic Union, suggested such a conference, believing that the question of life insurance clearly belonged to the social reform movement.[28] Many of these Catholic fraternal societies, he pointed out, had got off to a wrong start in that they were not organized by experienced or practical insurance men. If the Social Service Commission could map out for these societies a plan for a cooperative system that would be "bullet proof from a business standpoint," it would be doing a great service.[29] Besides increasing security for families at time of death, these fraternal societies, Heckenkamp pointed out, would also be a "vehicle" for uniting Catholic men and women.[30]

With the information supplied by Heckenkamp, Dietz prepared a circular letter suggesting for consideration at the proposed meeting in Baltimore the following six points: fraternal life insurance for children; competition between fraternal and old line insurance; readjustment of rates; legislation and fraternal insurance; the Church and fraternal insurance; the true prosperity of Catholic fraternal insurance societies.[31] Bishop Muldoon presided at the conference and called upon Father Dietz to give the keynote address.[32] Dietz pointed out the timeliness of the meeting since the American Association on Labor Legislation was preparing the draft of a bill embracing every kind of state social insurance, which would be presented shortly to forty-one legislatures.[33] Reminding the delegates of Leo XIII's warning not to let the state do what they themselves could do, Dietz proposed a discussion of the feasibility of adding to their present plan of life insurance old age insurance, children's insurance, and insurance against sickness and unemployment.[34] He questioned further:

> Could the fraternal insurance societies represented here agree upon some program in defending and strengthening their position either by the defeat of proposed adverse legislation or the advocacy of measures advantageous to them?[35]

Gertrude Beeks, director of the Welfare Department of the National Civic Federation, also addressed the group on the constructive phases of social insurance.[36] In the general discussion following these talks, the majority indicated disapproval of amalgamation, but deemed closer cooperation necessary. Accordingly, a committee comprising Bishop Muldoon, Father Dietz, and one representative from each society, was instructed to formulate a plan for a Catholic Fraternal Congress.[37] At the next convention in Toledo the Congress met again and Dietz recommended in his Secretary's Report that the Catholic Fraternal Congress be made a permanent part of future Federation conventions.[38]

For some time Dietz and other leaders in the American Federation of Catholic Societies had seen the need of federating the various organizations of Catholic women. The Columbus convention in 1911 appointed a committee of five women which reported on the question at Louisville the next year.[39] The committee opposed such a federation if it meant separation from the men's organization. Archbishop Messmer then proposed the formation of a National League of Catholic Women of the United States, which would be affiliated with the American Federation of Catholic Societies.[40] Following his suggestion, the women of Louisiana, Pennsylvania, and other states organized State Leagues of Catholic Women. Father Dietz guided the organization of one in Wisconsin.[41] By 1913, when the Federation met in convention at Milwaukee there were enough delegates from women's organizations to warrant discussion of a National Federation. At the close of a three day session, addressed by Archbishop Messmer, Bishop McFaul, and others, the women decided to postpone organization for one year, during which time Archbishop Messmer and Bishop Muldoon were to take charge of "preparing the way."[42]

Two years later, at Toledo, forty-two women delegates, with Dietz as chairman, made tentative plans for a women's section of the American Federation of Catholic Societies. Dietz appointed a committee of seven to prepare a program for the convention in New York the following year (1916).[43] With Helen Haney, chairman of the Women's Catholic Club of Randolph, Massachusetts, as chairman, this committee, with the aid of Dietz, drew up a petition for affiliation which Miss Haney and Sarah Conboy, international secretary of the United Textile Workers, presented to the Executive Board at the New York convention.[44] The Board subsequently passed the following motion:

> Owing to the wide scope of work connected with the women in the Federation and the many plans and great work that might be accomplished by a women's section, we respectfully ask the endorsement and cooperation of this Executive Board of the American Federation of Catholic Societies to the forming of a section of women as a unit in Federation.[45]

The women also requested space in the *Bulletin* for a "Woman's Department," and a lecture service to further the objectives of the new department. Pleased with the outcome of his efforts, Dietz devoted a *Newsletter* to the new movement. But he was taken to task by Muldoon and Matre for associating his school with the Federation in the concluding paragraph of his article, which read:

> To further the object of the Women's Department, a special social service course on practical organization work for women has been arranged at the American Academy of Christian Democracy to begin September 29.[46]

Bishop Muldoon's letter warned him:

> I cannot help the condition or situation, but it is in the air and and you must be careful not to associate the two even by implication. I realize to the fullest your missionary spirit in this regard, but that does not count in some quarters and you are

only building up distrust. You must treat the school in *Bulletin* and elsewhere as absolutely distinct. If you do not I am afraid that some action distasteful may be taken by the Executive Committee at its next meeting.[47]

Bishop Muldoon was aware that the problems harassing the officers of the Federation discouraged them about undertaking anything new. Perennially looming large was the question of finances. From the beginning of the Federation, a per capita tax was intended to provide sufficient revenue, but, with the added expense of the Social Service Commission, this was not sufficient. Even the *Bulletin* was not self-supporting, the subscriptions being few. The Commission adopted no specific system for finances until the Baltimore convention, which voted to grant it the ten dollar fee from the associate membership, henceforth to be called the membership for social service.[48] But the returns were still so small that Matre declared the matter "serious." A ways and means committee with Bishop Muldoon as chairman suggested borrowing money or doing away with the *Bulletin* entirely and taking up the proposal of *Our Sunday Visitor* to carry Federation news.[50]

The cost of renting the Commission's offices and reading rooms caused Archbishop Messmer some concern. He wrote Dietz:

I was assuredly much pleased to see these rooms . . . just what we want. I am anxious we should keep them. But unless we can succeed in getting other societies to join with us in placing their headquarters there, I don't know where the rent and upkeep is to come from.[51]

Added to lack of financial backing Dietz had to contend with criticism of his work. He seemed especially aware of the opposition after 1915. He complained to Muldoon:

You must allow that I have received scant sympathy and support from the Commission itself. . . . Sent them Newsletter every week. Not one of them has written a word of sympathy, or criticism, or encouragement. . . . Yet while they have nothing to suggest, why will they not at least support me and enable me to carry out plans that achieve results though they be tedious and gradual in the coming. . .[52]

This opposition and criticism reached a climax in the New York con-

133

vention in 1916. Dietz sensed some of it, for he wrote Hagerty:

> I have been trying to digest the convention. I was so busy . . .
> that I did not catch much of the current pro and con, yet it
> seems that there was some feeling against me. Somehow it
> grew on me. I do not know what it was. It was something in-
> tangible.[53]

Bishop Schrembs brought up some of these criticisms at the Executive
Board meeting during the convention, but Muldoon defended Dietz.
Heckenkamp, who was present, thought the opposition centered in
the "Boston Crowd," represented by Francis Slattery. But he assured Dietz:

> I know that the talk by Bishop Muldoon set the entire Executive
> Board, or at least some doubting members right. His talk was
> surely a credit to you and to your work.[54]

One of the criticisms stemmed from Father Dietz's constant agitation for a School of Social Science. In his first report to the Commission in 1913 he recommended such a school, where short courses
in "social-economic and political history, Christian ethics, public speaking and journalism" would prepare "secretaries, organizers, and lecturers" for Federation work. With the possibility of a "commodious
building with five acres of ground," at his disposal, Dietz expected the
Federation to provide only the equipment and running expenses. The
latter could be partly met, Dietz suggested, by scholarships offered by
state and county federations. He urged the establishment of this school
at each Board meeting until at Toledo, in 1915, he secured permission
to devote his spare time to a school. The Federation itself, however
refused to have any part in it.[55] Keenly disappointed over the refusal
of the Federation to back the school, Dietz wrote Heckenkamp:

> I feel tired not because of the work but because of the loss of
> genuine enthusiasm. And this comes from the lack of confi-
> dence in the things that are nearest to my heart. . . . Sometimes,
> I think I have done all I could and that I ought to resign
> and give someone else a chance. And then the idea of the
> "School of Christian Democracy" will not let my conscience
> rest. It was the thought that brought me into Federation and
> it is the one thing to which I cannot get; yet I can see how
> it is necessary beyond all telling, feasible and at the door.[56]

134

"Why is it," Dietz asked later, "that the biggest opposition and the most obstacles, and the greatest indifferences come from those whose support would be legitimately expected?"[57] He opened a school, his American Academy of Christian Democracy, at Hot Springs, North Carolina, in September, 1915, hoping that eventually it would win the support of the Federation.[58] But the Executive Board at the New York meeting in 1916 rejected his plea for recognition of the Academy as a training school for the Federation.

By 1916 some of the leaders of the Federation were aware that something was wrong with the organization. They could see what Dietz had seen long before—the need of a program of action to be carried out between conventions so that the organization would be doing more than passing resolutions midst band and parade once a year. Charles Daly of the Boston Federation wrote Matre:

> It is a feeling here of most of our representative men that the National Convention should adopt a working program which will mean work from the day the Convention closes until it assembles again in 1917. We believe today that the National Convention is without any special results except the good that comes from resolutions adopted and whatever much may be done by the press. The National Convention ought to evolve something which will help all of us Catholics everywhere to fight the different evils with which we are contending as bigotry, indifferentism, ignorance and other socialistic symptoms with which the country is now ailing.[59]

Bishop Muldoon asked for suggestions for making the Federation more effective. Dietz recommended the reorganization of the American Federation of Catholic Societies by bringing the various Catholic agencies under seven departments, each with its advisory board of seven appointed by the Executive Board of the Federation.[60] The National Conference of Catholic Charities would thus become the *Charities and Social Service* Department of the Federation; the Catholic Press Association would constitute the Federation's machinery for *Press and Publicity;* the Catholic Educational Association would eventually become the official Department of *Education.* The organization of *Public Morality* could be taken by the Federation itself, and Father Dietz thought he would have no great difficulty in working up an *Industrial Relations* Department. The last two—*Law and*

135

Legislation and *Health*—would have to await the coming of a Catholic Law Association and a Catholic Medical Association.[61]

Dietz incorporated this plan for reorganization in the fifty resolutions he sent Bishop Schrembs, chairman of the Committee on Resolutions. Others called for a "uniform system of reporting; segregation of visitors from the voting units on the floor of the convention; a more practical system of relations with the Labor movement."[62] When nothing was done with them, Dietz inquired of Schrembs what consideration, if any, the committee gave them.[63] Schrembs explained:

> I went over the entire book most painstakingly in person. It contains excellent matter for practical work by local Federation and societies, but the General Federation in its resolutions, can scarcely go into smaller details of social work as outlined in your book. . . . Besides the Right Reverend Muldoon stated that the resolutions prepared by you did not emanate from the Social Service Commission but were your own personal work.[64]

At the Convention Bishop Muldoon pleaded for a more tangible union among such organizations as the Federation, the Central Verein, and the National Conference of Catholic Charities. The delegates appointed a committee of five to draw up a tentative plan and report back to the Convention. The committee members, Dr. Kerby, Father Noll, Father Edward Garesche, S. J., Father Dietz, and Joseph Frey, drew up a preamble and by-laws which were adopted by the Convention. A committee of three from the three organizations was to implement the proposed program.[65]

At the convention in Kansas City in 1917, the reorganization of Federation was achieved, but not according to Dietz's plan. Foreshadowing the future National Catholic Welfare Conference, it ceased to be primarily a laymen's organization as its founders had intended. Dioceses replaced societies as the basis of the Federation, and a Commission composed of Cardinal O'Connell, chairman, Archbishops Messmer, Hanna, and Mundelein, and Bishops E. P. Allen, Regis Canevin, and James McFaul supervised affairs. Eight committees were responsible for Social Service, Resolutions, Organization, Law, Auditing, Public Morals, Press, and Ways and Means. To support the organization, henceforth known as "The Catholic Federation of

the United States," each diocese pledged one dollar for every thous-
and people.[66]

But by the time the convention met, the United States had entered the World War, and new and weightier problems engaged the
attention of the American people. The effect of the war on Federation unity worried Dietz even before America was in it. Critical of the
foreign policy of the United States, he wrote in the *Bulletin*:

> The atmosphere of America is vitiated with the suspicion
> that we are not a neutral nation, and the suspicion has as-
> sumed such psychological importance that the administration
> owes to large American minorities, much explicit confidence
> to re-establish faith.
>
> All the nations at war know it. Some openly rejoice in it,
> and some secretly resent it, and will now never consent to have
> America as an arbiter of peace when peace shall be on the
> wing.[67]

Because of the "various nationalities and racial prejudice" in the
Federation, Dietz questioned the advisability of holding a convention
in 1915.[68] Instead he suggested that the money thus spent, plus "a
collection taken up by Federation through the *Bulletin* and local committees," be turned over to the Holy Father.[69] But Schrembs feared
that "discontinuance of a convention even for one year would have
a tendency to kill the movement."[70]

When the anti-German sentiment in the country caused German-
American workers to be laid off, Father Dietz wrote to Gompers, urging their protection:

> Now if ever, solidarity is necessary, and I believe trade unions
> will be justified in striking, if need be to defend the rights of their
> members.[71]

On the other hand, he believed it to be to the best interests of trade-
unionism to "exact from German-American trade-union members, the
pledge that they will do nothing to discredit the labor movement."[72]

Shortly after America entered the war, Dietz devoted a *Newsletter*
to "The Holy-Spirit and War Time Charity." It initiated his "Asocia-
tion of Prayer for the Gifts of the Holy Ghost upon the Nation." Appealing both to those who were in sympathy with the war and to those
who were not, he urged them to pledge themselves to abstain from all

137

public discussion of war issues, to yield to no instinct of race antagonism and to "spend a lonely hour once a week before the Blessed Sacrament."[73] That Dietz himself was not too faithful to points one and two is evident from Bishop Muldoon's letter, written "only in kindness," about the complaint of John C. Shea, president of the Federation of Dayton, Ohio, that Father Dietz's talk before the Dayton Federation had been a "veiled defense of Germany in its war situation."[74] Muldoon wrote further:

> Now I feel confident that they have misunderstood and misinterpreted you—for I know your American sentiments, but it shows how very careful a person has to be as these are sensible times.[75]

Concern for the work of the Federation led Father Dietz to include a warning in his report to the convention in August, 1917, lest "many good works, having nothing to do with the war . . . be sacrificed or at least neglected," since works of charity and social service were "less sensational and striking in their appeal to the public" but "quite as necessary to the well-being of vast numbers of the American people."[76]

Whatever influence absorption in war work had on the fortunes of the Federation, it soon became evident that conditions were critical. Reorganization did not solve the Federation's financial problems. Funds were not forthcoming, and salaries and bills were overdue.[77] Bishop Muldoon wrote Dietz in late December, 1917:

> Saw Matre—Said he would send you all in treasury—only $200-$250. There is nothing on hand and I do not know what is to be done. It is deplorable. We had a small meeting of Federation (Messmer, Cannon, Flynn, and Matre). They all know the condition but have no solution to offer. Could you get a Chaplaincy for Mass near by your place to help you out?[78]

Apparently this was the only warning of things to come. In early September Archbishop Messmer learned of a meeting in Chicago of Bishops Muldoon and Schrembs, Thomas Flynn, president of Federation, Matre and Cannon, at which the financial conditions were discussed and the deficit reported. As a partial solution they decided to discontinue the Social Service Department, the services of the secretary of the Commission, and to publish the *Bulletin* bi-monthly. By reducing the salaries of the supervisor and the national secretary they could cut the budget from fifty-two hundred dollars to twenty-five hundred.[79] Cannon notified Dietz of this decision. "I regret that this action is necessary," he wrote, "but there seems to be no other way out of it."[80] Father Dietz expressed himself to Bishop Muldoon a few months later:

> I will not complain about the action of Federation; I have to this minute not opened my mouth to anyone about it. But will say to you that it was not the 'square' thing . . . 'dismissal' without any more ado than a brief note that there was not money . . .
>
> Now I am left high and dry in a foreign diocese with a debt of $10,000 and no income except Mass stipends.[81]

Yet he felt it best simply to forget about the Federation and what had happened. "I feel I have been exceedingly loyal to it and I yet feel that it is the forlorn hope of Christian Democracy in this country."[82] Dietz blamed the condition of the Federation on two things when he wrote to Thomas Burns of England:

> Federation is shot to pieces because it had no real policy and because the National Secretary whose chief business in the absence of any understanding of the times was to flatter the bishops instead of helping to make the bishops understand what was in the lay mind.[83]

Father Dietz was right in believing that the end of the Federation was near. War needs called forth new organizations that eventually absorbed the Catholic Federation of the United States. The first of these organizations, the National Catholic War Council, was set up in 1917 as the result of deliberations of a "General Convention of Catholics of the United States," called to consider how Catholics might best help the government win the war.[84] The delegates, representing most of the dioceses of the country, forty national Catholic organizations, and the Catholic Press Association, agreed unanimously that the need of the hour was a national organization to "study, co-ordinate, unify and put in operation all Catholic activities incidental to the war."[85] Appointed to the War Council's Administrative Committee— "a high court of general control and direction"—were two prominent

Federation prelates: Bishops Muldoon, chairman, and Schrembs.[86] Under the aegis of this Committee or its successors, many of the things for which Father Dietz had striven eventually came to pass. Most noteworthy of all its accomplishments was the official statement on the social question, "The Bishops' Program of Reconstruction," put forth February 12, 1919. Commenting on this program to Heckenkamp, Dietz had this to say: "If it is not a vindication of all that I suffer for and have been oftentimes blamed for, what is it?"[87] And to Bishop Muldoon he wrote:

> Your episcopal War Council document of recent date gave me much joy and on that program I surely have a mission. Will you not help me to it?[88]

With one part of the program, however, Dietz did not agree. That was the recommendation that labor participate in management and ownership through cooperative enterprises and ownership of stock. "How foolish," he wrote.

> to follow after all the 'altruisms' of profit-sharing, cooperation and other fine 'gestures' which don't bite 'capitalism' while they stab the workers in the back . . .
> Co-operation is almost as lofty an ideal as the Communion of Saints, but until the labor movement goes in for co-operation whole-heartedly, the other forces in that direction are worse than wasted; in that they delude, however well meaningly, those who believe them.[89]

Muldoon did all he could to secure a place for Father Dietz in the proceedings of the War Council, especially after the Federation dropped the Social Service Commission. He wrote to Dietz in December, 1918:

> I have on several occasions suggested to Dr. Cooper and Father Burke to have an interview with you and perhaps something agreeable on both sides might come out . . . I have written Father Burke again today.[90]

Later when Father Dietz asked to be made a regional director for the Cincinnati area should the War Council appoint one, Muldoon replied:

> Indeed personally I would be glad to see you in the work but

I cannot (and you would not wish it) force you upon committees.[91]

Ultimately the N. C. W. C. rejected Dietz because of his "pronounced stand on labor unions."[92]

Once the war had ended, it was a logical step from the National War Council to a permanent organization to look after Catholic interests in time of peace. When the Catholic hierarchy assembled in February, 1919, on the occasion of Cardinal Gibbons' jubilee, the members appointed a Committee on General Interests and Affairs, with Gibbons as chairman.[93] Bishop Muldoon, vice-chairman, was instructed to prepare a tentative program on which the bishops might act at their September meeting in Washington. He invited representatives of the mission field, the Catholic press, and Catholic social work to confer with him at the University of Notre Dame in July, 1919.[94] Muldoon attached to Father Dietz's invitation a personal note, urging him to come.[95]

By the time the group of experts met at Notre Dame, Dietz was at the height of his success in Cincinnati, with the American Federation of Labor and Archbishop Moeller giving full approval of his work.[96] He came to the meeting alert and confident about the labor question. When the labor problem had no place in the report of the Social Service Committee, Dietz "stated the case of labor and won the recognition that was accorded it in the program"—the creation of a section on Labor and Rural Problems.[97] Both Bishops Schrembs and Glass allegedly regarded his suggestion as the "most distinctive acquisition" to the program.[98] Dietz asked for the office of assistant director of the section on labor, in view of the work he had done "so laboriously and with so little encouragement."[99] The function of such a section as he saw it should be "to foster in each diocese a uniform policy toward the labor movement with a local priest assigned to its direction."[100] Dietz indicated some of the ways for securing such uniformity: Catholic attendance at union meetings; education work in and through the unions and Catholic societies; exchange of fraternal delegates in local central bodies; circulating literature in the unions; electing Catholics to local union offices.[101]

The September meeting of the ninety-two archbishops and bishops completed the organization of the Catholic hierarchy into the National Catholic Welfare Council.[102] An administrative committee of seven with Archbishop Edward Hanna as chairman established the following bureaus, each supervised by a committee member: Social Action under Bishop Muldoon, Lay Societies managed by Bishop Schrembs, Education in charge of Archbishop Dowling, Legislation supervised by Archbishop Dougherty, and Catholic Publicity and Literature under Bishop Russell.[103] How familiar these purposes of the Council must have sounded to Father Dietz:

> Not a centralization of authority but a unification of Catholic effort. Not the master but the servant of the Catholic activities and organizations of the country. What is being done in one state or diocese should be known as a matter of information and guidance to every other diocese. We are wasting our efforts and our opportunities if, through lack of unity and conference, our voice in matters of public concern expresses one opinion in one place and another in another place.[104]

A national coordinating committee of representatives from each bureau with the Reverend John J. Burke, C.S.P. as chairman was to be located in Washington.[105]

When Bishop Muldoon was ready to organize the Social Action Department, he solicited the opinions of those who had been at the Notre Dame meeting. His first letter covered the following points:

1. Suppose the social section is allowed $50,000 for the year's work, what would be the most practical questions to take up and work at this year?
2. Where would be the best location for the central headquarters?
3. Other than those who were at . . . Notre Dame (and Dr. Kerby has been elected a member) whom would you suggest for membership on the reorganization committee?
4. . . . Please indicate those whom you would deem fitted by education and experience to act as Chairman of the . . . committee. Your suggestion need not be confined to the clergy.[106]

Dietz answered the letter point by point. The most practical work for the year, he believed, would be to create and organize the Bureau, to develop its Christian (Supernatural) Morale; and to make proper provision for the education (according to the supernatural morale) of the prospective social workers, agents, secretaries, etc., and to actually initiate this work of education.[107]

Quite naturally he selected the American Academy of Christian Democracy as the headquarters of the Department. At the school, Dietz assured Muldoon, available at a minimum of expense were a library, living quarters, a hall for meetings, and a chapel for the convenience of the clergy.

As additional members to the group that met at Notre Dame, Dietz suggested George Gillespie, president of the St. Vincent De Paul Society, as a member ex officio; Dr. Charles Bruehl of St. Charles Seminary, Overbrook, "a social scholar as great as he is modest"; and Matthew Woll of the Executive Council of the A. F. of L. As an alternate to Woll, "if such official connection should be prejudicial," he recommended William P. Clarke, president of the Flint Glass Workers of America.[108] For chairman of the Social Action Committee, Dietz selected Gillespie, since "historically our social activities have grown from the seed of this organization." His second choice was Dr. Kerby. To these Dietz added "if a subdivision for labor is contemplated I should regard myself as a candidate for the sub-division."[109]

At the December meeting the hierarchy named Bishop Muldoon chairman of the Social Action Committee.[110] Muldoon called a meeting in Chicago at the Loyola School of Sociology to organize the Department.[111] Two of the men Dietz had recommended were invited—Father Bruehl and George Gillespie—but neither representative of labor was there.[112] Father Dietz had no place on the Executive Committee; Father John A. Ryan and John A. Lapp assumed immediate charge of the Social Action Department.[113] Its comprehensive program covered the "whole field of citizenship and social and industrial relations."[114] It was to be a "clearing house for the distribution of the best Catholic study on these matters," through lectures furnished gratis to Catholic colleges and seminaries, through releases to the Catholic press on industrial facts, through explanations of the encyclicals of the Popes and of the Bishops' Program of Reconstruction, and through encouragement and advice to social study clubs.[115]

Ironically, Dietz was selected to open a series of lectures on social subjects at Mt. St. Mary's Seminary. In the letter of invitation, the Reverend Raymond A. McGowan, assistant director of the Social Action Department, wrote:

> We thought, Father, that you might consent to speak upon the subject, 'Industrial Relations,' and since you are so thoroughly versed on this subject, we suggested that you be first on the program. . . . We feel confident that you will consent to speak upon this subject . . . since we know how close it is to your heart.[116]

Father Dietz accepted the invitation, but the seminary decided to postpone the series.[117]

Since Father Dietz had no place in the directing of the N.C.W.C.'s policies, members of the A. F. of L., concerned about the relationship between the two organizations, wrote to Archbishop Hanna, the chairman, asking that the policies of the A. F. of L. be "understood and interpreted properly at Council deliberations." The letter continued:

> Father Dietz has for years made it his business to understand the Labor movement by direct contact and has proved himself not undeserving of our confidence. In matters before your body affecting the labor movement it would surely be gratifying to see Father Dietz so situated that his knowledge and experience, may have practical value and consequences.[118]

Although this request was not granted the labor leaders retained their confidence in Father Dietz. When Father John A. Ryan launched his plans for a Catholic Industrial Conference, Matthew Woll, invited to take part, asked Father Dietz for opinions on the nature of the conference. Dietz suggested that only Catholic employers in "contractual relations" with labor be invited. Since *Rerum Novarum* declared for trade-unionism, he argued, "Catholic employers have in conscience no legitimate excuse for not being in contractual relations with the workers and the Church therefore cannot consistently dignify by invitation non-union Catholic employers who brazenly flout a known Catholic position."[119] Later Woll sent Dietz a copy of his letter to Ryan, as-

144

suring him: "I have followed your suggestions almost literally."[120]

Father Dietz remained a member of the Social Action Department of the National Catholic Welfare Council for a number of years, but leadership in its affairs fell to others. In a few years, the N. C. W. C., which enjoyed ecclesiastical and financial backing Dietz never had, realized much that he had labored for as Secretary of the Social Service Commission. An official statement from the hierarchy, a national school of social service, Catholic Industrial Conferences, incorporation of laymen in Catholic social action, and the co-ordination of all Catholic social endeavor through a national clearing house were all part of his dream for the American Federation of Catholic Societies.

For all practical purposes Father Dietz's active participation in the Catholic social movement as represented by the American Federation of Catholic Societies and its successor, the National Catholic Welfare Conference, ended in 1918, when the Social Service Commission was discontinued. That year likewise marked the close of the pioneer period of Catholic social reform. Dietz had broken the ground and planted the seed, leaving the harvest to others.

Chapter Seven

Launching
a School
of Social Service

THE AMERICAN ACADEMY of Christian Democracy for Women opened in Hot Springs, North Carolina, in September, 1915—the culmination of years of agitation by Father Dietz for a school of social service. In 1909, when editing the English section of *Central Blatt and Social Justice,* he planned a school for the Central Verein.[1] Again in 1911 he discussed with John Mitchell the desirability of a school patterned after the Rand School of Social Science in New York, to train secretaries for the American Federation of Catholic Societies.[2] Such a school, he declared, could

> give a business course of one or two years preparation in the political sciences and history, the labor movement, sociology, economics, philosophy, oratory and journalism.[3]

Failing to persuade the Federation to sponsor the school, Dietz struck out on his own. The "commodious building with five acres of ground" to which he referred in his first report to the Social Service Commission, in 1913, was in reality a sixteen-room Mission House in Johnson City, Tennessee, offered him by the Reverend Emmanuel F. Callahan, a Tennessee missionary.[4] Callahan had approached the Right Reverend Thomas S. Byrne of Nashville, in whose diocese Johnson City was located, about the proposed school and reported to Dietz that the Bishop would welcome him with "open arms."[5]

Subsequent correspondence between the Bishop and Father Dietz disclosed, however, that the Bishop could give no title to the property, only "temporary possession," and that, on condition that the priest in charge of the school look after the surrounding small

146

parish.[6] Byrne was not entirely discouraging, however, assuring Dietz that he would "be pleased to give any workable proposition a favorable hearing."[7] The Carolina, Clinchfield and Ohio Railroad offered another possibility — a grant of land in Johnson City or Newport, Tennessee.[8]

In the meantime Dietz cast about for donations toward the ten thousand dollars he figured as the minimum for launching his school.[9] Judge Morgan O'Brien of the Supreme Court of New York, consultant for Thomas Fortune Ryan, financier, seemed a likely prospect.[10] The Judge encouraged Dietz to put his ideas "on paper" and, if they seemed feasible, promised that he would try to interest Ryan and his associates.[11] Dietz likewise asked James Flaherty of Philadelphia, Supreme Knight of the Knights of Columbus, Archbishop James Blenk of New Orleans, and Cardinal O'Connell of Boston to contribute.[12]

At the time these negotiations for a site and for money (1913) were under way, Dietz planned to remain in Milwaukee and turn the direction of the school over to someone else. His first choice for the post of Director was Dr. John A. Ryan. Dietz wrote:

> Several years ago, I wrote you in the matter of a school for Catholic social workers at Oberlin. Perhaps the matter was premature. Since that time there have been various developments, not always the way that I anticipated or desired, but yet in the direction that promised results.[13]

Telling of the Johnson City offer and of Bishop Byrne's sympathy, Dietz continued:

> If you would take hold of the school, its success would be assured from the start and Federation would soon be the power through which Catholic Social Plans could be promptly realized.[14]

Ryan's repy was final "As to the school proposed, it will be impossible for me to consider it."[15]

Dr. Charles Bruehl of St. Francis Seminary, Milwaukee, who was second choice, responded with enthusiasm:

> Glad to learn plans assuming concrete form. As to my part in the matter, I am willing to accept the position in question, provided

147

it offers some permanence and some security of a livelihood. The cause pleases me well. You may reckon on me, if the plan really becomes possible.[16]

Father Dietz hoped that ultimately the American Federation of Catholic Societies would sponsor his school. Important to Dietz, then, was the support of the members of the Social Service Commission as entree to the Executive Board of the Federation. He could not afford to ignore their opinion of the Tennessee venture. Professor Hagerty preferred Chicago or Milwaukee to Johnson City.[17] Bishop Muldoon thought Tennessee a long way to bring young men. Furthermore he cautioned Father Dietz:

When you go there look over the entire proposition with a business eye—remember that a gift horse is sometimes a dear one, and also that scenery however grand is only an incident. The financial end is the greatest.[18]

Muldoon was hesitant about taking up any project that would necessitate the Commission's taking a "back step." Willing to admit that the training of secretaries for the Federation was "a most important item," he thought it was hardly in the "direct field" of the Commission but more in the "general" work of Federation.[19] Muldoon, however, discussed the matter of a school with Monsignor Thomas J. Shahan of the Catholic University and found him "very sympathetic."[20]

Eventually Father Dietz abandoned the plan to settle in Tennessee accepting instead the offer of an estate in Hot Springs, North Carolina, secured through Father Callahan from Mrs. Bessie Safford.[21] She was a wealthy convert, a member of the Rumbaugh family with a philanthropic bent. By May, 1914, Dietz was planning his school for the training of field secretaries, men who were to be "placed in charge of the Catholic lay movements in every part of the land."[22]

But the Social Service Commission and the Executive Board did not share the enthusiasm of Father Dietz over Mrs. Safford's offer. When the matter was presented at their meeting in Chicago in 1915, it was agreed that a school, not in Hot Springs but in Chicago, affiliated with the Loyola School of Sociology, would greatly aid the

148

Federation's work. When Dietz threatened to resign rather than accept such a plan, the Board dropped the matter.[23]

Father Dietz, however, continued his connections with Mrs. Safford, suggesting that he rent one of the houses on her estate and move his office down there where he would be free from the distractions unavoidable in Milwaukee.[24] When Mrs. Safford offered him the use of a house, Dietz applied to Archbishop Messmer for a leave of absence for as long a time as he should be engaged in the work of the Social Service Commission. He based his request on his need of "leisure for study and undivided and undistracted time" and the impossibility of paying further rent for the Milwaukee offices.[25]

Fortified with Messmer's permission, Dietz asked the blessing of Bishop Muldoon on his move.[26] The Bishop wrote:

> As we have not provided you with a home, I do not see how we can require you to live in Milwaukee or any particular place. Hot Springs seems far away but if you can do your work to better advantage I cannot interpose any objections. Of course, if you intend to give part of your time to other efforts than the weekly letter and the Bulletin I would object. The Committee understands that you are to give all your time and talent to these two things and nothing else—and you have more than enough in these two. So if you go, it is understood that you initiate no new work then even on your own responsibility.[27]

Before this letter reached Dietz, however, he had already taken further steps in the direction of a school in Hot Springs, as his letter to Mrs. Safford revealed:

> I may, from the Hot Spring's publication office make my plan so plain and acceptable as to silence adverse opinion. I may even gather 'unofficially' a few young men, part students and part collaborators, and the school in 'embryo' will be born by the time of the convention.[28]

In this same letter he suggested that Mrs. Safford make a definite disposal of her property by designating that at her death it be devoted to the "educational, charitable and social purposes of the American Federation of Catholic Societies," with the "*bishops* of the province" as executors.[29] By this property arrangement, which never materialized, Dietz hoped to forestall the objection made at Chicago that the Safford offer was too indefinite.

To give further security to his position, Father Dietz obtained the approval of the Right Reverend Leo Haid, O.S.B., Vicar Apostolic of North Carolina. This Bishop wrote sympathetically:

> Your endeavors to found a school to prepare young Catholics properly for social work must meet the approbation of all who understand your aims and know the necessity of trained workers to carry them out. Should you desire to choose a home for such a training school in North Carolina you have my fullest approval, and I will always beg God's choicest blessing on your noble work.[30]

Father Dietz moved to Hot Springs in late April, 1915, and for a time everything went well. He sent a glowing account of his reception to Bishop Muldoon, stressing the great relief he experienced in being free from the cares and worries that had surrounded him in Milwaukee. In the peace and calm of his new home he could pray and meditate again and could relax spiritually.[31]

One of the fruits of his prayer to the Holy Spirit for light and guidance was a new idea for his school, this time not for men but for women. Important in this new plan was the cooperation of Mrs. Safford, to whom he wrote:

> This work ought to be started now and by yourself. You may be willing to give it a certain encouragement, but without personal service, such as you can and should render, it cannot succeed.[32]

The details of the plan were nebulous at that time. He gave some thought even to the organization of a religious community to "handle the modern woman problem." He sent a general sketch of his idea to Dr. Bruehl. There would be no religious habit, unless at home or in chapel the sisters chose to wear one. Their home would be in the "downtown districts of the cities" where they would do

> friendly visiting among the sick, the sick poor and especially recent immigrants in their homes, *direct* guidance for sodalities, women's Trade-union leagues, consumers leagues, child welfare, etc., in fact have charge of the social reform work for women.

> They could live at priests' houses or sisters' convents or at any place provided by bishop or the women's organizations, and in time they could develop a central institution like the Y.W.C.A.[33]

He abandoned this idea, except in so far as it operated in the White Cross Nurse organization, in favor of a school for girls. The *Newsletter* for July 26, 1915, carried the announcement of a plan

> which is expected to fill many a gap in Catholic endeavors, to contribute to the co-ordination of various Catholic activities among women and, incidentally to raise them to a higher plane of efficiency.

This was the proposed American Academy of Christian Democracy for Women, at Loretta Chateau in Hot Springs, where a first course would begin September 8. The article gave the Social Service Commission credit for a "new approach to social problems." Father Dietz presumed on the Commission's collaboration as his letter to Bishop Muldoon showed:

> The last news-letter may come somewhat as a surprise to you. Circumstances over which I have no control and of which it is difficult to write made me take action quickly, if action were to be taken at all. I would ask you to take this on faith until I can discuss it with you in person.[34]

Nevertheless, Dietz went forward with his scheme and when the convention of the American Federation of Catholic Societies met at Toledo in the summer of 1915, he had a prospectus ready to present to any who were interested. In his report to the Commission he again brought up the question of a school for men and added:

> The Secretary here wishes to call attention to another enterprise for women undertaken under the lead of the Social Service Commission by Mrs. Katherine M. Safford, a socially prominent Southern convert to the Faith.[35]

The Commission discussed the question in two sessions and finally agreed to let Dietz give any spare time he had to the proposed Academy, provided the Commission and the Federation were not associated with it in any way.[36] Muldoon further instructed him to "make it clear in the next issue of the Bulletin that the school is an individual venture of Mrs. Safford."[37] When Dietz sent his report to the printer he changed the above quoted section to read:

> The Secretary here wishes to call attention to another similar enterprise for women, undertaken upon his advice and responsibility by Mrs. Katherine Safford.[38]

Muldoon did grant him permission to use the *Bulletin,* however, to appeal for students, provided he was careful not to give the view "that Federation is in school work."[39]

Although Dietz was grateful to Bishop Muldoon for the "square deal" he had given him by defending him, he felt that Muldoon could have done more for him. He protested:

> By failing to give the support that your influence commands it seems to me you have handicapped my best opportunities for marketing the potentialities of Federation. In the main I am either right or wrong. I am not afraid of the logic of facts and I do wish to realize how far I square with the "objective" truth. . . . My only ambition now, if I can speak of such at all, has been to invest the light of grace that God has given me, especially upon the field of Divine Social Redemption.[40]

Attempting to explain his position, Muldoon wrote:

> Whilst admitting the necessity we do not see alike as to feasibility just now—besides I must be guided by the sentiment of the Executive Committee which at times is not too friendly and is very sensitive when it is a question of funds in any fair amount. Up to the present it has not been with me what ought to be done, but what could be done amid the surroundings and circumstances.[41]

He gave three reasons why the Social Service Commission did not "take very kindly to the Hot Springs adventure":

> 1. Manner of approach — either consciously or unconsciously you committed Social Service to Hot Springs venture before consulting them—tactical mistake
> 2. You had no definite contract with the owner, and could only state 'oral promises' . . .
> 3. Ways and means not very apparent or well worked out.[42]

Forced to be content with the reluctant sanction of the Federation, Dietz concentrated on arrangements for the opening of the

152

school in September. One of his problems was the securing of teachers, limited as he was financially. During the summer Mrs. Safford had entertained seven Sisters of Our Lady of Mercy from Charleston, South Carolina. They were interested in the proposed school, and two of them were willing to teach Social Education, Charities and Practical Nursing.[43] At first it seemed as if the plan would work out, but Bishop Henry Northrup decided that the Sisters could not go, first, because they were moving to another diocese which might have sisters that could do the work just as well, and, second, because since there were only two of them, they would not be able to keep up the "spirit, life and regulations of their Community."[44] Dietz finally secured the services of a Dr. Alphonse Lange, a masseur connected with the Hot Springs Hotel, and a Dr. Peck, who gave lectures on health.[45]

Seven young women representing six states enrolled in the first course, which began on the Feast of the Exaltation of the Cross: Virginia Morrissey of Antigo, Wisconsin; Margaret Tucker of Philadelphia; Susan Frawley of Knoxville, Tennessee; Mary Marvick of Tampa, Florida; Marie Kanzler of Bay City, Michigan; Catherine Germershausen of Milwaukee; and Theresa Dietz, sister of Father Dietz, of Oberlin, Ohio. This first course of fourteen weeks was largely experimental. Dr. Lange taught the medical aspects fundamental to the training of a practical nurse. Father Dietz used Monsignor Henry Parkinson's *The Primer of Social Science* and *Rerum Novarum* as basic texts in his courses, amplifying them with his personal experiences. Simple and limited as this beginning was, Dietz could see the possibilites of a great future for his school. He wrote to Heckenkamp:

> Just think what this will mean in the course of years. People scattered all over the country understanding the philosophy of organization, the scope of its possibility, the methods of Catholic society, intelligent co-operation with existing agencies, ready to grasp every situation and to make use of every opportunity, and above all fired with true Catholic zeal.[46]

The location at Hot Springs was particularly suited to the purpose Father Dietz had in mind. It was far from the distractions of

153

a large city, a veritable "social service novitiate," where young women could prepare their minds and hearts for the work. Living a disciplined community life, strengthened by daily Mass and Holy Communion, the students, while becoming "technically efficient," learned also that the "soul of reform is the reform of the soul" and "that he who would uplift others must first uplift himself."[47] Symbolic of this spiritual emphasis was the sixteen-foot white cross of Iona, erected on top of a mountain one thousand feet above the valley.[48] Significant, too, to the founder, was the mystical number seven of the first enrollment of students. Even the name of the school had not been chosen at random. Each word in the title had meaning, the implications of which were developed on a special card:

American: Devoted to the ideals, institutions and history of the American people in the development of their social, economic, political and religous life; a devotion, however, not exclusive, and working no prejudice to international ethics, brotherhood and law.

Academy: A practical scholastic method of regular social study courses of moderate duration, for those, who, lacking earlier opportunities want to understand and interpret social facts with a view to shaping present conditions and future events.

Christian: Building a modern civilization upon foundations of the perennial intellectual and moral code, which protects especially the weak and the lowly from the snares of evil and the brutal forces of might in the battle for a commonwealth of justice on earth.

Democracy: Vindicating the prior native and original right of organization and union to freedom from undue restraint, equality of opportunity for self-determination and fraternity of purpose against autocratic aggressions and impositions of capitalist statecraft.

The manifold cares of the school never completely dimmed Father Dietz's vision and he communicated that great spirit to the students.

154

The first course was scarcely under way when personal differences with Mrs. Safford necessitated a change of residence. The original plan for the girls to live in Mrs. Safford's spacious "Chateau" was changed just before the girls arrived, because she was afraid of exposing her fine things to breakage. Instead, the girls lived in the much smaller villa of Mrs. Baker, and only the chapel in the Chateau was open to the students. Since Mrs. Baker's home was too small for living quarters and classes, the latter had to be held in the "hermitage," where Father Dietz had the Commission offices, a quarter of a mile from the villa.[49] Adding to this inconvenience, Mrs. Baker apparently wanted to live with the girls and supervise them. This Father Dietz would not permit as she was "always on the verge of a nervous collapse" and inclined to interfere unduly in the school's arrangements. He found her of "no value as instructor or matron or disciplinarian or advisor." A "superannuated butterfly" was his name for her.[50] Some misunderstanding arose, too, over financial arrangements, when Mrs. Safford failed to contribute the expected amount.[51] All seemed relieved when the separation took place with "apparent good-will and without loss of dignity on either side."[52] Father Dietz rented a larger house in the center of town, fixed a room for a chapel for which Bishop Haid provided an altar stone, and the work of the school continued through the first course, which ended in December.[53]

Obviously two faculty members were not sufficient to offer a variety of courses. Father Dietz had hoped to send the students to the Southern Normal College in Hot Springs for the courses necessary for social work and planned to supplement these by giving the Catholic point of view.[54] The plan to affiliate fell through when the president, Dr. William Hastings, insisted that special as well as regular students attend daily chapel.[55]

Every attempt to secure other teachers failed. Mrs. Honor Walsh, associate editor of the Philadelphia *Catholic Standard and Times* had agreed to teach the practical work in charities.[56] When she did not appear, Dietz appealed to Dr. Kerby. Kerby thought he had a "clever and experienced young lady," but, when they went over the schedule carefully, he decided she was "too poorly acquainted with

Catholic principles and distinctive Catholic policies to undertake the work."[57] This young lady was the only one Kerby knew in Washington, which led him to observe: "All of which shows with distressing force, how necessary instruction in social work has become."[58]

Father Dietz invited Dr. Bruehl to come for the course beginning in June, 1916, but the dates interfered with lectures he was giving at the Cliff Haven Summer School.[59] Bruehl regretted the conflict, for the set-up at Hot Springs was quite to his taste:

> You have a very fine and exhaustive schedule of lectures and with some good will and attention the students ought to be able to take home with them a whole lot of valuable information.[60]

For a short time John E. Kent taught a class in anatomy and physical training.[61] He had been in charge of physical training at Battle Creek and had come to Hot Springs to teach in the Southern Normal School.[62] But for the most part Dietz had to rely ultimately on the students to help him with instruction. Margaret Tucker had sufficient experience to handle certain phases of "Charities," and Virginia Morrissey and Marie Kantzler were preparing to teach "Working-girls Problems" and "Practical Nursing."[63]

Essential to the success of the school, of course, was a continuous supply of students. To insure this, Father Dietz inaugurated an advertising campaign of some proportions. Many of the Catholic papers carried the story of the new Academy, and circular letters went out to bishops, to forty women's Leagues, and to over one hundred academies and convents. All were asked to send students and to provide scholarships for those otherwise unable to come. In the course of three years (1915-1918), over two hundred applications, and inquiries from thirty-two states and Canada indicated the scope of this campaign.

On the whole the school was well received by those associated with Catholic social welfare. All agreed on the need for such a school under Catholic auspices. The following opinions are typical of many of the women's organizations. Theresa Molamphy, president of the Catholic Women's League of Pittsburgh, wrote:

156

We are pleased to learn that an effort is being made to train Catholics along this line as it is next to impossible to secure trained Catholics for our social work and we are at a disadvantage competing with the trained non-sectarian workers.[64]

Mary Workman, founder of Brownson House, Los Angeles, rejoiced that Catholics were preparing to meet the social needs of the times:

The need is only in its infancy, much as we feel it, and our Catholic lay-workers must be trained and soundly grounded in the true Christian philosophy of life. We Catholics should be leaders not followers.[65]

Martina Johnston, president of the Catholic Social Betterment League of Seattle, expressed pleasure and surprise on reading of the new Academy:

It seems almost too good to be true. For years while I was editor of the diocesan paper here *The Catholic North West Progress,* I urged upon the Catholic public the necessity of concerted action along the lines of social service and calling pointed attention to the fact that we are far, far behind our non-Catholic fellow citizens in this regard.[66]

Several ecclesiastics admired the bravery of Father Dietz in starting such a venture. Almost the only one, however, who tried to supplement approval with material support was the Reverend Joseph M. Corrigan of Philadelphia, later Rector of the Catholic University and Bishop.[67] He wrote Dietz:

The impressions made on me by your daring experiment have convinced me that your zeal and pioneer spirit should have every possible support. I accordingly took the occasion of my stay in Pittsburgh to lay before His Lordship, Bishop Canevin, a full explanation as far as I was able of your purposes and of the means you are so bravely taking to accomplish them. You will be glad to hear the Bishop was deeply interested and I was able to correct certain wrong notions he had of the work.[68]

Corrigan stressed with the Bishop the significance of the school as a pioneer movement.[69] Undoubtedly, Corrigan's finest tribute was to send his sister, Mrs. Mary Dolan, who had worked for organized charity for over four years, to take the second course.[70] He wrote later: "She is delighted with the place, especially with your instructions . . . I would be further pleased if you could permanently interest her."[71]

To aid financially, Corrigan tried to interest Mrs. Edward de V. Morrell, a member of the wealthy Drexel family. After several interviews he dropped the matter, largely because Mrs. Morrell hesitated to contribute toward a general fund "without knowing just what elements were also cooperating to success."[72] Considering the lack of Catholic interest in social work, she was "inclined to doubt, not the need for such a school, but the demand for it."[73]

The opinions of other ecclesiastics are interesting. Father Joseph Brock of Carry, Pennsylvania, wrote Father Dietz:

> To be honest with you, Dietz, I must admire your zeal and your letter just rings with the sentiment I feel myself, but I fear that your ideas are premature.[74]

The Right Reverend Denis J. O'Connell, Bishop of Richmond, assured Father Dietz:

> I believe you are doing a really good work and are meeting modern needs in your training school.[75]

Many objected to the location of the school. Some, like Father Corrigan, could understand Dietz's "novitiate" idea, but others, like Bishop Canevin, could not see how such a school could exist isolated from the industrial and urban areas.[76] Father Dietz was aware of the drawbacks of the site in its limited opportunities for field work and the impossibility of obtaining teachers. Again, as with his Militia of Christ, he broached the question of affiliation with the Catholic University. Dr. Kerby investigated the matter for him and transmitted three opinions: his own, Bishop Shahan's, and that of Dr. Edward Pace, director of studies.[77] Kerby thought it unwise for the University to take on any new responsibilities, since it was already carrying so many lines "that its strength and resources" were "tested to the limit." A type of affiliation in which Father Dietz retained complete autonomy would require his showing "a pretty good corps of instructors with definite standards of scholarship, and a satisfactory financial backing."[78] Bishop Shahan did not see how he could take up the proposal under the present circumstances, while Dr. Pace based his objections on the school's poor location, far from "social problems and experienced teachers."[79]

Father Dietz did not abandon the idea of moving from Hot Springs, in the meantime continuing to organize his courses and begging everyone he knew to send students. During 1915 and 1916 the school offered five courses varying in length from six weeks in summer to twelve, sixteen, and eighteen weeks during the regular school year. The enrollment varied from four or five to twelve or fifteen students. Sometimes the students stayed on for more than one course, or became a part of the faculty, like Margaret Tucker and Anna Hourigan, or part of the administration, like Mary Marvick and Mary Dolan, prefects of discipline.

The Fourth or Women's Federation Course, typical of those offered at the school, provided "professional training for secretarial work as organizers, lecturers, correspondents, field agents, etc., under the auspices of Catholic Association, league and federation."[80] Twenty-one hours a week were devoted to a program covering seven fields: Education, Law and Legislation, Industrial Relations, Charities and Social Service, Public Morality, Press and Publicity, and Organization.[81] A theoretical and practical approach placed significant emphasis on the social and political rights, duties, and obligations of Catholics.[82]

The Fifth General Course, the last offered at Hot Springs, differed somewhat from the others as the general introduction indicates.

> The foundation of this General Course is the study of the Christian philosophy of society, the principles thereof, and there application to church, state, family and associations of every kind. In addition to this structural work on society, and its relations, there is a medical course equivalent to the first years university course in medicine, including physiology, hygiene, sanitation and nursing. Other courses will deal with charity and correction in all their phases; with organized co-operation; social and state agencies; collecting social statistics; public speaking, writing and parliamentary practice and organization.[83]

Ordinarily, only young women eighteen years of age who were high school graduates could enroll, but both requirements for age and for education were waived when a pastor or some equally qualified per-

159

son recommended the students. As a matter of fact some of the most valuable students were older women like Mrs. Mary Dolan or Elizabeth Lenz, whose maturity and experience contributed much to the school. The fee for tuition, board, room and laundry varied from one hundred and twenty-five to one hundred and fifty dollars, depending on the length of the term.

Limited as Father Dietz was financially, the library facilities seem to have been quite adequate, if the opinion of one student has any weight. Veronica Hanley recalls.

> We had a gorgeous library to use, and I think every periodical ever published on the labor question, and all the Catholic papers came to us regularly.[84]

Opportunities for field work were limited, however, because of the location of the school. To give the students some practical experience Dietz sent two of them, Ruth Norris and Marguerite Fitzgerald, to Anderson, South Carolina, to "study the labor problem as it is."[85] A strike in the textile mills there involved three hundred women employees who were demanding a ten percent wage increase.[86] Dietz instructed Mary Keller, organizer for the United Textile Workers, about the two students:

> Let them understand how the working girls live and if possible, arrange for them to stay at the home of some working girl. . . . Let them get as much insight into the conditions of the workers as possible.[87]

It was literally true that the students lived "a disciplined community life." With the exception of Wednesday and Saturday afternoon, which were free, practically every minute of the day was scheduled, from the rising hour, which varied from five to six-thirty with the seasons, to lights out at nine or ten at night. Study, recreation, and prayer had their place in the order of the day. Spiritual motivation was further supplied in conferences by Father Dietz and in posted exhortations which encouraged meditation, examination of conscience, and spiritual reading.

Early in the first course, October 7, 1915, Father Dietz organized the students into an association which he called the "White Cross

160

Nurses." The word "nurse" used here, he explained, meant one who "nourishes, fosters, and manages with care and economy." The association chose no specific field for its work "beyond the encouragement of existing works, the raising of the standards of organized efficiency and general co-ordination of Catholic efforts in the light of a basic Christian philosophy of society."[88] It was not a religious order, though religion was the "prime and all-pervasive motive of their work." For those who did not wish to enter a religious order, yet felt a special vocation to serve humanity in the role of the social worker, the White Cross Nurse Association offered a certain security and fellowship. A pension plan, the White Cross Nurse contract system, required six months of service at some assigned duty, followed by the "regular White Cross service" at a monthly salary of forty dollars for the first year. This salary increased each year for seven years, when the White Cross Nurse became eligible for a pension.[89] A grey and white service uniform and a silver ring engraved with the letters FVT, signifying the motto of the organization, *Fiat Voluntas Tua,* distinguished the members.[90]

Special devotion to the Holy Spirit was the spiritual bond uniting them. On a specified day of the week each made a Holy Hour asking for one of the Gifts of the Holy Spirit for herself and the Academy. Slips drawn from an urn on the Chapel altar designated the time for the Holy Hour and the special Gift to be invoked. Some of the members continued this practice of the weekly Holy Hour for many years, even though the White Cross Nurse organization ended with the closing of the school.[91]

The White Cross Nurse, a quarterly dedicated to the "social, civic, and charity Ideals of American Womanhood," offered articles by the members and others on a wide range of social subjects.[92]

Three evenings a week the White Cross Nurses met in parliamentary session to discuss the outstanding social problems of the day. The chairmanship rotated alphabetically, and the Secretary kept the minutes scrupulously. Following the discussion, the group drew up resolutions which were referred to a committee for further study with the view to reconsidering them at subsequent meetings.

In this way the students made practical application of the theories

161

learned in the classroom. Father Dietz liked to think of this meeting as a "Catholic Congress in continual session."[93]

Dietz sent some of these resolutions to Bishop Schrembs for consideration at the convention of the American Federation of Catholic Societies.[94] A resolution denouncing the distribution of propaganda in favor of birth control received notice from several Catholic papers.[95] It was the basis also for a resolution unanimously adopted by a large meeting of the Brooklyn diocesan branch of the Catholic Federation.[96] By general protests and writing to their representatives, Federation members hoped to forestall the repeal of the laws prohibiting such propaganda in New York. The White Cross Nurses went further and exhorted Catholic women to

> sever all connections with clubs and societies already vitiated, and to organize in their associations, departments of morality, one of whose functions shall be educational propaganda of Christian sex morality.[97]

They sent copies of the resolution to bishops and to the Catholic press, and the members agreed to "boycott all journals, magazines, and publishers who have become partisans of the propaganda." The titles of other resolutions indicate the scope of the discussions carried on by these young women: protection for working girls; playgrounds under Catholic management; securing women's rights through the ballot; labor unions among women; the morality of peaceful picketing; establishment of vocational trade schools; and correct use of lobbying.

Even apart from the strict discipline, life at the American Academy of Christian Democracy was not easy. Lack of funds involved the sacrifice of many of the ordinary comforts. As one of the students described it:

> Our meals were so frugal, our housing so plain, our recreations so simple that day by day, we wondered that the other girls could stand it. . . . The house was not heated and night after night we slept with our coats on. The cold baths can be remembered to this day and the funny remarks of Margaret Tucker on that subject made life worth while.
> We took long (eight or nine mile) hikes through the woods, discussing our own private theories, and eating cheese

and crackers, which we were able to buy at a little mountain store (when neither Father Dietz or Theresa would see us). We all had the feeling that no matter how hungry we were, we must not let them know. They worked so hard and had such a little to do with, that we were constantly amazed that things continued as they did.[98]

After a visit to Hot Springs Father Corrigan commented on these conditions to Dietz:

> The exacting conditions I saw, while inspiring to one of zeal, are absolutely prohibitive as far as the ordinary willingness to suffer privation for 'uplifts' sake goes.[99]

Yet withal there was a spirit of cooperation among the students. Veronica Hanley tells how each contributed her talents (she taught typing) to keep things running. They wrote letters to every bishop or prominent clergyman they knew, trying to spread information about the school in order to secure backing "which was so sorely needed."[100] Many of these "pleading" letters they placed on the altar before mailing, but Miss Hanley concludes: "We worked and we prayed and had little encouragement."[101]

Perhaps no one thing demonstrates the courage of Dietz so well as the condition of the ledger in which he kept the financial record of the Academy. From the first course which ended with a deficit of four hundred and sixteen dollars, until the end of the fifth course when there was a deficit of four hundred and ninety dollars, the books never balanced. The five donations recorded range from twenty dollars from Bishop Muldoon to some one thousand dollars from anonymous donors.[102] The apparent approval and applause afforded the school were not expressed in terms of tangible help.

Father Corrigan revealed a segment of opinion when he reported the following conversation, although he identified only one of the parties—Dr. Kerby. Wrote Corrigan:

> All seemed to agree that whatever chance your academy had in the beginning it had practically none now that the Catholic Colleges were taking up courses on social topics. The institutional nature of the Academy I found did not appeal at all. Then Kerby delivered a statement. The Academy should

not be carried on as it kept you from what he believed would prove your vocation. He declared he knew no man of such high inspirational power and believed that . . . you should use your free time in going from seminary to seminary throughout the country delivering courses on these so badly neglected social reform topics. . . . You would leave inspiration behind you everywhere and do untold good.[103]

He agreed that Kerby's idea was "sensible and feasible," adding:

You gave of your best to the Academy and perhaps have been, in the wise designs of Providence, the instrument of bringing about the decidedly unusual activity in sociology in our Catholic colleges.[104]

Opinions like these had little influence on Father Dietz. He believed that the ultimate test of the school would be the ability of its graduates to secure and hold positions. Soon they were demonstrating that they could meet that test. Susan Frawley Eisele, the youngest of the original group of seven students, is a well-known rural columnist today. Mrs. Eisele credits Father Dietz with discovering her ability to write and forcing her to do so, often against her will. No doubt she would echo the opinion of most of those who came under the influence of Father Dietz, when she writes:

I had lived in a fairyland until I met Father Dietz. Life was one grand sweet song. He showed me for the first time how serious life is, and how necessary it is for each of us to be our brother's keeper. . . . He made me aware of the suffering and injustice which men inflict upon each other. . . . He taught me the dignity of labor and the duty of an employer to his employees.[105]

The St. Vincent de Paul Society offered a field of activity for several of the White Cross Nurses. Cecilia Hourigan, after a time at Santa Maria Institute in Cincinnati, transferred to Detroit in 1917, to become supervisor of the Homes Department of the Society. Her supervisor wrote of her to Father Dietz:

Miss Hourigan is all that you recommended her to be and more. She has proven herself to be a very capable person with children, and an efficient Home Investigator.[106]

Her place was taken by Theresa Dietz in 1919. Before coming to Detroit Miss Dietz had been executive secretary for the Catholic Women's League of Pittsburgh. Two years later she accepted a position with the Mothers' Pension Department of the Juvenile Court, transferring in 1925 to the Public Welfare Department of Detroit.[107] Theresa Winters, a graduate nurse who had come to the Academy for the Catholic training it offered, served as directress of the Vincentian Auxiliary in Cumberland, Maryland.[108]

Some of the graduates were interested in helping the working girl. Elizabeth Linthicum of Washington, D. C., wrote enthusiastically of her work and of her appreciation of the Academy:

> I often recall the time spent there and the splendid work you are undertaking. I've opened a Home in Washington for working girls and am most anxious to do other work along the social line. We will move into larger quarters . . . and I wish to open a real social center.[109]

Veronica Hanley of Coshocton, Ohio, was also interested in this type of work. After graduation from the Academy in 1916, she served as assistant to the Secretary of the Associated Charities of Coshocton.[110] Later, as secretary of the Catholic Community League of Canton, Ohio, where she did follow-up work of court cases dealing with delinquent children, she wrote Father Dietz of her special interest:

> I have been working on 'girls' friendly clubs' for strange girls and hope to be encouraged in the idea of starting a Girls' club with gymnasium, etc. . . . There is much need for protective work for girls in a place like this that attracts so many small town girls with its big wages and lack of facilities for caring for them when they get here. We have a room registry and were able to furnish forty-seven rooms to the Pennsylvania Railroad office which was trying to locate Catholic employees here.[111]

Miss Hanley's continued effort to carry out his principles of social action pleased Father Dietz very much and led him to remark to his sister, Theresa, many years later (1943), "It was all worth while, anyway, wasn't it?"[112]

A call for medical social workers found White Cross Nurses capable of filling such positions. When the supervisor of Mercy Hospital in Wilkes-Barre, Pennsylvania, wrote for a "good social worker" who could follow up patients after they left the hospital and take care of any situation, Dietz recommended Anna Hourigan of Schenectady, New York.[113] When he called her back to the Academy to teach, Ann Murphy replaced her in Wilkes-Barre. Because of Miss Murphy's "very good work," her supervisor, Sister Mary Celestine, wrote Dietz two years later, asking for another medical social worker.[114]

When Miss Hourigan's classes were discontinued in 1920, she secured a position through Frank Morrison with the United States Veterans' Bureau Vocational School.[115] The Bureau later asked to use her "plans and outlines" for the curriculum of two new training centers.[116]

Elizabeth Kuhlman of Quincy, Illinois, did social work at St. Elizabeth Settlement in St. Louis, founded by Frederick P. Kenkel. About a year after she came to St. Louis (1918), Mr. Kenkel declared his "trust and faith" in her were such that he wanted her to take charge of a settlement he planned to open in Chicago after the war.[117] This plan never materialized, however, and in 1925 Miss Kuhlman transferred to Springfield, Illinois, where she did social work for five years, cooperating with Monsignor J. C. Straub in organizing the Ladies of Charity.[118]

These young women represent the type of work Father Dietz was doing at Hot Springs. Their letters to him asking for advice, recounting their successes and failures, and expressing an interest in his welfare indicate more than anything else the spirit that prevailed in the American Academy of Christian Democracy for Women.

In the meantime Father Dietz realized more and more the desirability of a change of location for the school. What had seemed advantages in the beginning—Mrs. Safford's benefaction, the beautiful mountain scenery, and the location fairly central to Illinois, New York, Florida, and Louisiana—were offset by certain disadvantages. North Carolina was not Catholic and did not contribute to populating the school; the environment was "full of false social and economic theories," which inevitably affected Catholics living there; there was no opportunity for practical work, and, finally,

166

a change in location might induce the Social Service Commission to adopt a more favorable attitude toward the Academy.[119]

An offer of one hundred and seventy-five acres of land at Black Mountain appealed greatly to Father Dietz, though it would have meant remaining in North Carolina. Through Bishop Haid, he had become acquainted with R. G. Alexander, a cotton merchant of Charlotte, North Carolina, who was handling the disposition of property belonging to Mrs. Florence Weatherly of Birmingham, Alabama. The lady offered the land to the Catholic Church for a summer playground.[120] The Episcopalians, Presbyterians, Baptists, and Methodists had already constructed cottages and hotels in the area. In the center of these a group of "musical people" under the leadership of Walter Damrosch planned to build an auditorium that would hold twenty thousand people.[121] Somehow Dietz thought this would be an ideal setting for his school. The correspondence over this gift ran all through 1916 and part of 1917, in an effort to adjust the "strings" attached so that the integrity of the school could be maintained and episcopal jurisdiction could be safeguarded.

Negotiations reached the point of drawing up a deed, with Bishop Haid and Father Dietz as trustees. This arrangement was to hold until the New York Convention of the American Federation of Catholic Societies, when Dietz hoped the Federation would "take action one way or another."[122] But, as has been noted, the Federation's Social Service Commission rejected the offer and remained unmoved by Father Dietz's plea for "recognition of the American Academy of Christian Democracy as a training school for Federation Social Service."[123] He was left free to use the Black Mountain offer, however, provided the Federation was in no way committed.[124] For a time Father Dietz continued to plan his building at "Credo Cove" as a permanent home for the White Cross Nurses, but inability to arrive at a satisfactory agreement with Mrs. Weatherley, as well as lack of funds, kept him from taking definite steps.[125]

Bishop Haid, who thought Black Mountain the best if Dietz were staying in North Carolina, advised him to reject other offers at Flat Rock, Waynesville, and Pinnacle Mountain.[126] But even when arrangements were made to move to Cincinnati, Dietz still clung to the idea of a "novitiate" in western North Carolina to which the students could come for three or four months during "the slack part of the year in the cities."[127]

While negotiations were going on for Black Mountain, Father Dietz was sending out "feelers" to cities in the Middle West and East. As an approach to Indianapolis, he wrote to Father Francis Gavisk about the possibilities of establishing a center for practical work. Since there were no "Catholic social enterprises" of the character Dietz was interested in, he would have an open field there and, more important, the city was a trade union center. But he especially wanted to know the attitude of the Bishop toward such work.[128] Father Gavisk agreed that Indianapolis would be a good place since there was a great deal of interest in social work among the general population. But he added:

> I have found it quite difficult to interest the Catholic people in matters of this sort. As for the Bishop, the Coadjutor, he has not shown any interest in these matters. The clergy generally, I suspect, look with good natured tolerance upon me as crotchety . . .[129]

He suggested, however, that Father Dietz see the Bishop. This he did in mid-June. Dietz followed up the interview with a letter asking permission to use St. Joseph's Industrial Home, which the Sisters told him was to be closed, for a six months' experiment beginning with his summer course in July.[130] Bishop Joseph Chartrand, the Coadjutor, refused the permission:

> After deliberation and consultation, have concluded that Indianapolis is not now the place for the work suggested.[131]

Further importunings by Dietz and Bishop Muldoon left the Bishop unmoved.[132]

Since Pittsburgh seemed another likely place for his Academy, Father Dietz got in touch with the Reverend Thomas F. Coakley of that city. But Duquesne University had just completed plans for a school of social service similar to the one Dietz planned and Coakley thought "it would scarcely be possible for Pittsburgh to sustain two such schools."[133] Nevertheless Dietz wrote to Father

J. A. Dewe, professor of Economics and Sociology at Duquesne and president of the Diocesan Commission of Labor, about the possibility of cooperation.[134] Dewe explained that although "inspired and directed" by himself, the school was actually under the Catholic Associated Charities, and concluded:

> I much regret to say that as far as this locality is concerned any cooperation between ourselves is impossible. I greatly admire the work you are doing and would not at all mind cooperating with you in your general work throughout the states, but as far as this place is concerned, an additional person would only mean further friction, and disappointment to yourself.[135]

When Father Dietz learned that the Sisters of the Poor of St. Francis were reputedly giving up their work at St. Elizabeth's Hospital in Dayton, Ohio, he wrote Archbishop Henry Moeller of Cincinnati, offering his White Cross Nurses in their place.[136] Moeller was not certain that the Sisters were giving up the hospital, and if they did, he would prefer that diocesan Sisters take charge of it, but he added:

> If they cannot, I might consider allowing the Hospital management to be placed in other hands. Before considering in any way the White Cross Nurses, I should have more information. Under whose control, and what authority would the Bishop of the Diocese have over them?[137]

Dietz's reply to these questions eventually won him a place in Cincinnati:

> My purpose is, that the White Cross Nurses compete with the secular Charities, much like the parochial system competes with secular education on the basis of less expense and more consecration. I would wish the White Cross Nurses to be subject to the bishop in their work . . . with one proviso . . . the right to appoint or withdraw individual White Cross Nurses as circumstances may make necessary.
>
> I do not want the White Cross Nurses to acquire or to own property or institutions, with the exception of one central place, to which those who are infirm or superannuated may retire . . .[138]

169

Before the Cincinnati site materialized, Dietz sent the following letter "to a select number of bishops":

> The enclosed "White Cross Nurse" explains itself. The work that it stands for has taken root. Its beginnings have been very insignificant. There is nothing wonderful even now in the way of development. It is growing, however, and I have been enabled to place nearly all students of the present course which concludes February 22nd.
>
> The next course beginning a month later, could be inaugurated in a much bigger way if I had a large building and better equipment. I have not the means to do this here on rented property. I can only accommodate 12 students at best, and that without the proper comforts.
>
> Besides, now that our work has definite shape, it can well afford, and perhaps ought to come out of its isolation. Is there not in your Lordship's diocese some building that is not being used to any great advantage, and which could be put at our disposal for the immediate needs of this work, entrusting the farther future to Divine Providence?[139]

Only a few of the replies to this letter are available. The secretaries of the Bishops of Wheeling, West Virginia, and Covington, Kentucky, reported the regret of their respective Bishops that no building was available.[140] Praise of the work of Father Dietz in meeting modern times, already quoted, preceded the Right Reverend Denis J. O'Connell's regret that he had no building to offer.[141] Bishop N. J. Hoban of Scranton said that he would be very pleased to have a "social service academy established in the diocese."

> We need trained s o c i a l w o r k e r s very badly as our volunteers cannot do the work as well as thoroughly paid workers, who can give all their time to the work, after having been prepared for it. We need some here in Scranton . . . a practical nurse with common sense could do an immense amount of good.[142]

Shortly after these letters arrived, a telegram from Sister Blandina of the Santa Maria Institute in Cincinnati assured Dietz that the Archbishop and Father Francis Gressle, director of Catholic Charities, were favorably impressed with his aims.[143] She wrote Dietz further of her visit with the Archbishop:

His Grace wishes to say—if you can conduct your school of Christian Democracy without appealing for aid to the public here and that the Archbishop of Cincinnati maintains a certain supervision over the school, the place is open to you.[144]

By March, 1917, an abandoned hospital, the Good Samaritan, was available for the use of Father Dietz. He wrote Archbishop Moeller:

Thank your Grace for giving the work of the White Cross Nurses a welcome to the Archdiocese of Cincinnati. I do not hesitate to place this work under your patronage and supervision, feeling confident that it will be no burden either upon your Grace or the diocese. On the contrary, God continuing to bless our weak endeavors, we have some hope of being of real assistance in your apostolic mission.[145]

The two people most concerned in his sojourn in Hot Springs reacted very differently at news of his departure. Bessie Safford expressed all her pent up feeling in her note to Father Dietz:

I am so happy to know you, and the atmosphere made by your life, is removed from this section of the country, for the influence of it will be a slur on the Catholic priesthood for years.[146]

The letter Dietz wrote in reply was brief and classic. After acknowledging her letter and declaring the incident closed, he concluded:

I have left behind me at Hot Springs, the White cross on the mountain. It is sacred. I lay upon you as a burden of conscience the upkeep of this cross. It should receive every year a coat of white paint. I ask you to do this not for my sake, but for the sake of everything in your life that might have been and is not. He who died upon the cross, however, can fill every void.[147]

His letter to Bishop Haid, on the other hand, revealed their friendly relationship and Dietz's deepest gratitude:

I do wish to thank you from the bottom of my heart for the faith that you have had in me. Without this faith, I would never have been enabled to do as well as I have done, surrounded by numberless difficulties. You have not been disap-

171

pointed in your faith, and I go back to Cincinnati with all priestly integrity. . . . As long as I live there will be a prayer in my heart for you.[148]

Sincere appreciation and confidence were apparent in the Bishop's reply:

> I am glad to learn (what I anticipated all along) that remarkable success crowned your labors. I know you began under difficulties, and various obstacles met you at every step. . . . You will certainly enjoy a wider field, have greater opportunities, and meet fewer difficulties in Cincinnati. Your aims and work were not understood in North Carolina. . . . I hope you will reap a rich harvest in Ohio, and that your graduates will carry the good effects of their training far and wide.[149]

Twelve students transferred with the school from Hot Springs to Cincinnati. The transfer, completed in March, 1917, ended the pioneer period of the American Academy of Christian Democracy for Women. Father Dietz had demonstrated the need and the demand for such a school where short courses in the social sciences, parliamentary law, and practical nursing prepared young women to fill competently a wide range of social positions. He had demonstrated, likewise, his ability to organize and maintain, virtually single-handed, an institution that imbued its graduates with a deep understanding of the spiritual implications of social service. With the removal to Cincinnati, a wider range of opportunity opened to him among the labor groups and Catholic social agencies. But old problems were accentuated, and new ones, eventually insurmountable, arose.

Chapter Eight

Developing
a Labor College

FATHER DIETZ MOVED his twelve students into an unprepossessing building. Good Samaritan Hospital, or "Old Sam" as the girls called it, was over seventy-five years old. Abandoned by the Sisters of Charity when they moved into a new hospital, it had been vacant for some time, and now only the front part of the building was at all habitable. In this wing Dietz set up the new school, planning at some future time to renovate the whole building.[1] His experience in painting, carpentering, and paper hanging stood him in good stead, as he described the process of renovating to one of his former students:

> Nearly all of us have spent a great deal of our time washing, scrubbing and cleaning of every kind and description. We have had wagon loads of dirt and rubbish removed. Most of the floors had two or three layers of worn out oil-cloth. Even when this was ripped up, the innumerable tacks that remained behind proved an almost impossible test of patience. So it was with everything all the way down the line. I have established a paint shop and carpenter shop from which a number of beneficent activities radiate in various directions.[2]

He offered the first Mass as soon as a superficial cleaning of the chapel made it possible. Large sheets of wrapping paper served as a carpet and an assortment of broken chairs substituted for pews. But the altar was in good condition, its whiteness strongly contrasting with the dirty walls and ceiling.[3]

Sixteen girls enrolled for the sixth course, which began in early April. Father Dietz maintained all of the features of the school

173

at Hot Springs, except for an increased faculty which the new location permitted. Besides Ann Hourigan, who returned to teach "Charities," Elizabeth Hocker and Anna Crotty, two local physicians, had charge of the medical work. Several "public spirited citizens" interested in social work agreed to give occasional lectures.[4]

Opportunities for practical field work were many. Sister Blandina of Santa Maria Institute was most cooperative in affiliating the students with its work among the poor and unfortunate, especially the Italian immigrants.[5] The Associated Charities Bureau allowed the girls to attend case conferences held twice a week, and the Bureau of Catholic Charities, under the direction of the Reverend Francis A. Gressle, permitted the students to go out every day with visitors from the Bureau.[6] Available also were the Juvenile and Domestic Relations Courts, the Consumers' League, and the Central Labor Union.[7]

Father Dietz was especially attracted to the three-year experiment inaugurated in Cincinnati in December, 1917, by Mr. and Mrs. Wilbur Phillips.[8] They selected thirty-one blocks in the Mohawk-Brighton district of the city to set up a social unit, the idea being to break down the popular distrust of the trained professional social worker. By creating a community spirit in a limited area, the experiment would lead the people to become conscious of their common needs and would lead them to cooperate more readily, it was thought, with the agencies prepared to help them meet those needs.[9] Two local committees, a citizen's council of thirty-one (one member from each city block), and an occupational committee representing nine occupational groups guided the investigation.[10] Since the Mohawk-Brighton district included a large Catholic population, Father Gressle of the Cincinnati charities thought Catholics should take an active part in the experiment.[11] He wrote Dietz:

> Mr. Dinwiddie desires priests on the Occupational Committee. . . . Let me know if you are willing to serve. . . . I shall be delighted if at any time in the very near future, you will confer with me about this matter, so that we can properly organize ourselves to watch the interests of the Catholic people in the District selected.[12]

The Reverend John Schopp, pastor of St. Augustine's parish, which was part of the social unit, and the other Catholic leaders concerned, including the Archbishop, approved Dietz's representation on the committee.[13] Accordingly Dietz called a meeting of the young men of the parish and suggested the organization of a Catholic Social Unit Co-operative, with Father Schopp as chairman, to see that "all questions that came up in the social unit board, would be decided from a Catholic point of view."[14]

Shortly after the organization of the social unit, however, Mr. and Mrs. Phillips were suspected of being Socialists, and local organizations withdrew their support.[15] Archbishop Moeller ordered Dietz to withdraw also.[16] That he obeyed is suggested by a letter from Phillips:

> The social unit is now well under way. . . . Will you not, as one who took an interest in seeing the plan launched, express your continued sympathy . . . by becoming one of our thinking membership?[17]

In August, 1917, Father Dietz and two of his students undertook the organization of a project somewhat similar to this—a social survey of the city of Covington, Kentucky.[18] Dietz had proposed the initiation of surveys in various centers of the Federation to ascertain "on the basis of existing facts the Catholic problems coming within the scope of lay activity."[19] He pointed out that a "systematized plan" of this kind was the only one "worthy of so great and comprehensive an organization as the Catholic Federation."[20] At the New York convention in 1916, the Executive Board gave Dietz permission to work out a plan, but lack of funds prevented any action on the idea except in Covington, under the auspices of the Covington Federation.

The Right Reverend Ferdinand Brossart, Bishop of Covington, cooperated with Dietz by sending the following letter to his pastors:

> The Reverend Father Dietz, who has charge of a social survey in various dioceses of the country and of the American Academy of Christian Democracy in Cincinnati, will call upon you at my request and unfold to you a system of work in the social order of our people that has become a necessity in

175

many places and may be such also here. I desire that every pastor give Father Dietz every encouragement possible so that an experiment may be made in our city and later on throughout the Diocese.[21]

The original plan for the survey had seven divisions: education and entertainment; civics and law; social and industrial relations; charities and social service; public morality; press and publicity; and organization and central bureau. The Directorate (seven members from each division), and the Common Council (seven field agents from each parish), formed the administrative body for the survey.[22] At the initial meeting, August 1, 1917, in the Guild Hall, Anna Hourigan explained certain phases of social service, such as child-welfare clinics, medical supervision in home and school, hospital extension, the sick poor, and friendly visiting.[23] The group at this meeting decided to limit investigation to two divisions: charities and social service, and social and industrial relations. However, reports of committees on education and entertainment and public morality are among the Dietz papers.

The recommendations of the committees provided an enlightened program of social action for the Covington Federation. Included in those of the committee on education and entertainment were the organization of evening classes for illiterates (Kentucky ranked thirty-seventh in literacy), a night school for adults, the establishment of parochial school social centers in every parish, and a course in "Parliamentary Law for young men and young ladies . . . that they may present and uphold in a convincing and logical manner the Catholic view-point on subjects of the day, especially when associated with non-Catholics."[24]

The committee on charities and social service secured promises from several doctors and dentists to contribute their services to the care of school children. Other needs brought to the attention of the group included the organization of Mothers' Clubs to care for "the poor widow's children while she is away at work," about thirty cases of sick poor, and the enforcement of the curfew laws to prevent young boys from collecting in pool halls.[25]

Shortly after the completion of the survey Father Dietz moved the Academy again, this time to a ten-acre tract near Ault Park, purchased from the Jacob Feck estate.[26] Jacob Feck had been a grower of fine grapes and at one time had operated a winery there. Situated on the estate was a large seventeen room stone building used originally as a private residence. Like the "Old Sam," it was in disrepair, but again by dint of hard labor Dietz and two of his students made it livable.[27] Because of its "peculiar sidelong location" on a hill, the house had two basements. The lower one, about twenty-five by fifty feet, made a unique chapel. With the floor cemented and chandeliers and an altar added, its vaulted ceiling and "catacomy effect" reminded Father Dietz of the chapel of San Pietro in Vinculis in Rome.[28] His old friend and counsellor Very Reverend Thomas Frederick Price, M.M., co-founder of Maryknoll, who stopped in Cincinnati for this purpose while enroute to China as head of Maryknoll's first departure group, dedicated the Chapel on September 9, 1918.[29]

This new and more pretentious venture brought financial problems greater than Dietz had yet encountered. The situation became particularly critical when his income from the American Federation of Catholic Societies, already in arrears, stopped altogether in September, 1918.[30] He exploited every possible source to secure financial help.

Bishop Muldoon, unable to help him personally or to secure for him part of the funds of the National Catholic War Council, wrote Father Noll in his behalf:

> Perhaps you know more about Father Dietz's work than I do, but I do think it is a very good work and capable of expansion. He thinks that possibly you could find a way of assisting him in his present difficulty. I hope so.[31]

Father Noll sent Dietz one hundred dollars and notified him that he had placed three thousand dollars in a Cincinnati bank for a loan.[32]

Ultimately the representatives of labor unions offered him the greatest help and encouragement. During the intervals between courses and while the new location at Ault Park was being put in readiness, Dietz had contacted labor leaders in Cincinnati. His attendance at A. F. of L. meetings for so many years made him a familiar figure

177

to many of them, and they gave him permission to attend meetings at Labor Temple. Frequently after these meetings interested trade-unionists would gather around Dietz for further discussion of labor problems. As they were all interested in his American Academy of Christian Democracy, it was not surprising that the Central Labor Council petitioned the Committee of the War Chest Fund of Cincinnati for a grant for the Academy.[33] To add strength to the petition Dietz solicited recommendations from leading trade-unionists for what he was already calling his "labor college." Frequently accompanying an endorsement was a contribution, sometimes a personal donation, sometimes a union donation. W. D. Mahon, International President of the Amalgamated Association of Street and Electric Railway Employees, gave both; his personal check for ten dollars and a union check for fifty.[34]

Necessary for any success along this line were the approbation and support of Archbishop Moeller. In the letter requesting a recommendation Dietz revealed some of his personal anxiety when he wrote:

> Something akin to despondency prompts this letter and I have struggled so hard and so long.[35]

It put the Archbishop on guard and brought the unsympathetic refusal to endorse his work:

> From the tone of your letter, it appears that your enterprise is on the verge of a failure. By giving it moral support, if a crash should nevertheless come, I would in a measure be held responsible. I cannot afford thus to compromise myself.[36]

To make his position secure, the Archbishop directed a second letter to Father Dietz on the same day reminding him that he was allowed to remain "simply as a visitor" in the diocese. And to clarify the situation still further the letter concluded:

> I hereby request you to secure from your Bishop and to submit an authenticated copy to me, papers showing that you have and for how long a time, a leave of absence from your diocese, and to inform your Bishop that you have no prospects whatever of being incardinated here.[37]

Archbishop Messmer's delay in sending the papers brought a second letter from the Chancery, threatening the withdrawal of Father Dietz's faculties if the papers were not forthcoming within two weeks.[38] The tension was finally eased when, with Bishop Muldoon's help, Archbishop Messmer was pressed to respond, and Moeller "assumed something of an atmosphere in which it was possible to breathe."[39]

In the midst of these distressing circumstances a fire at the Academy partially destroyed the roof, causing an estimated damage of five or six thousand dollars. The fire necessitated breaking up classes for some time, but Father Dietz wrote optimistically to Bishop Muldoon:

> It matters not; I am too anxious and God is determined that I bide my time. It will come and I am not at all discouraged.[40]

In the course of repairing the damage, an entire third floor as well as personal apartments for Father Dietz were added. For this work he had the help of members of the building trades, who contributed their services gratis.[41]

When the Committee on the War Chest Fund refused the grant, the Central Labor Council redoubled its efforts to advertise the Academy. A circular letter to its affiliated unions called attention to the fact that the Academy had been endorsed by the Council on December 10, 1918. The letter continued:

> This Academy can be of much value to the Trade-union movement, and we believe that the trade unionists should take some interest in it and find out for themselves just what its work is and what its mission means for the workers.[42]

Father Dietz was kept busy through June, 1919, and part of July filling requests from the various locals to explain his Academy.[43]

Labor's endorsement on a national scale was accorded during the convention of the A. F. of L. at Atlantic City in the summer of 1919. As never before, Dietz appreciated his many friends among the men of labor. For the first time he felt free to use his own judgment without fear of repercussions from either the Executive Board or the Social Service Commission of the American Federation of Catho-

179

lic Societies.[44] Reporting on events to Muldoon, he listed the following achievements:

1) The Federation of Labor endorsed the Academy. . . .
2) Those particularly friendly to me revived the organization I started some years back and which the Federation of Catholic Societies refused to let me develop.[45]
3) They pledged themselves to support the institution financially, by encouraging scholarships and providing students.
4) They regard it as a national plan and will support no similar movement started under other auspices.
5) They will not branch out locally until I am well enough established to institute branches and foster them in the one agreed policy.[46]

In the midst of his great satisfaction over events at the convention, a letter arrived from Archbishop Moeller. Anticipating trouble, Dietz delayed opening it. When he finally summoned sufficient courage, he was totally unprepared for its contents. The Archbishop assured Father Dietz that he appreciated and sympathized with his years of effort to solve the social and industrial questions. From "reliable sources" Moeller had learned that Father Dietz's views on these matters were "strictly in accord with the sound principles of theology." But in order that Dietz proceed "with the greatest possible safety" the Archbishop had appointed an advisory committee of three—the Very Reverend Francis J. Beckman, S.T.D., Reverend M. Mulvihill, and Reverend Louis J. Nau, S.T.D. Moeller approved the American Academy of Christian Democracy as meeting "a much needed want" and promised to "encourage and foster" it to the best of his ability.[47]

To these encouraging approbations, Father Dietz wanted to add one more. Convinced that "authority should not be divided, nor jurisdiction questioned, nor varying policies adopted," he asked Bishop Muldoon to secure for him the protection of the "hierarchy and Catholic organization."[48] In short, he wanted recognition from the bishops of the United States when they assembled in September, 1919. With that he would be able "confidently and securely to look forward to a development" he was not "permitted to have before."[49]

Instead of recognizing Dietz's school, the War Council established a school of its own in Washington, which brought the complaint from Dietz:

> I had forty four graduates out in positions before the War Council in Washington started its school for which it had the unhistorical hardihood to claim that it was the first of its kind in the country.[50]

The financial pledges given at Atlantic City by the labor men netted Father Dietz over six hundred dollars. They varied in amount from two hundred and fifty dollars sent by P. H. McCarthy, president of the State Building Trades Council of California, to five dollars contributed by the Cincinnati local of the Amalgamated Sheet Metal Workers.[51] Matthew Woll's contribution of twenty-five dollars (he was sorry he could not give more) held special interest since he had declared a few months before that he was opposed to labor colleges because of their radicalism.[52] With this relatively substantial backing Dietz announced the "Tenth Social Institute," a ten-week course for working girls, including the study of English, Parliamentary Law, Public Speaking, Charities and Social Service, and the History, Policies and Methods of the American Labor Movement.[53]

The Institute marks a turning point in the nature of the American Academy of Christian Democracy. Emphasis from this point on was more on labor and less on social service. At the first meeting of the Advisory Committee appointed by Archbishop Moeller, Dietz outlined his three-point proposal:

1) The executive authority to deal with the industrial situation in Cincinnati (not academically but executively); the right, in your name, to deal with the industrial questions as Father Gressle deals with the charity problems.

2) The organization of a voluntary industrial Council composed of representatives of the Chamber of Commerce and of the Central Labor Council for the purpose of diagnosing the situation and planning the preventive, educational, conciliatory measures which tend toward a policy of peace rather than the industrial war which we now suffer from almost constantly.

3) My most intimate plan whereby I want to get the interested and concerned parties and friends to spend week ends at the Academy in order to give them special and personal treatment and for this purpose mobilize the vast storehouse of Catholic treasure in books, doctrine, and devotion. The materials (human) that must be dealt with in these matters are stubborn often and only that which comes from the heart of Christ can make them malleable; there is no other way and it contains my most fundamental solution for labor troubles.[54]

To insure solidarity among the Catholic trade unionists, Dietz wanted to organize them on parish lines irrespective of crafts. At a joint session, say four times a year, members of these parish societies could discuss the "doctrinal and moral" implications of labor matters.[55] Members likewise could attend the Academy through a common fund set up for that purpose. In time Dietz wanted to see published a Catholic labor journal, an organ for the Christian interpretation of controversial issues.[56]

The Archbishop agreed enthusiastically to all of these points, even asking for the withdrawal of Father J. Reiner, S.J., from Cincinnati so the labor field could be left entirely to Father Dietz.[57] He again assured Dietz that he believed his work was "very good and timely" and was convinced that he would "conduct the same along safe and well balanced lines."[58]

Fortified by the long-sought approbation of Archbishop Moeller, generally and specifically given, Dietz proceeded confidently in his program for labor. It was a time when labor needed a champion as never before. At the close of World War I the clash between labor and capital, held in abeyance during the war when labor found support in a sympathetic President, was on again. In the fall of 1920 the United States Chamber of Commerce launched another "open shop" campaign, in what it chose to call the "American Plan of Operation," but which was aimed primarily at smashing the unions. As a champion of the union shop, Dietz took part in labor's "campaign of education" to acquaint the public with the true state of things.[59]

For some time Father Dietz had been recognized as an official labor mediator, holding credentials from the Central Labor Council and Trades Assembly permitting him to attend all meetings of the various unions of Hamilton County.[60] Frequently he was called in to mediate labor disputes like that of the six-weeks-old strike of two hundred and fifty members of the International Capmakers' Union. They demanded the reduction of a fifty-hour week to forty-four, a two dollar per week wage increase, pay without work on the six national holidays, and recognition of their union. Three large firms and several smaller ones were opposing these demands. Within two days after Dietz was called in, a compromise settlement was effected, by which the companies agreed to recognize the union, granted the pay increase, settled for a forty-seven hour week, and holidays with no pay.[61]

About this same time Dietz became interested in the plight of the Cincinnati firemen, who had sought affiliation with the A. F. of L. When four firemen admitted membership in the International Association of Fire-Fighters and were discharged, five hundred firemen resigned and were out for a week. A committee of mediation met with the mayor and the safety director and drew up a written agreement, on the strength of which the men returned to work. But, contrary to the agreement, there were demotions with decrease in salary, while those who had not resigned were promoted. Furthermore, reinstatements were slow and were not made according to seniority. Dietz, at the request of Captain Moorman, had attended the meetings of the firemen, encouraged them in their desire to unionize, and cited the government's attitude during the war as proof that unionism was not un-American. He also addressed a letter in their behalf to the Honorable John Galvin, mayor of Cincinnati, assuring him that there was "nothing socialistic or bolshevistic" about the firemen who had pledged themselves to honorable conduct which he was sure they had kept and intended to keep.[62] Recognizing that "in principle it would be hard to choose between the natural right of association lawfully guaranteed and the obligation of securing the public safety," Dietz still thought it would be better to "direct the current" than to dam it.[63] He explained that the "crux" of the difficulty lay in the interpretation of Rule 55. This rule, which recognized the *"poten-*

tial" right of the men to affiliate with the A. F. of L., was *"actually controverted,"* the firemen believed, by the influence of the Metal Trades Association. As a solution, Dietz suggested an armistice reinstating all the firemen but one, whose case might be "benevolently litigated with the understanding of eventually abiding the decision of the courts."[64]

Opposition to trade-unions was especially bitter among the machine tool manufacturers who belonged to the local Metal Trades Association, notably the R. K. LeBlond Machine Tool Company.[65] When a strike for union recognition occurred in the plant, the strikers came to Father Dietz for advice. The company claimed that of the one hundred and thirty-three men out on strike only forty per cent really wanted to strike; the rest had left their work because of "malicious representations from Union Headquarters."[66] In a protracted correspondence with Richard K. LeBlond, head of the firm, Dietz tried to educate him in the possibilities of trade-unionism. He suggested for settling the strike a contract with the machinists on an open shop basis, and he offered to stand between the men and the company "for the life of the contract."[67] LeBlond rejected the idea because there was no "such thing as a contract on an 'open shop' basis" and furthermore contracts were "always one-sided" because the "various labor organizations" did not respect their contracts.[68] LeBlond warned Father Dietz against being used "as a tool by the unions" to further a purpose which he did not comprehend.[69] Ignoring the warning, Dietz raised the question whether the breaking of one or more contracts made it reasonable to denounce all contracting and pointed out that there was a "splendid record here also of contracts kept."[70] Furthermore, the record of contract breaking was not limited to labor, and he cited the most recent case in Cincinnati where the guilty ones were the garment Trades Employers.[71]

When LeBlond tried to impress upon Father Dietz the economic loss through strikes, the latter countered with the thought that loss and gain were not fairly estimated in dollars and cents, for, he continued

> these contests bring out much that is in the human mind and heart of intelligence and wisdom or ignorance and folly; qualities of weakness that otherwise remain dormant are

smoked out and psychologically a strike may mean much to humanity's truer interests that ought not to be discounted by the money aspect.[72]

Father Dietz condemned the use of the injunction, though he realized it was the "livest issue" in the land and would have to be fought out. But he believed

> when the smoke of battle is over, it will be apparent here too, that the hopes of its abettors lacked democratic foundation. There will be no government by injunction in America.[73]

As in the case of contracts, Dietz could see no logic in LeBlond's belittling arbitration as a method of settling differences just because it had failed in certain instances. What could be substituted, he asked, but "steel Trusts and Russias?"[74] Dietz emphasized the importance of the arbitrator, since every good man was not a good arbitrator. Among his important qualifications, Dietz believed, were the "courage of conviction" and the ability to distinguish between "principle" and "opportunism," for where the arbitrator "merely splits the difference he fails in argument, sacrifices principle and looks to circumstances for the easiest way."[75]

Dietz made no claim that trade-unionism was flawless. He admitted all the irregularities pointed out by LeBlond, and more, such as charging for the same service twice on the railroads, charging for services never performed, and the employment of more men that the need required. On the other hand, he questioned:

> How am I to apply the remedy? By denouncing and interdicting the *principle of association?* Then my logic would be at fault and I could not hope to profit by error. But if I devote what poor energies I have to baptize and ennoble associations of working-men, then I am doing something that is not only avoiding the extremes of the I.W.W. and the Chamber of Commerce . . . but I am doing that sensible and constructive thing which roots in nature but has the hope of reaching to high heaven.[76]

To Dietz the desire on the part of employers to destroy trade-unionism could be accounted for in no other way than that they found it easier "to condescend and treat with a weak enemy than with a

185

potential rival for power who must be negotiated with rather than dictated to." And, he observed, there was one certain characteristic of trade-unionism — "it loves to negotiate." But, he warned, if the time ever came when labor refused to negotiate "tyranny" would be "supreme."[77]

Finally, Dietz assured LeBlond that

> capitalism will not be murdered by the labor unions; if it goes the way of death it will be by suicide. . .[78]

That might be a fitting end, he suggested, for "some exponents of it who figure prominently in contemporaneous industrial history: witness especially the Steel Trust and some Coal Barons."[79]

Richard LeBlond did not consider Father Dietz an enemy, but showed an understanding of what Dietz was trying to do. On two occasions he made contributions of five hundred dollars—one time outright, and another through the Community Chest as a "designated gift."[80] One letter expressed his attitude very well; he wrote:

> I sincerely hope that you will in your teachings try to place yourself in the other man's point of view occasionally. In other words, I feel that it is your mission to heal rather than to aggravate the wounds brought about by the present conditions; and heal them through the channels of honesty and justice.[81]

To heal the industrial "wounds" through the "channels of honesty and justice" was exactly what Father Dietz tried to do by bringing together into peaceful conference the groups most interested in industrial peace: the Cincinnati Chamber of Commerce, the Central Labor Council, and the public. The confidence of the Central Labor Council he already had. The cooperation of the Chamber of Commerce remained to be won. His plan was to form an industrial Council made up of seven representatives of each organization plus seven chosen by those fourteen from the public at large. This Council was to be "a fraternal association for purposes of conciliation, industrial evolution, voluntary arbitration, social welfare and Christian democracy."[82]

The Chamber of Commerce repeatedly denied his requests to

address it. Apparently the only concession was permission to attend a special meeting of representatives of business organizations and associations, on November 23, 1920. He secured this through the influence of Joseph G. Steinkamp, an architect.[83] The representatives adopted the Constitution of the Industrial Division of the Cincinnati Chamber of Commerce, subject to amendment by the Executive Committee within ninety days.[84] During the course of the meeting Dietz heard the leaders of labor referred to as a "lot of bulls riding around in Packards overawing a mass of unwilling men" who were "dying to get out of the labor movement" and were waiting for the help of the capitalists to do it.[85] In language such as Father Dietz had yet to hear at any meeting at Labor Temple, management, secure in its "holding the whip hand" once again, with labor "scared to death," planned its "Americanization" of the labor movement.[86]

According to its Constitution, the object of the Industrial Division was:

> To promote and protect the best interests of the community. To constitute a clearing house for all questions of common interest.
>
> To recognize that the rights of the public are paramount and take precedence over the interests of any trade or class, and in any industrial disturbance we demand that the law must be enforced and order maintained, and that no citizens desirous of working shall be interfered with or in any way prevented from following their chosen vocation.[87]

The Executive Committee ratified the Constitution on November 27, 1920.[88] After the Cincinnati *Times-Star* of that date published the proceedings Dietz addressed the following open letter to the editor:

> In Saturday's Times-Star all too meager if interesting "publicity" was given to the Proceedings of the Industrial Division, Cincinnati Chamber of Commerce.
>
> The perfectly "safe for democracy, openly diplomatic" statement addressed to the public contains the germ, very probably, of very serious consequences for our city.
>
> As a citizen of Cincinnati, interested in industrial peace—

187

aggressively so—may I not raise my voice in a public (since a previous private appeal was denied) to ask the Chamber of Commerce for an open meeting and to afford a hearing to the public before the plans of the Industrial Division, consummated last Saturday, are finally ratified by the Board of Directors of the Chamber of Commerce?

The Constitution of the Industrial Division is said "to promote and protect the best interests of the community; to constitute a clearing-house for all questions of common interest;" also it sets forth that "the rights of the public are paramount and take precedence over any trade or class."

With this last dictum I find myself in complete accord. May I again, however, ask in the light of my "public rights" which are confessedly "paramount" why the Chamber of Commerce ought not at least to consult with "the public" whose "best interests" it proposes to "promote and protect," and why it ought not to afford in advance of final action "a clearing-house for certain questions of common interest" in the premises?

I cannot be blamed for being just a little suspicious of a powerful organization that undertakes to "promote and protect my best interests" without even giving me a chance formally to delegate them to it. If this is the "American Plan" I want to know more about it. Maybe some other Cincinnati citizens feel a kindred impulse.[89]

Naturally labor was pleased with this letter, which was reprinted with approval in the *Weekly News-Letter* of the A. F. of L.[90] But the Chamber of Commerce reacted quite differently. A committee of Catholic business men, members of the Metal Trades Association, approached Archbishop Moeller, protesting against the article in particular and the work of Father Dietz in general, insinuating that he was teaching Socialism and harming the best interests of the Catholic Church.[91] Episcopal repercussion came soon after in the following letter:

You acted very imprudently in writing the article. It is of a nature which might fan into mighty conflagration the flames of excitement existing between employers and employees. . . . Wherefore in virtue of Canon No. 1386 of the new Codex I hereby forbid you in future, to publish in the papers, any article, no matter on what subject, without having first submitted it either to the Right Reverend F. Beckman, D.D., or Right Reverend William D. Hickey, Censores Librorum, and obtain their nihil obstat and my permission to publish same.[92]

The source of the Archbishop's information was no secret to Father Dietz. Accordingly he addressed this letter to the Board of Directors of the Chamber of Commerce:

> There have been several verbal as well as written requests to your body for a hearing by you on matters over which you claim jurisdiction but which touch other jurisdictions as well as your own.
>
> My attitude toward you was Christian and your attitude toward me was Socialist. For you must know that the Socialist says that he is not going to negotiate with Capitalism but wipe it out and that is just what you are attempting to do to me.
>
> I have some things to say to you, gentlemen, that would be well worth your time to listen to. I want harmony between Capital and Labor: you want war between Capital and Labor and in that you again find yourself in accord with the principles of Lenin the Dictator of the Russian proletariat.[93]

The letter was turned over to P. W. Drackett, head of a chemical manufacturing firm, who invited Dietz to his office "to go over the situation in a personal way."[94]

Failure to influence the employers as a whole through the Chamber of Commerce was offset by success in bringing labor and management together in the Building Trades through the Wage Board Conference. Based on the "practical recognition of the worker's right to organize and to negotiate through spokesmen of his own choosing" these conferences discussed wages and shop conditions. Decisions were subject to the "ratification of constituent units."[95] Thus only through collective bargaining and trade agreements, which presupposed organization, could the workers hope to secure a "fair share of the fruit of their toil." Dietz wrote many of the building trade agreements "without either employer groups or unions making any fuss" and there were no strikes.[96] Because of his work the Ohio State Building Trades Council endorsed the American Academy of Christian Democracy.[97]

Fundamentally this Wage Board Conference was an improvement over most of the existing relations between labor and capital in the other trades, but Father Dietz could see the possibility of making it even more effective. Basing the representation of the crafts on their strength and importance, he wanted certain crafts to have more delegates than others. Weekly or bi-weekly meetings, where business was carried on in strictly parliamentary fashion, would give opportunity for a program that would expand beyond the problems of wages and working conditions to include "all elements that enter into building operations from the production of the material and its costs to the finished product."[98] This Conference or Parliament of a semi-public nature would find the way to actual legislation for the industry, and the power to punish violations of that legislation—a power "essentially moral in its nature and flowing from the sources of idealism: culture, patriotism, religion, honesty and business sense."[99] Dietz submitted these suggestions to the several employers in the building trades. The comment of one of them is indicative of the attitude of many Cincinnati employers toward the aims of Father Dietz. Tyler Field, vice-president and treasurer of the Ferro Concrete Construction Company, wrote:

> I am returning to you the article which you left with me the other day. I have read it carefully.
> Your suggestions . . . are interesting to me, and if you at any time would care to drop in and talk this over, I would be very glad to have any further suggestions that you have on this subject.[100]

This plan bore witness to the belief of Father Dietz that the problems of workers had a larger significance than formerly. Workers were coming into their "estate," and a place must be found for that estate as an "integral part of the modern commonwealth." To help the workers establish that estate and fit themselves into it was, he believed, the duty of every patriot.[101]

In the meantime Dietz continued his personal influence over groups of trade-unionists through class instruction, one or two nights a week at Labor Temple, in correct English, parliamentary procedure, and trade union problems. At first some of those who attended came out of curiosity and had no serious interest in study, but gradually the number of earnest students increased until between twenty-five and thirty attended regularly.[102] On week ends they came to the Academy at Ault Park for conferences on the Christian principles underlying trade-unionism.[103] Twenty-five years later, one of these trade unionists recalled how earnest the men were and how Father Dietz inspired them.[104]

Still convinced, however, of the superiority of the boarding school plan which removed the students from the distractions of everyday life, Dietz offered the Eleventh Trade Union Course to begin January 18, 1922, at Ault Park. An intensive five weeks' training followed the lines of previous courses, except for the omission of Charities and Social Service. By this time the Ohio State Federation of Labor had joined the other labor organizations in endorsing the Academy and asked its affiliated unions to cooperate in making this course a success.[105] The Federation suggested that scholarships be made available for deserving young trade-unionists or a small endownment fund created bearing sufficient interest to care for a student each year in perpetuity. The benefit derived would be the availability of "a body of enthusiastic, zealous enlightened young advocates of labor progress, whose services will be inexpensive and yet of inestimable value."[106]

By a natural process of development the American Academy of Christian Democracy moved from the social service emphasis through the trade union courses and conferences, to the announcement in March, 1922, of a National Labor College, the first of its kind in the country, undertaken by the American Federation of Labor at Ault Park.[107] The first course of seven weeks, beginning May 4 and continuing through the convention of the American Federation of Labor in June, was largely experimental, depending on the "previous education, experience, and reading of the students."[108] Through John P. Frey, president of the Metal Trades Department of the A. F. of L., Dietz secured several professors from the University of Cincinnati, who agreed to lecture gratis. John C. McCarthy, a "brilliant young lawyer," likewise agreed to lecture without fee on law as it affected labor. Frey was to handle trade-union

191

methods.[109] The students for the first course were principally those who held scholarships from the Central Labor Unions of Ohio and Pennsylvania, selected in most instances through competitive examinations and the vote of local members.[110]

Naturally the new venture aroused much interest. Among those writing for verification, further information, or to congratulate Father Dietz, was Daniel E. Doran of the Department of Publicity, Press and Literature of the National Catholic Welfare Conference. Doran wrote:

> This news is of course of vital interest to the Catholics of America and we write to inquire as to the reliability of the dispatch and for any further details that you may be able to furnish us, with a view to possible release through this Bureau.[111]

But the Labor College never materialized. At the height of his success, recipient of the highest mark of confidence organized labor had yet bestowed upon him, Father Dietz received orders to close the Academy and to leave the Archdiocese. Since the visit of the men from the Chamber of Commerce to Archbishop Moeller in the fall of 1920, Dietz's actions had been suspect.

Prior to the reprimand regarding his letter to the *Times-Star*, Dietz was taken to task for his part in the election campaign of Warren G. Harding. He had gone to Marion for a personal interview with the candidate, and later "did very good work" for the Party under Will Hays, Republican Chairman.[112] When a reception for Harding was held in Cincinnati, Dietz was named to the reception committee. However he protested to the chairman that he thought it would be better not to have "the Roman-collar in evidence at the depot and en route to the Hotel Sinton."[113] But he did say Grace at the dinner held there.[114]

An article on the League of Nations published in the *Times-Star* really brought the admonition from the Archbishop. In the article Dietz warned the people against accepting the League of Nations simply because the propaganda of the press made Cardinal Gibbons "lend the weight of his personal and ecclesiastical influence"

to it, or quoted the Pope as favoring a league.[115] Father Dietz
opposed the League because it was built on force and linked to

> crucified peace built upon dishonorable repudiation of all the
> idealism that surged behind the 'Four Minute-Men, the 'Lib-
> erty Bonds,' conscription and the cheerful suppression of cher-
> ished American Liberties.[116]

Following the publication of the article, the Archbishop claimed he
had asked Dietz "fraternally" not to write for the papers, but Father
Dietz claimed he had asked him not to "mix in politics."[117] The
seriousness of sending the subsequent letter about the Chamber of
Commerce to the *Times-Star* depends entirely upon which claim is
correct.[118]

After Father Dietz received the letter invoking Canon Law against
him, he wrote a long letter to the Archbishop trying to clarify himself and make Moeller understand his position. He complained about
how needlessly difficult his position in the diocese had been.[119] The
"various injunctions" which ultimately proved to be "impractical
or useless" had prevented him from developing his work "with security." Even in things that surely met with the Archbishop's approbation he had been denied the consolation of knowing it. When
"anonymous propaganda" militated against his best endeavors, Dietz
felt that the Archbishop had "cherished the anonymity." He wrote
the letter about the Chamber of Commerce, Dietz explained, only
for "a complete showdown on the often repeated charge that the
Catholic Church is controlled by capitalism," and in that he was on
Catholic ground. Dietz assured the Archbishop that in spite of this
explanation he held himself "frankly subject" to the discipline im-
posed, but asked the Archbishop to reconsider. The explanations
and petition were fruitless. Far from reconsidering, Archbishop Moeller took the next step to end once and for all his difficulties with
Father Dietz. Interpreting Dietz's letter as one more evidence of his
impulsiveness and ingratitude, Moeller urged Dietz to "wind up"
his affairs in Cincinnati and move to some other diocese, preferably
Milwaukee, where conditions would be more to his liking and where
he would be under the control of his own Ordinary.[120]

Father Dietz could not accept this turn of events and tried in

193

every way to induce the Archbishop to change his mind. To withdraw now when he was so involved, he argued, would be "Christian cowardice."[121] Aside from the heavy financial outlay, other reasons made it difficult for him to move elsewhere easily. Chief among these he counted the fact that his Academy was "now known to the labor movement the country over," and to change its location would mean a great loss of prestige.[122]

Meanwhile Dietz continued his work, reaching the high point of success already noted. Shortly after he sent the announcement of the National Labor College to the press, however, he received the following formal mandate from Archbishop Moeller:

> December 15, 1920 I requested you to arrange for leaving the Archdiocese of Cincinnati.
>
> At the last interview I had with you, you admitted that since you received the above notice, you made improvements on your property at Ault Park. Moreover according to the statement that appeared in the Catholic Bulletin of Cleveland you have already closed a contract . . . for the construction of a three-story brick and stone building at Ault Park.[123] It is evident from the foregoing facts, that you are making no efforts to leave Cincinnati, but on the contrary you are taking independent steps to establish yourself more firmly in the Archdiocese; and to carry out your enterprises.
>
> Wherefore, after due consideration, and after conferring with the Diocesan Consultors, we hereby command you under the pain of suspension, to be incurred ipso facto, to desist from making the proposed improvements at Ault Park, or in any other part of the Archdiocese with a view to carry on your American Academy of Christian Democracy, and your College of Labor.
>
> Moreover, we hereby notify you that you must leave the Archdiocese of Cincinnati on or before May 15, 1922 and that on this date the permission to say Mass and the right to exercise the faculties granted you will ipso facto cease.

The "showdown" which Dietz hoped would not come had arrived at last.[124] His first impulse was to "fight it out" when he informed Archbishop Moeller that he would have "Recourse to Higher Authority."[125] But further investigation disclosed that he had no basis in Canon Law for such an appeal, since he was not a member of that diocese, and hence had no claims there.[126] He might approach it only on the financial angle. Dr. Kerby suggested that since he had "entered the plan and bought a place, with approval," withdrawal did involve him and he ought to have a chance to protect himself.[127] But deciding that he "must not do as the world does," Dietz informed Archbishop Moeller that he would "comply not only with the letter" of the mandate but as far as he could "also with its spirit."[128] Since it would take some time to wind up his affairs, he asked permission to say Mass as long as he was in the Archdiocese. The Archbishop granted an extension of his faculties to June 15.[129] When that extension of time was not sufficient, Archbishop Messmer asked Bishop Brossart to permit Father Dietz to say Mass in Covington, explaining:

> Unfortunately Archbishop Moeller has for some time shown a very hostile spirit towards the institution and wished me to recall Father Dietz. This I would not do as I believe he is doing a splendid work in making the laboring world and its unions understand the principles of the Church that should govern this mighty labor movement.[130]

Not knowing the "reasons for the action" of Archbishop Moeller and not wishing to embarrass him, Bishop Brossart refused the request.[131] Ultimately Dietz secured an extension of faculties to January 1, 1923.[132]

In the meantime leading trade-unionists had taken matters into their own hands. They refused to stand by and watch the end of all Father Dietz's labors and not look for some way to induce Archbishop Moeller to reverse his decision.[133] Opportunely the convention of the A. F. of L. met in Cincinnati that year, from June 12-23, and gave opportunity for a more concerted program of action.[134] A committee of three, Frank Duffy, Matthew Woll, and Daniel Tobin, acted for the group. Since Archbishop Moeller had gone to Europe shortly after he issued the mandate, the committee's first contact was by cablegram. It read:

> The undersigned national officers and members of the Executive Council of the A. F. of L., in behalf of organized labor were amazed at the order to close Father Dietz's Academy of

Christian Democracy which has come to be known as a national institution. Stop. In behalf of these trade unionists we petition you to withdraw this order, at least to suspend it until we can confer with you on your return to Cincinnati. Stop. This subject is of national importance and is causing grave concern and you will greatly strengthen hands of national and conservative trade unionism if you will comply with this request. Stop.[135]

Two days later the Archbishop cabled:

Weighty reasons convince me that I should not change my decision.[136]

In the absence of Archbishop Moeller, the men had a short interview with Monsignor Hickey, the Vicar General, in the course of which he allegedly stated that Father Dietz had undertaken his work in the Archdiocese without permission.[137] With that the commitee promptly sent him a copy of the Archbishop's letter of approval written in 1919.[138] But the Monsignor refused further conferences on the plea that he was too busy.

After a consultation with President Samuel Gompers, the committee drew up the following petition, signed by over sixty trade-union officials and delegates, and sent it to Archbishop Moeller, lately returned from Europe:

Having learned that influences, inimical to organized labor, have been conspiring against the maintenance of the American Academy of Christian Democracy, conducted by Reverend Peter E. Dietz, at Ault Park, this city, we beg to be permitted to ask the kindly consideration of Your Grace for the following petition:

The adjustment of the relations between Capital and Labor, on principles of justice, is one of the most vitally important questions now demanding solution by the American people, as well as by the world at large.

Delay in settling this question is threatening the very existence of civilized society. It is recruiting the armies of Anarchism and all other radicalisms.

It is now pretty generally recognized that the solution of the Social Question cannot be brought about by civil laws. Practical men on both sides realize that only through mutual confidence, good will, friendly conference and free agreement can the difference between Capital and Labor be settled satisfactorily. This was the advice of Leo XIII.

The logical, practical procedure, therefore, would seem to be to dissipate the prevailing distrust, and replace it with sincere trust on both sides, with a disposition to be mutually fair and just.

To start this procedure it is necessary to obtain the services of devoted men, personally disinterested from a viewpoint of either wages or profits, and dominated with a keen sense of justice and a strong love of humanity, who can mediate between the opposing parties, bring them to the point of composing their differences in a spirit of mutual forbearance, and engender in them a willingness to make mutual concessions and sacrifices for the general good of the community.

Father Dietz is pre-eminently one of these devoted men. He has consecrated his life to precisely this kind of service. He has made an intensive study of the Social Question for more than fifteen years, and has settled a number of industrial disputes satisfactorily to both sides. He is intimately acquainted with all the prominent leaders of the A. F. of L., and is known to many of the officials of organized labor in Europe. These men have the utmost confidence in his sincerity, his judgment and his integrity; and his conscientious regard for his vocation as a priest should be a guarantee, sufficient for employers, that he would not allow his sympathy with labor to lead him to connive at the violation of the just rights of Capital. There is not another man in the entire country as well qualified as Father Dietz to aid in the solution of the Social Question.

Even handicapped as he has been since his advent here, Father Dietz has been a power for good in Cincinnati. He has been a tower of strength against the advances of impractical and dangerous radicalism; and he has labored unceasingly for a more widespread knowledge of correct ethical principles.

May we not, therefore, respectfully petition Your Grace to permit Father Dietz to continue his important work in this community, as we feel certain that such action will conduce toward industrial peace and order, and to general prosperity and happiness.

We might mention that Cincinnati is the logical center for Father Dietz's activities, because two-thirds of the national and international officials of organized labor are residents of this city or of Indianapolis.

They sent a copy of the petition to Archbishop Messmer who was then in Rome. In an accompanying letter the three members of the committee requested Messmer to secure the Holy Father's approval of their petition.[139]

The last hope of the committee was a conference with Archbishop Moeller. While he did not refuse to see them, Moeller let them know that he did not think they should interfere, since his action was prompted not "by any hostility to organized labor," but by reasons that concerned Father Dietz's "status in the Archdiocese."[140] The interview on August 19 consequently bore no fruit except to confirm the labor leaders in the belief that Archbishop Moeller, for all his protests to the contrary, was in reality a reactionary and hostile to organized labor, basing his attitude toward Father Dietz on the ideas he received from the Catholic employers who visited him at the start of the trouble.[141]

Meanwhile Father Dietz remained in Cincinnati casting about for some way out of the predicament. Ever since the letter of December 15, 1920, asking him to leave, he had not been unmindful of the possibility of having to give up his work in Cincinnati. He considered transferring to the Cleveland Diocese, but Bishop Schrembs advised him to "put an end, once and for all," to his attempt at "specializing in Sociology," since he "had not succeeded in this work to the satisfaction of any of his ecclesiastical superiors."[142] Schrembs did not charge there was anything wrong with his teachings nor his personality but, he insisted

> Somehow you stand apart and alone while all those that are engaged in sociological work along Catholic lines—among them many sincere friends of yours—look askance of your work.[143]

Certainly Archbishop Messmer was one ecclesiastical superior of whom that was not true, the one who, in the last analysis, was really responsible for Dietz's work. Early in 1921 when Father Dietz was trying to secure a position with the Harding government, es-

GRAVE OF FATHER DIETZ

pecially as a member of a Commission to draft an alternative to the League of Nations, Messmer's letter of recommendation to Senator Irwine Lenroot expressed the greatest confidence in Father Dietz.[144] It read in part:

> He is a priest in my diocese, but years ago I gave him permission to devote himself entirely to sociological work, as he is extremely well fitted for such work not only by natural inclination, but also by long study and practical experience. . . . He has had remarkable success with a number of American labor organizations in holding them aloof from the more radical and socialistic influences. Among Catholics I know of no other man, priest or layman, who has such a thorough theoretical as well as practical knowledge of the labor question.[145]

Later events in Cincinnati did not lessen that faith.

At the advice of a friend, Dietz appealed to the Right Reverend Hugh C. Boyle of Pittsburgh for permission to come there and organize the Catholic trade-unionists of the diocese along the same lines he had suggested to Archbishop Moeller.[146] Bishop Boyle was not ready for the plan proposed but had alternatives to offer. One was that Father Dietz take a "chair of social science or some other study" in one of the schools of the diocese and in time he "might gradually begin to influence the industrial situation and to win it in the direction of conciliation."[147] The other was to get in touch with Charles J. Jaegli, editor of the *Pittsburgh Observer* and see if they could make some arrangement wherein Father Dietz would have "a channel through which his teaching and influence would flow into quarters in which it was needed" without being "construed as hostile and provocative."[148] Two attempts to contact the editor led Father Dietz to observe ironically:

> In a way all these experiences and disappointments are amusing; in days now gone when I seemed somebody, old Jaegli like others whom I had occasionally the opportunity to meet, would make a great show of friendliness and yet today I am not worth the poor homage of even an answer.[149]

After several unsuccessful attempts to move Archbishop Moeller Dietz wrote Archbishop Messmer pleading for a "word of consolation or direction."[150] He had a certain refuge in an Italian parish, but the pastor was due to return soon, leaving him "stranded altogether." He revealed something of his mental state when he wrote:

> In the last few days I have become exceedingly pessimistic; I have thought of giving up my program altogether and devoting the rest of my life to strictly ecclesiastical work on the basis of complete self-abnegation. I could devote myself to the work of spiritual direction at the seminary . . . or if that were not agreeable to you, to do whatever you suggest in blind obedience.[151]

Archbishop Messmer did not intend that Father Dietz give up his work at that point. He explained that he had not written to Dietz from Europe because he did not know what to say. He had been reasonably sure that Archbishop Moeller would be sufficiently influenced by the appeals from the committee of the A. F. of L. and the publicity the affair had gotten to reconsider the whole matter.[152] Instead Moeller had asked Archbishop Messmer to recall Dietz because he was "creating a lot of trouble."[153] This Messmer refused to do, at least until he had found a suitable place for Dietz to carry on his work. The general offices of the N.C.W.C. seemed to be just the place, but, ironically, Bishop Muldoon did not agree because of Dietz's "pronounced stand on labor unions."[154] Being "too much of a laborer's man" militated, too, against his acceptance by one of "the most active Catholic leaders" in Milwaukee, whom Archbishop Messmer had approached about the feasibility of bringing Dietz there to continue his work along lines similar to those he had developed in Cincinnati.[155] Despite these discouraging refusals, Archbishop Messmer's advice was to "trust to God and don't give up the good work."[156]

One last attempt to interest the N.C.W.C. in the case was made at the meeting of the Social Action Committee in Chicago in late December, 1922. Matthew Woll, representing the committee from the A. F. of L., brought up the "Dietz situation," but Father John A. Ryan, who answered him, was "inclined to favor the Archbishop rather than Father Dietz."[157] Nevertheless Dietz appealed to Ryan to intervene with Archbishop Moeller in his behalf.[158] Dietz had hope of a favorable outcome when he learned that the Archbishop had refused to see a committee from the Chamber of Commerce which had hoped to counteract the influence of the earlier group, on the the grounds that the difficulty had nothing to do with the industrial situation.[159] Ryan made an effort to see Moeller, but the latter's illness prevented an interview. An informal talk with Monsignor Hickey brought no results, although Ryan had suggested to Dietz that his best approach to the situation would be "through a frank and friendly conference with Monsignor Hickey."[160] But Dietz knew that it was on the advice of Hickey that Moeller had taken the stand that to reverse his decision would mean a loss of authority.[161]

Linus G. Wey, editor-in-chief of the Catholic Press Union and editor of the *Catholic Bulletin* (now the *Catholic Universe Bulletin*) of Cleveland also intervened in Father Dietz's behalf. A long-time friend and admirer of Father Dietz, Wey had hailed the opening of the National Labor College as one more evidence of his "blazing the trail again."[162] Later when the rumor of the mandate was circulated, Wey took occasion to denounce his "fellow Catholics" who were the "instigators" of the story that Father Dietz was a Socialist, and cited it as a case in point that proved Father John A. Ryan's contention that "among our hierarchy and clergy are many whose individual ideas on labor, economics, sociology, etc., are far from those of Leo XIII."[163] Learning that his editorials had not helped Father Dietz's cause, Wey hastened to write Archbishop Moeller stating his regret that anything in his paper had contributed to the hardships of the priest. Reminding Moeller that numerous students of labor problems had for years appreciated the enviable position of Father Dietz, he reiterated the practical value of his influence on the "better element of trade unionism" and declared his belief that

> if the Church in America were ready to follow Leo XIII . . .
> Father Dietz would soon find an army of priests following his
> example.[164]

The same day, Wey wrote Messmer suggesting Dietz for the editorship of a projected Catholic daily. Since Nicholas Gonner's

203

death, Wey had been urged to get busy on propaganda for such a daily, but because of ill health he would not be available for six months and more. In the meantime he strongly recommended Dietz, suggesting that

> perhaps God has delayed the work Father Dietz had mapped out, so that the new daily would become a fact and also have a strong and brilliant editor to inaugurate it.[165]

But that Catholic daily never got beyond the propaganda stage. When Archbishop Messmer called Father Dietz to Milwaukee to take charge of an Italian parish while the pastor was in Rome, he did suggest the possibility of a position on the editorial staff of the *Catholic Herald*.[166]

Once Father Dietz had accepted the fact that Archbishop Moeller was not going to change his decision, there remained the problem of disposing of his property. He offered it to the Maryknoll Superior, Very Reverend James A. Walsh, M.M., for use as a subsidiary establishment for mission purposes, and to the Discalced Carmelites on condition that they offer their prayers and good works in perpetuity for the welfare of the American labor movement.[167] Finally he settled it on the Catholic Students' Mission Crusade, a new and struggling organization whose director was his good friend, Monsignor Francis Beckman. There was an outstanding debt on the property of four thousand dollars, fifteen hundred of which was owing on the loan Father John F. Noll had made. At the request of Dietz to remit the obligation "in whole or in part, in favor of the Crusade," Noll agreed to make the loan a gift.[168]

In his last letter to Archbishop Moeller announcing the disposal of his affairs and his readiness to depart, Father Dietz still maintained that reparation and restitution were owing him.[169] But the Archbishop could not see that any great harm had been done to Dietz. In asking him to leave, the Archbishop harbored no "ill will" against him but believed that his departure was for the "best interests of the Diocese."[170]

Before Father Dietz left for Milwaukee, his loyal friends Daniel Tobin and Matthew Woll addressed a letter to Archbishop Messmer, reviewing the whole situation, evaluating the work of Dietz, assuring Messmer that they had thoroughly investigated all the accusations made against him by Moeller and others, and expressing their deep regret that he was forced to give up his work in Cincinnati. It was a sort of letter of recommendation preparing the way for the return of Father Dietz to his own diocese.[171]

Thus ended the second period in the history of the American Academy of Christian Democracy. It had been in existence approximately seven years (1915-1922), but it had demonstrated many things. Through it Father Dietz had the opportunity of actualizing two ideas which he had cherished throughout his life: to provide social workers trained in a knowledge of Catholic social principles and to bring to the trade-unionist, Catholic and non-Catholic, the social doctrine of Leo XIII. His sufferings and travail in the process showed how unready still many churchmen and laymen were to face the practical problems and the risks involved in translating social theories into action.

Labor had bestowed a great mark of confidence on Father Dietz when it made him Director of its first National Labor College. Though he might be accused of a lack of tact on occasion, Dietz could hardly be branded as dangerous, having as he did the respect of the broader-minded type of employer who was willing to recognize the right of men to form associations and the consequences flowing therefrom—a right insisted upon by Leo XIII. His every plan had been submitted to Archbishop Moeller and to the committee appointed to guide him, and full authority had been given him to proceed after alleged assurance "from reliable sources" that his views were "strictly in accord with the sound principles of theology."[172]

With the closing of the American Academy of Christian Democracy, Father Dietz withdrew from active participation in the labor movement. Subsequently assigned to the mission of Whitefish Bay in Milwaukee, he spent the rest of his priestly life (1923-1947) building it into a thriving parish. But his great knowledge of the labor movement in America and his years of experience with its key men made him a valuable source for advice and guidance to those who carried on his work in the Catholic social movement.

Chapter Nine

Continued Activity
and Influence

WHEN ARCHBISHOP MESSMER recalled Father Dietz to Milwaukee, he had no idea of making him a pastor. His assignment to the Italian Church of the Blessed Virgin of Pompeii was only temporary in the absence of the pastor in Rome.[1] But when representatives of the thirty Catholic families of Whitefish Bay in north Milwaukee, petitioned the Archbishop for a resident pastor, Messmer named Father Dietz.[2]

About mid-December, 1923, Dietz took up his residence in a summer cottage at the north end of the village of Whitefish Bay. Constructed for summer use, the house was little protection from the winds of Lake Michigan, and during the severest weather he was forced to move to the home of one of his parishioners. Lacking a church of any kind, Father Dietz said the first "official" Mass of the parish in the village hall on Christmas day.[3]

Not one to let such conditions prevail for long, Dietz purchased a farm in February, 1924, for twenty thousand dollars, making the initial payment with the gift of twenty five hundred dollars which the Executive Council of the A. F. of L. had given him in appreciation of his many services to the labor movement.[4] The farmhouse on the property became the rectory. Not far distant he located a soundly built barn, moved it to the property, and with the help of a few of the men and boys of the parish, converted it into a church. Dubious at first about worshipping in a barn, the parishioners became enthusiastic when they saw the transformation. A contemporary description of the church tells why:

206

In the church interior much of the original structure remains unchanged. Hayloft has become choir loft with the addition of benches and reed organ; horse stalls are now glorified with a tile floor and form the church vestibule. The massive rafters span the nave of the church, lending a remarkable air of intimate warmth. The wood has all been left unfinished and has been dyed a warm olive-brown. On the altar and in two niches at the rear of the nave are a number of sacred figures, beautifully carved from the natural wood by a family of artisans who live in the Tyrolian Alps. . .[5]

The church was completed in about a month at a cost of less than six thousand dollars and was dedicated on May 4, the Feast of St. Monica, patroness of the parish. This small church remained a center of devotion even after the new church was begun.

In these first years the financial problem was acute, since the parishioners were unable to pay Father Dietz a salary, and the collections were small, that of the first month totalling only twenty-five dollars.[6] Again his friends in the labor movement came to his assistance, the women taking the initiative. Anna Neary and Sara Conboy, secretary-treasurer of the United Textile Workers of America, sent to about seventy-five trade-unionists a letter which read in part:

> During a recent visit in Washington, it was brought to our attention that our good friend, Father Dietz, is in need.
>
> He is in Northern Milwaukee starting a new parish in a very humble section of the city. I know if you knew that, you would help him in every way possible.
>
> I feel sure too that the prayers we will all receive in return, will indeed repay amply for the small amount we contribute. Could you donate ten dollars or more to a fund we are trying to raise for him?[7]

The most interesting contribution came from Harry Rosenberg, a Jew, who gave Sara Conboy a check for five hundred and eighty-one dollars, the current price of a Ford.[8]

The parish developed rapidly. With characteristic foresight Father Dietz, in 1926, added another farm to the property.[9] A school, begun in 1927, opened in September, 1928, with the Sister Servants of the Immaculate Heart of Mary, of Monroe, Michigan, in charge.[11]

207

In July, 1928, Dietz began work on the basement of a new church which he hoped to make the most beautiful Catholic church in the Middle West. That he did not live to see it completed was one of the sorrows of his later life. Since Father Dietz planned and supervised the building, there was an architectural similarity between Crusade Castle and the buildings at St. Monica's. Four bells were blessed and installed in 1929. One of these, named Peter, was moved from Crusade Castle, the gift of Mayor Galvin of Cincinnati in recognition of Father Dietz's part in settling the firemen's strike.[11]

By 1929 the parish had increased in size from thirty to one hundred families.[12] The organization and administration of the parish grew likewise, as Father Dietz tried to put into practice some of the ideas he had talked about for so long.[13] Believing that religion should be supported freely and "not cheapened by circus or theatre methods," he permitted no bazaars, or "ticketing peddling," no pew rent, no money at the door, no school money, just the collection at the Offertory of the Mass.[14] As a substitute he had a unique plan— each member of the parish contributed one day's income a month to the support of the parish.[15] Of the two hundred and fifty-five contributing members, married and unmarried, in 1929, Dietz reported that thirty-three per cent supported the plan fully; twenty-five per cent with a good average, and the rest "more or less deficiently."[16] But "moral suasion from the altar" was the only "leverage employed," there being no published list of contributors. In return Father Dietz was available to all for any service, "even if they never contributed a penny."[17] And never so long as he was pastor did he accept for his own use any Sunday, Christmas, or Easter collection.[18] He wanted the school run on the principle that "the Church exists for service, especially for the service of the needy and ignorant," and he would tolerate nothing that smacked of the commercial.[19] Consequently he regulated the price of books, music lessons, and other fees.[20]

Ever conscious of the financial needs of his parishioners and anxious to protect them from loan sharks, Dietz organized in 1928 the first Parish Credit Union in the State of Wisconsin.[21] Under the jurisdiction of the State Banking Department, this savings and loan association stated its objectives to be to promote thrift among its members, especially school children, to loan its funds to parishioner‑ members for worthy purposes, and to invest funds not required for personal loans in obligations of St. Monica's Congregation, repre‑ sented by time notes, or other securities of the Archdiocese of Mil‑ waukee which are legal investments for trust funds.[22] By contribut‑ ing twenty-five cents a week, school children could accumulate two paid shares (five dollars each) in the course of a school year.[23] By 1931 the treasurer reported assets valued at five thousand dollars, three thousand two hundred representing "loans made to and se‑ cured by mortgage on St. Monica Parish property," and sixteen hundred representing personal loans to credit union members.[24]

Convinced that the project was worth while, Dietz suggested to Archbishop Samuel Stritch that he appoint a priest to organize sim‑ ilar unions in schools and parishes throughout the Archdiocese.[25] In this way an archdiocesan fund would eventually be available for many worthwhile purposes. Recalling his own experiences in or‑ ganizing St. Monica's, when he had no place to stay, no place to say Mass, and no property, Dietz made this observation to the Arch‑ bishop:

> In that I have done no more than thousands of priests before me. But it ought not to be in these days; our organization has not grown apace; here is a gap that requires filling and I really believe that if an extension service were provided dozens of new and needed parishes would get under way easily and happily . . .[26]

By such a plan, he believed, the Church could protect its independ‑ ence and dignity in not having to depend on banks, to say nothing of the "sums of money saved every year that go to waste for inci‑ dental fees, commissions, high rates of interest, *etc*."[27]

As interest in credit unions increased, others wanted to profit by the experience of Father Dietz. When Reverend William McGuire of Genoa, Illinois, was assigned a paper for the 1934 National Catho‑ lic Rural Life Conference on "The Pastor's Views on the Parish Credit Union," he asked Dietz to suggest some important points that should be included in such a paper.[28] Henry Ohl, president of the Wisconsin State Federation of Labor, also requested material on the

St. Monica Credit Union, and asked Father Dietz to advise him on "launching such credit unions for labor groups."[29] The St. Monica's Credit Union functioned for ten years; then as the parish grew wealthy and the need for it lessened, it was liquidated.

Still interested in social service and charities, Father Dietz made several attempts to establish institutions in Milwaukee. Always devoted to the work of the society of St. Vincent de Paul, he organized the St. Monica's Conference in May, 1929. Charles O'Neill, present executive secretary of the Archdiocesan Central Council of Milwaukee, recalls Dietz's interest in setting up a program of preventive charity, by which people could be helped to help themselves.[30] He had in mind a co-operative home for housemaids on the east side of Milwaukee, where they could go on their days off, and where they could live during periods of unemployment.[31] The Society of St. Monica, a sort of Vincentian Auxiliary, affiliated with the Paris office of the Ladies of Charity.[32]

In 1926, Archbishop Messmer appointed Father Dietz president (*Praesis*) of the Kolping Society to be established in Milwaukee. His letter of appointment read in part:

> I am very thankful to you for accepting this office and for volunteering your services for this praise-worthy Society. To my mind it is somewhat of a doubtful problem whether the Society will find a proper and successful field here in Milwaukee. But it is worth trying.[33]

There were at that time Kolping Societies in fourteen countries, including twelve branches in the United States.[34] Headquarters for the American branches were in Chicago. Named for their founder the Reverend Adolph Kolping, the Societies (*Gesellen-verein*) were patterned after the first one he founded at Cologne in 1849. Before he became a priest, Father Kolping was a traveling shoemaker. Observing the moral pitfalls to which the young journeymen were exposed in the inns of his day, he determined to establish homes for them.[35] He organized young men between the ages of eighteen and twenty-five under a priest-president on a family basis. He established technical schools, libraries, reading rooms, and employment exchanges wherever it was feasible.[36] Numerous hostels or lodges were set up where such journeymen could secure supper, bed, and breakfast free of charge.

Father Dietz had something like this in mind when he purchased a home at 108 Prospect Avenue to house the Society.[37] It was a fifty-eight thousand dollar investment for which he paid but one thousand dollars.[38] A loan of five thousand dollars from the Kolping Society in New York City, of which his boyhood friend, Leonard Heuser, was executive chairman, helped ease the great burden of indebtedness.[39] The institution, placed under the patronage of Our Lady of the Holy Spirit, was to be "primarily an educational institution, designed to enable the members of the society to perfect themselves in their respective trades."[40] Here, also, young men who were working away from home could find companionship and protection.[41]

The venture did not succeed. About a year after the purchase Dietz had to relinquish the property with the mortgage not liquidated.[42] One opinion advanced for its failure was the location of the house in a neighborhood where men with dinner pails felt out of place.[43]

Another project which never seems to have developed was the establishment of a trade school (*Kunstgewerbe Schule*) for orphan boys. At least Father Dietz inquired about buildings on Port Washington Road to be used for that purpose.[44] Archbishop Messmer gave Father Dietz permission to "engage the Franciscan Sisters of the Immaculate Conception, of Little Falls, Minnesota, for the erection of a hospital, maternity and nursery" on the property of St. Monica parish.[45] Though neither of these projects materialized, the work at St. Monica's along the lines of Catholic Social Action merited the following comment:

> St. Monica's parish is at least one place in Milwaukee where the social philosophy of the recent Popes is translating itself into an actual program, and where the arts are again being put to the service of religion as they were in the Cathedral building days of the Middle Ages.[46]

Though engrossed in the development of his own parish, Father Dietz did not forget the needs of the Church elsewhere. One of the recipients of his benefaction was the Most Reverend Anthony J.

Schuler, S.J., Bishop of El Paso, Texas, who was most grateful for the donations and Mass stipends sent to the fifty-five Mexican refugee priests under his care.[47]

Deeply interested in foreign missions as well, especially in China where his brother Fred had been at work as a Maryknoller since 1920, Dietz wrote to the Reverend William Quinn, national director of the Society for the Propagation of the Faith, suggesting the "adoption system" as a means of helping to finance the missions.[48] Many a well-established parish in the United States, he believed, could, with a mere pittance of its annual finances, sponsor a struggling parish in some mission country and derive much spiritual profit thereby. Father Quinn was impressed with the idea and wrote Dietz:

> I shall bring your note to Rome next month to the meeting of the Consilium Generale a Propagatione Fidei and shall ask if there is not some way by which your suggestions can be carried out . . .[49]

Actually Dietz had begun putting the idea into execution some years before by having St. Monica's parish send occasional contributions for his brother Fred's mission at Tungchen. When the latter was placed in charge of Maryknoll's South China Language School for missioners, he suggested that St. Monica's adopt the mission at Chikkai. Bishop James E. Walsh, M.M., acknowledged "the splendid gift of one thousand dollars" sent to "St. Monica's" mission by Father Dietz.[50]

Apparently cut off from contact with his previous life, Father Dietz soon received proof that his work was not forgotten. John Frey, for one, found it hard to accept Dietz's retirement. Shortly after Dietz arrived in Whitefish Bay, Frey wrote:

> You were thrown into contact with the trade-union movement in a manner such as has been experienced by no other clergyman. . . . I cannot believe that your contact with the trade-union movement was a matter of accident and of no importance, and that the knowledge you acquired is to be retained within your mind, closeted there instead of being used for the benefit of your fellow men.[51]

Later, when Frey asociated with John A. Ryan and the Reverend Raymond A. McGowan, he wanted Dietz to complete the triumvirate. "Having some idea of the splendid work which both of these men are doing," Frey wrote:

> I feel that you, too, with your wide knowledge of men in the trade union movement should be in some such center as Washington where your special knowledge would be of such great value.[52]

He was wrong, however, in believing that Father Dietz would again become active in trade-union affairs. Whatever sharing of his "special knowledge" he did after 1923 took second place after his work as pastor of St. Monica's parish.

Interest in organizations similar to Father Dietz's Militia of Christ and his Labor College was reawakened and stimulated in 1931, when Pope Pius XI wrote his great Encyclical *Quadragesimo Anno,* in which he reiterated Pope Pius X's precautions regarding Catholics in neutral trade unions. Wrote Pius XI:

> Side by side with these trade unions, there must always be associations which aim at giving their members a thorough religious and moral training, that these in turn may impart to the labor unions to which they belong the upright spirit which should direct their entire conduct.[53]

Six years after the Encyclical appeared, the Association of Catholice Trade Unionists (A.C.T.U.) was organized in "the slums of the lower East side of New York City" by eleven Catholic laymen, aided and encouraged by the Reverend John P. Monaghan. Though the founders of A.C.T.U. disavow any historical continuity with the Militia of Christ its purposes expressed in its Articles of Federation echo those of the Militia. A.C.T.U. aims to bring "all Catholic working people into the unions of their occupations and choice," to make "all Catholic union members" belong to A.C.T.U., to help labor unions, "wherever feasible" to secure their just demands and "to spread among all people the social teaching of the Church, and the idea that it is a religious duty to aid the reform of society."[54] A.C.T.U.'s program of spiritual activities likewise resembled those of the Militia of Christ, with its retreats, days of recollection, and especially its daily "personal devotion to the Holy Ghost."[55]

In its organization year (1937) A.C.T.U. launched its first Workers' School with the help of Fordham University.[56] Schools like this one under various auspices became common, recalling to others the work done by Father Dietz twenty years before. The following are cases in point.

Richard L. G. Deverall, then co-editor with Norman McKenna of *The Christian Front,* a monthly magazine of social reconstruction, wanting to "profit by the experience of the pioneers in this field" when he was helping organize a labor college in the Detroit Archdiocese, wrote Father Dietz:

> While attending a Catholic Workers' Colloquium at Detroit . . . we heard from Father Siedenberg, S.J., of a Catholic Workers' College held at Cincinnati years ago. . . . Would you care to tell us where we can find out more about it?[57]

Dietz sent him the three issues of his *Social Service* magazine, about which Deverall had this to say:

> After reading carefully these three magazines now yellowing with age, it is quite plain that you were apparently about 25 years ahead of your time. It was simply thrilling to realize that what we think is so 'new' and so 'radical' was being done by your group back in 1910-1911.[58]

Desiring to outline the historical background of A.C.T.U., the Reverend Sebastian Erbacher, O.F.M., chaplain of the Detroit Chapter, recalled the "good work" done by Father Dietz in Cincinnati when he was a student there.[59] He wrote:

> I am very much interested in what has been done in the past for our Catholic workers. I knew that you were a pioneer in this field with your *Militia Christi.* . . . I would like to point out to our younger generation that not all modern ideas are new; but that they existed long ago; and that the heroic attempts were made by priests like yourself to do what the Popes have so strongly demanded. . .[60]

Father Dietz sent his last copies of *Social Service* to Father Erbacher. He briefly reviewed the circumstances that ended the Militia when

Archbishop Moeller ordered him to leave the Archdiocese. About the affair he made this comment:

> I obeyed because I wanted to be a good soldier myself; neither did I want to fight the Archbishop's decision—because he was old and already had had a stroke. . . . I know he was a *good man* at heart and these matters were entirely outside his purview.[61]

There is reason to believe that Father Dietz might have had a direct influence on the organization of A.C.T.U. for he had been agitating for similar groups on parish lines ever since he first suggested them to Archbishop Moeller and Bishop Hugh Boyle in 1920.[62] When the Catholic Industrial Conference met in Cleveland in October, 1926, Dietz addressed the group on the subject: "Pope Leo's Encyclical and the American Labor Movement."[63] He regretted that the Encyclical received so little attention. Its need "should be less optional, more profound, more compelling, more sure of its purpose." Too many of the best intentioned Catholics were still satisfied with maintaining "a benevolent neutrality on vital problems." These same people would grant to the priest the role of preaching and administering the sacraments, but would oppose any of his attempts to "meddle" in their private affairs and business pursuits. But to Dietz it was clear that

> if there is to be any salvation for America industrially as well as socially and politically, the polar social principles of Christianity must have their rightful entree into the deliberations as well as the acts of every society, party, labor union and Chamber of Commerce.[64]

One of the great needs of the times, Dietz declared, was the integration of the "doctrine" of *Rerum Novarum* with the organized endeavors of American trade unionists. This could be done by organizing in every parish Catholic trade unionists who would "digest" Pope Leo's teachings and make them the basis of action in trade unions to which they belonged.[65] To those who resented the Church's recognition of the trade union movement, especially the Catholic employers, Dietz would offer the same recognition and method:

215

Let them organize into a Catholic society of employers to encompass the aims of the Encyclical. . . . As they are earnest and true Catholics they will make the Encyclical a live and real thing from the employer's standpoint.[66]

Occasionally these two blocs of a "solid Catholic unionist and a solid Catholic employers' opinion" should meet and from the ensuing discussions and inevitable clashes would merge an "organic opinion" based on the Encyclical. Then both groups formed in Catholic thought and principle would go to their meetings, the laborer to his union, the employer to his Chamber of Commerce, "not as a neutral figure but as the advocate of the well defined manner of procedure," having something to say on every question arising whether local, national, or international in outlook.

In the discussion that followed this address, Father John A. Ryan criticized Dietz's plan for organizing Catholic trade unionists and employers as likely to arouse the opposition of labor union leadership on the grounds that it was setting aside Catholic union members from the rest.[67] The Reverend J. W. R. Maguire, C.S.V., on the other hand, favored the organization of parish groups as a way to "help break down the attitude of the employer that the Church has no right to speak to him regarding his duties to his employees."[68] Apparently Dietz did not stay for the rest of the discussion for he wrote Elizabeth Kuhlman:

I was very anxious to see the end of the discussion I started. I have no word from anyone how it ended. It all shows how little we matter and what we say. We must keep plugging along just the same and do what we can.[69]

Before Father Dietz addressed another industrial conference in 1936, two significant events occurred: Pope Pius XI issued *Quadragesimo Anno* on May 15, 1931, and John L. Lewis organized the Committee of Industrial Organization on November 9, 1935. The Encyclical seemed an answer to Dietz's plea that *Rerum Novarum* be "less optional" and "more compelling," for after summarizing the "beneficent results" of Leo's encyclical, Pius continued:

Nevertheless there are some who seem to attach little importance to this Encyclical. . . . These men either slander a doctrine of which they are entirely ignorant or if not unacquainted with this teaching they betray their failure to understand it, or else if they understand it they lay themselves open to the charge of base injustice and ingratitude.[70]

The Pope's order to Catholic trade unionists to organize separate societies has been noted. Likewise Pius XI especially favored conferences of employers and employees, similar to those Father Dietz had fostered in Cincinnati in the Building Trades, when those groups came together for the "common interest of the whole group" and the "directing of the activities of the group to the common good."[71]

In the fall of 1934, Dietz's old friend, Archbishop Francis Beckman of Dubuque, invited him to speak on the history of the Labor movement at an Industrial Conference there, but ill health prevented his going.[72] The Right Reverend Monsignor J. M. Wolfe, general director of the Catholic Youth Organization for Catholic Action made all the arrangements for the meeting. Disappointed that Dietz could not come, Wolfe wrote:

> I wanted you very badly because his Excellency, the Archbishop had spoken many times about you, and I of course had known you in the long years gone in relation to the A. F. of L. and your views regarding Labor organizations and their rights, long before Dr. John A. Ryan began to interpret the Catholic view and theories regarding the equities of labor.[73]

Two years later Dietz was invited to Dubuque as principal speaker on a program sponsored by the Holy Name Societies during Catholic Social Action Week.[74] In his address, "Labor Organizations and the Modern Menace of Communism," Dietz berated those Catholics who through sloth or cowardice failed to realize their responsibility toward social reform. This failure, Dietz believed, was one of the causes for the rise of the "modern universal heresy" of Communism. He asked:

> Is the Church merely an institution for the protection of capitalistic interests or has she a right to ask that their temporalities be put into the service of God and the Commonwealth?[75]

The Committee on Industrial Organization he viewed simply as the recurrence of the "one big union" issue of the past. Communists encouraged and abetted its spirit of "rebellion against the constitutional authority of the A. F. of L." as a "breaking through the bulwarks of established solidarity."[76] Because of this, Dietz deemed the merits of the arguments for and against the C.I.O. as of lesser importance than the necessity of unity in the labor movement. Again he stressed the importance of every Catholic worker's belonging to the union of his craft or trade, attending its meetings, introducing and fighting for the enactment of the principles of the great encyclicals.

Events in Spain further impressed Father Dietz with the importance of the Church's leadership in the struggle for social reform. Under the stress of this conviction he wrote to the Most Reverend Amleto G. Cicognani, Apostolic Delegate to the United States. Briefly reviewing his past efforts with the labor movement, Father Dietz confessed alarm at the "accelerated pace" with which the A. F. of L. was moving to the left.[77] But the battle-fronts, he averred, were not "where political noise and confusion" were loudest, but in the "local meetings of every labor union and Chamber of Commerce." Accordingly he pleaded for the specific appointment by bishops, especially in industrial dioceses of priests who would attend these local meetings regularly, in order to understand at first hand the agitating issues.[78] Father Dietz warned against those in the American Church who so misunderstood the European social cleavage as to regard it as foreign and as inconceivable in this country, for he declared, "We are more European than we own and none of the European ferment is alien to us."[79] In view of this he begged the Apostolic Delegate, by the prestige of his office, to induce at least a few of the bishops "to pastorize *intensively* on the industrial battle-front."[80]

What influence this may have had on subsequent events is difficult to determine, but in May, 1937, His Excellency, Archbishop Samuel Stritch sent a circular letter to the priests of the Archdiocese of Milwaukee, which read in part:

> In November, 1936, the Administrative Committee of the NCWC sanctioned the establishment under its authority in proper centers of the United States Priests' Summer Schools for Social Action to offer to priests special training in fitting themselves for responding to the call of the Holy Father al-

ready voiced in previous letters. It was our good fortune to have Milwaukee chosen as a center.[81]

It pleased Father Dietz that Father Haas suggested that he be invited as one of the "pioneers" to give two lectures on the American Labor movement.[82]

About one hundred and thirty priests attended the Summer School. When Father Dietz gave his lectures during the fourth week he found his audience predisposed toward the C. I. O. as a result of previous lectures.[83] Accordingly he reminded these priests that labor history did not begin with the C. I. O. and that the record of the past ought to be seriously studied and appreciated. Especially did he impress upon them that it was the priest's business to "reconcile the rivals rather than become intensely partisan."[84] This experience gratified Father Dietz, giving him a "touch of the old days."[85]

Archbishop McNicholas of Cincinnati provided the climax to these opportunities for Father Dietz to vindicate himself when he invited Dietz to return to Cincinnati to resume his leadership in the labor world.[86] Almost at the Archbishop's door in Norwood, twenty-one hundred workers at the plant of Chevrolet and Fisher Bodies had gone on strike, December 31, 1936.[87] The claim of the employers in Norwood that they had lived up to their agreements "most scrupulously," complicated the problem. Furthermore, rumor in Cincinnati hinted that this labor disturbance was part of a war carried on by John L. Lewis to "replace the old system of craft unionship with his newer plan for organization of workers along industrial lines."[88]

Archbishop McNicholas wanted no bloodshed in Cincinnati, but he did not know what position to take. Since Catholics were on both sides in the Lewis-Green quarrel, some thought the Church should be silent on the matter.[89] But Chancellor Thill wrote Dietz:

> The Archbishop is not sympathetic to this point of view. If Mr. Lewis is wrong, the Archbishop feels that every Bishop has an obligation in conscience to instruct the workingmen of his jurisdiction, to warn them, and to use every means available to save the country from the chaos of economic rebellion.

219

The Archbishop feels that you are entirely conversant with the situation. His Grace wants your advice.

The Archbishop will call upon your Ordinary to return you to us for this work, if you will undertake it.[90]

In giving advice, Dietz, with his limited knowledge of the men and the issues, was averse to making any pronouncement regarding the local scene, but he did "risk an opinion" on the Lewis-Green controversy.[91] First of all, the "original sin" of the automobile industries was their refusal to deal with organized labor in the past. Had they cooperated whole-heartedly with the crafts, their position would be much stronger. John L. Lewis, Dietz believed, was "insincere, theatrical and undemocratic." By over-emphasizing a "structural weakness" in the A. F. of L.—a weakness Dietz had seen long before—Lewis was splitting the labor forces. Facing the possible outcome of the controversy, Dietz continued:

> Supposing that Lewis succeeded with a plan of industrial unionism nothing could brake the extravagances of mob psychology for a period; then it would either fall apart or if any sort of real leadership obtains, it would rebuild groupings according to a hierarchy of function.[92]

He saw no reason for the Church to take a stand either way since there was no moral issue involved, but he did believe Catholic leadership should insist on union:

> The big idea is to *compel* the factions to get together—to *compel* them to do it *themselves;* if public opinion could be aroused to the extent that they know they must do it, they will do it.[93]

Archbishop McNicholas' plan was to appeal to the strikers in Norwood, hoping other bishops would imitate him until eventually the Administrative Board of Bishops of the N. C. W. C. might appeal for union.[94] A direct request to the Board could be made, but, McNicholas observed: "It is so hard to get such a statement, and it usually takes a very long time."[95] Dietz approved of this local appeal to the strikers, for he believed

> the people have a right to their bishop's direction. We are going into proletarian futures, and the place of the Church is

out in front. France, Spain and other countries stayed in the back-ground, though called by the Holy Father to accept the new eras; they did not profit by staying behind the lines. Our traditions are not fossil and there is hope that we may achieve a Christian Democracy. But it won't be without a battle and without the Church in the thick of it.[96]

The Archbishop incorporated these thoughts of Father Dietz's into a letter he addressed to the workingmen of the Archdiocese. He wrote appreciatively to Dietz:

> May it please God to do something in this labor situation and may He also be pleased to use one with your humility, knowledge and experience as a potent factor both in composing difficulties and in making clear the guiding principles.[97]

The bishops did not follow the lead of Archbishop McNicholas as he had hoped they would, although Dietz observed that Monsignor Joseph Smith of Cleveland had been "hailed as a major prophet" by the Cleveland press for suggesting rapprochement between the two labor groups at a C. I. O. meeting.[98] Once again Father Dietz advised McNicholas to appoint two priests to attend local meetings of the unions and the Chamber of Commerce. From this beginning could come "sodalities or confraternities of trade and labor unionists and of Catholic business men," at least one in a city at first, under the direct authority of the bishop.[99]

A few months later Archbishop McNicholas selected twenty priests of the Archdiocese for a Conference on Industrial Problems. Monsignor Edward A. Freking, chairman of the Priests' labor group, extended the Archbishop's invitation to Father Dietz to address the priests since he was "the best informed priest in the country on the labor question."[100] One of the first fruits of the conference was a special Mass for laboring men and women at St. Mary' Church each Sunday, with a short sermon on the rights and duties of the working man.[101]

Father Dietz did not accept the invitation to return to Cincinnati to reopen his labor school. He was well established in his pastoral duties by that time and felt that the other work should be undertaken by younger men.[102] Perhaps it was better that way, for he had only a few more years to live. Never robust, he was by 1946 severely handicapped physically and mentally. The hypertension under which he lived had so effected his sight that, at the time of his death, October 11, 1947, he was practically blind.[103]

The second span of his life (1923-1947) brought to full cycle Father Dietz's striving for the cause of social justice. His devotion to the common people and his desire to help them meet the vicissitudes of life was as sincere at the end as it had been in the beginning of his life. His Parish Credit Union, his St. Monica's Conference of the Society of St. Vincent de Paul, his plans for a Kolping House, a hospital, a nursery, and the unique way he supported the parish were all expressions of his concern for the social welfare of others.

Unlike most pioneers, Dietz had the satisfaction of seeing his work appreciated as fundamental, fifteen yars later, and was privileged to guide and advise the younger men who carried on his work of organizing Catholic trade unionists and establishing labor colleges. The inscription on the cross-shaped monument erected over his grave in Wauwatosa, Wisconsin, perpetuates Father Dietz's two great accomplishments: "Champion of Labor" and "Founder of St. Monica's Parish."[104]

Chapter Ten

Thirty Years After
–An Evaluation

PETER E. DIETZ met the challenge of his times with an enthusiasm, energy, and courage seldom surpassed. He grew to manhood under the influence of Cardinal Gibbons and Leo XIII. Leo died in 1913, his social program for the most part unrealized. At least in America, *Rerum Novarum* was still largely the concern of scholars when Father Dietz took up his priestly work in 1904. Yet the Church faced tremendous social problems. The rapid industrialization of the country created a whole new class of people—landless, urban, foreign, poor, and exploited. A large percentage of them were Catholics. The dangerous philosophy of Marxian Socialism made inroads among them at an accelerating pace. Its program of social reform was daring and attractive. The Church, in contrast, advanced no program. Catholic workingmen were inclined to believe the Socialist gibe that the Church was friendly to the capitalist but indifferent to the needs of the laborer.

Father Dietz was one of the first to see the need of unifying and organizing Catholics in support of a positive and comprehensive social program. No one was better prepared to inspire and guide such a program. Dietz was well grounded in Catholic philosophy and theology and was familiar with the writings of European and American social thinkers. He was no academician, however. He did not write books or articles for the great Catholic reviews. He was not a brilliant pulpit orator. He was, rather, an agitator, an organizer, and a journalist. From boyhood Dietz had experienced the social injustices recounted in the writings of Leo XIII. His desire to uplift the masses and solve the problems of the workingman were an essential part of his vocation to the priesthood. In Dietz's own words, he wanted "to bring *Rerum Novarum* to the people *in practice.*"

With dynamic enthusiasm Father Dietz attempted to overcome the inertia, the conservatism, and the opposition he met in the three organizations he used to realize his life's ambition—the German Catholic Central Verein, the American Federation of Catholic Societies, and the American Federation of Labor. He persuaded the Central Verein to add an English section to its social reform journal (*Central Blatt*) to make it *The Central Blatt and Social Justice,* and brilliantly edited it for a time. He organized the Verein's first Social Institute, the model for those that came after. He prevailed upon the American Federation of Catholic Societies to set up a Social Service Commission. As its secretary Dietz turned the Federation to a serious consideration of his social program. His yearly reports repeatedly urged the unifying of all Catholic social agencies through a Bureau of Catholic Social Statistics, a Catholic Social Yearbook, a training school for Catholic social leaders, and a national clearing-house for Catholic social opinion. At the yearly conventions of the American Federation of Catholic Societies he pushed through resolutions that merited recognition and applause from the leaders of secular social agencies.

He advocated an articulate Catholic press as a necessary supplement to his program. Dietz was responsible with others for the development of the Catholic Press Association. His own weekly *Newsletter* distributed to hundreds of Catholic and labor papers won national recognition for its editorial judgment. As editor of the Federation's *Bulletin,* Dietz reported and interpreted, warned and exhorted. Had his program received the support it deserved, a national Catholic social movement would have antedated that of the National Catholic Welfare Conference by several years. But the war interfered with Dietz and his plans for social reform. The National Catholic War Council and the National Catholic Welfare Conference supplanted the almost defunct American Federation of Catholic Societies. Even in the organization of the Social Action Department of the latter organization, however, Dietz played a significant role in en-suring a place for labor in its program.

Dietz knew the complexity of industrial society and the necessity for study as a prelude to its improvement. No longer could charities be left to the haphazard though zealous ministrations of parish ladies with leisure time. The new type of preventive charity required a trained lay personnel. But Catholics were not ready for the role Dietz assigned to the layman. Religious communities such as he envisioned in his "Militia of the Divine Will" are only now receiving official sanction by the Church. Even the paid social worker was frowned upon by Catholics generally. To prove that professional social work and spiritual dedication were compatible, Dietz set up his American Academy of Christian Democracy for Women, hailed as the first of its kind in the country. Unsupported, the Academy soon closed, but over fifty of its graduates, as White Cross Nurses, competently demonstrated the wisdom of its founder.

Father Dietz is best remembered for his work with the labor movement. He declared many times that in an industrial society "the great problem of social reform is largely the problem of trades-unionism."[1] Beginning on the local scene in Ohio as union organizer for the Ohio State Federation of Labor, Dietz soon attended regularly the yearly conventions of the American Federation of Labor. The personal friend of key men like John P. Frey, Daniel Tobin, Matthew Woll, and Philip Murray, Dietz exerted a greater influence directly on the labor movement than any other priest before or since. After twenty-five years, these leaders gratefully recall his work. Wrote Murray: "He strongly voiced the rights of labor to organize and bargain collectively. This he did at a time when few public figures were willing to do so."[2]

Dietz's closeness to these labor leaders gave him opportunity to observe the "boring from within" tactics of the Socialists. The damaging effects of radical influences on trade unionism were only too apparent. Yet when others advocated separate Catholic trade unions, Dietz spoke out forcefully against them. Instead he urged Catholics to join neutral unions, attend union meetings, serve on committees, and run for union offices. In the tradition of Cardinal Gibbons and in the spirit of *Rerum Novarum,* Dietz organized his Militia of Christ for Social Service, an ally not a competitor of the A. F. of L., and prevented the labor movement from splitting over the religious issue as it had done in Europe and Canada. Under the spirited leadership of Father Dietz, this Militia exposed the false position of the Socialists who exploited for their own ends the "neutral" character of the American labor movement. Dietz impressed upon trade unionists that only in so far as it was Christian was the labor movement truly progressive and American. Unlike other Catholic labor associations of its day, the Militia of Christ, or the American Conference of Trade Unionists as it was later called, set in Catholic trade union strategy a precedent followed by the present day Association of Catholic Trade Unionists.

The first to see the necessity of an official Catholic policy toward labor that would clarify the current confusion of Catholic opinion, Dietz petitioned Cardinal Gibbons for a labor pastoral eight years before such a pastoral was finally issued. As an important adjunct to this official policy he urged the calling of Catholic Industrial Conferences similar to those which, since 1923, have become part of the social program of the National Catholic Welfare Conference.

The confidence of trade unionists, non-Catholic as well as Catholic, in the sincereity of Father Dietz made him an effective mediator. His work along this line was especially significant in the important trade union city of Cincinnati. Dietz's friendship with many right-thinking employers helped to bring labor and management together in peaceful relations during the turbulent twenties. Averse to anything that savored of welfare capitalism, Dietz persuaded employers that only by recognizing labor as its own estate could cooperation succeed. His excellent industrial council plan, still a desideratum, set up among the Building Trades of Cincinnati, was pioneering of the highest order.

The independence Dietz demanded for craft unionism he denied, however, to the unskilled, although he had recognized the weakness of craft exclusiveness in the A. F. of L. as early as 1913. He urged the extension of the benefits of organized labor to the unskilled, but through a sort of craft paternalism rather than through industrial organization. His failure to influence labor leaders in the direction of industrial organization was in the light of later development one of the serious weaknesses in his trade union policy.

The power house for Father Dietz's influence in Cincinnati was his labor college at Ault Park, his American Academy of Christian Democracy transformed. His lectures, conferences, and retreats gave him the opportunity to imbue trade unionists with correct social principles, which exerted a mellowing influence on labor relations. The A. F. of L. officially recognized the importance of the school to the trade union movement when it made the Academy its first National Labor College. No greater mark of confidence has ever been conferred by that organization. After World War I, however, with the resurgence of capitalism, Dietz met an opposition he could not brook. Hostile Catholic factions among employer groups in Cincinnati prevailed upon the aging and sickly Archbishop Moeller to order the closing of the school and the withdrawal of Father Dietz from Cincinnati.

On the international front, the work of Father Dietz was no less significant. By preventing the affiliation of the American Federation of Labor with the Socialist-dominated Amsterdam International, Dietz again saved the labor movement from radical influences. He persuaded the Executive Council of the wisdom of closer relations with the International Federation of Christian Trade Unions, whose organization Dietz had helped inaugurate. He saw these Christian unions as a bulwark against the anti-democratic forces in Europe.

Any consideration of the career of Father Dietz raises the questions: Why was he unsuccessful in launching his social program? Why was it that his ideas now so obvious and orthodox failed to receive the support they so richly deserved? Unquestionably Father Dietz was many years ahead of his time. Only a few of the bishops and priests of his day had the courage to brave the implications of his program. Hostile forces among so-called better class Catholics, especially the employer groups, obstructed his efforts for labor. And beyond a doubt the personality of the priest had much to do with his lack of permanent success. Dietz was an individualist. He had no taste for compromise. Unwilling to yield a point here to gain one there, he

227

had to have all or nothing. Consequently he was harshly intolerant of those who did not see eye to eye with him. This was especially true of his fellow priests who were not yet educated to the plans he advocated. Even those who admired him greatly wished that he could have had some of the "sweet reasonableness" that would have won more to the support of his program. Dietz admittedly was bored with the details of organization and found it practically impossible to persevere through uninteresting periods of development. Yet he could not confidently delegate such work to others. This weakness prevented his taking deep root anywhere. On the other hand, many of these characteristics are those of a pioneer. Had he been content to wait for things to happen, or been defeated by the first sign of opposition, Dietz would never have been a trail blazer.

That he was a trail blazer no one can deny. Most of the important Catholic social organizations existing today find their antecedents in the work of Father Dietz. He organized the first Catholic labor college in the country, if not in the English-speaking world. He petitioned for an official Catholic program of social reconstruction. He pointed out the advantages of yearly industrial conferences under Catholic auspices. His school for social workers was the first of its kind in the country. His Militia of Christ for Social Service was a forerunner of the Association of Catholic Trade Unionists.

The work of Father Dietz lives on. So, too, does the memory of the man. His dynamic personality made an indelible impression on all who met him. Even those who disliked him heartily never forgot him and still wax emotional over their grievances. His many friends recall his high idealism, his deep faith in the providence of God, and his willingness to bear the dark night of failure in the hope of tomorrow's sunrise. But all, friend and enemy alike, remember Peter Ernest Dietz as a priest who in the sphere of virtue as in that of nature was essentially a fighting man.

NOTES TO CHAPTER ONE

[1] Henry S. Spalding, S.J., *Social Problems and Agencies* (New York, 1925), p. 22.

[2] Frederick C. Dietz, M.M., to author, Jan. 15, 1949.

[3] Unless otherwise indicated the events in the life of Father Dietz are taken from his two-volume *Diary*, loaned by the Very Reverend Frederick C. Dietz, M.M. his brother.

[4] Peter E. Dietz to Aaron I. Abell, May 8, 1945.

[5] Peter was a top-ranking pupil. The family still preserves a framed picture, "The Old Mill," which he received as a prize. Cf., Theresa Dietz to author, April 12, 1949.

[6] That he discontinued in good standing is certified to by the Reverend August Drooper, C.SS.R., Rector, August 31, 1896. This certification is among the Dietz family papers supplied by Frederick C. Dietz, M.M.

[7] Mulry to Rt. Rev. J. M. Farley, V.G., July 10, 1900. Dietz Family Papers.

[8] Leonard Heuser to Dietz, May 5, 1901. Dietz Family Papers.

[9] Dyer to Dietz, May 5, 1899. Dietz Family Papers.

[10] Dietz met the Rev. F. Joseph Butler, O.F.M., president of St. Bonaventure's Seminary, in Washington, D. C., on the occasion of the dedication of Mount St. Sepulchre, which had been erected by Father Godfrey, O.F.M.

[11] This composition, dated Nov. 13, 1899, is among the Dietz Family Papers.

[12] Dyer to Dietz, Dec. 7, 1899. Dietz Family Papers.

[13] Dietz to Peil, Sept. 30, 1901. (Copy) Dietz Family Papers; *Diary*, September 30.

[14] Cf., A private notebook in the Dietz Family Papers.

[15] Cf., *Ibid.* Weil ich *Meister* der Engl. Sprache; Literatur; Theol. u. Volkcharacter werden muss; Ich will eindringen in das Wesen u. den Geist des werdenden Amerikaners um ihn *richtig* verstehen zu koennen gleich von Anfang an.

Es laesst sich nicht laeugnen (sic) dass der Amerikaner die socialen Probleme der Gegenwart leichter erfasst u so weit am Besten geloest hat obwohl allgemein bekannt ist dass die schliessliche Loesung noch weit in der Ferne liegt. Meiner Ansicht nach haengt diese Loesung nicht im geringsten Teile vom Wirken des Kath. Clerus ab. Wir wissen ja alle das Amerika auf intellectuellen gebiete nichts ueber das Mittelmaessige bisher geleistet hat; das ist zunaechst ganz natuerlich denn Amerika ist noch in seinen Flegeljahren; trotz dem aber sprudelt ueberall sporadisch die urwuechsige Energie empor. Dieser Energie die Richtung zu geben mitwirken zu duerfen, ist eine herrliche Aufgabe. Dietz to Peil, December 14, 1901. (Copy) Dietz Family Papers.

[16] *Ibid.*

[17] August 11, 1902. (Copy) *Diary*.

[18] The plans for this Congregation are written in full in the *Diary* for October 20, 1902.

[19] Dietz to Spalding, December 25, 1902. (Copy) *Diary*.

[20] *Diary,* April 10, 1903.

[21] Godfrey to Dietz, April 26, 1903; Elliott to Dietz, June 1, 1903. Bishop P. J. Garrigan of Sioux City, Iowa, agreed to adopt Dietz at Dr. William Kerby's request. Garrigan to Kerby, November 17, 1903. All in Dietz Family Papers.

[22] Elliott to Dietz, July 12, 1903; September 14, 1903. Dietz Family Papers.

[23] Dyer to Dietz, April 20, 1904. Dietz Family Papers.

[24] John C. Murrett, M.M., *Tar Heel Apostle* (New York, 1944), p. 61.

[25] Dietz to Horstmann, Oct. 7, 1904. (Copy) Dietz Family Papers.

[26] Horstmann to Dietz, January 11, 1906. Dietz Family Papers.

[27] Cf., John R. Commons and Associates, *History of Labor in the United States* (New York, 1935), III, 294-302.

[28] The census of 1890, in an investigation of 44,225 industries in 165 cities, employing 757,865 males, 16 and over, reported that 51% were receiving less than twelve dollars per week; in 1891 the Annual Report of the Commissioner of Labor showed that 73% of 28,127 males working in iron, steel, and glass, received less than two dollars per day. Cf., John A. Ryan, "The Underpaid Laborers of America; Their Number and Prospects," *Catholic World,* LXXXI (May, 1905), 144. The children in the cotton mills of the East received less than four cents a day. Cf., John Talbot Smith, "The Children at Work," *Catholic World,* XLIII (Aug., 1886), 619.

[29] Richard T. Ely, *The Labor Movement in America* (New York, 1886), p. 60.

[30] Henry J. Browne, *The Catholic Church and the Knights of Labor* (Washington, D.C., 1949), p. 38.

[31] Cf., Ely, *op. cit.,* p. 209. The Socialist Labor Party was founded in 1876 under the name of the Workingman's Party of the United States. The next year the name was changed. Cf. also Browne, *op cit.,* pp. 83-90.

[32] Cf., Richard T. Ely, *op. cit.,* pp. 229-276; Nathan Fine, *Labor and Farmer Parties in the United States* (New York, 1928) pp. 147-154; N. I. Stone, *The Attitude of the Socialists Toward the Trade Unions* pamphlet, (New York, 1900), pp. 4-5; S. F. Markham, *A History of Socialism* (London, 1934), p. 254 ff.

[33] Parsons was a member of the International Working People's Association and McGuire was active in the Socialist Labor Party. Cf., Browne, *op. cit.,* pp. 89-90.

[34] *The Religious Mission of the Irish People and Catholic Colonization* (New York, 1880), p. 204. The Bishop modified this view later. Cf., "Socialism and Labor and Other Arguments," *Catholic World,* LIII (1891), 791-801.

[35] Cf., Browne, *op. cit.,* especially Chapter III, "The Attention of the Hierarchy," pp. 70-104, for the various opinions of ecclesiastics on the Knights of Labor and trade unionism; also Aaron I. Abell, "The Reception of Leo XIII's Labor Encyclical in America, 1891-1919," *Review of Politics,* VII (October, 1945), 468; John Tracy Ellis, *The Life of James Cardinal Gibbons* (Milwaukee, 1952), I, Chap. XII, pp. 486-546.

[36] Browne, *op. cit.,* 104.

[37] For a complete text of the memorial Cf., Browne, *op. cit.,* Appendix II, pp. 363-378; also Allen S. Will, *Life of James Cardinal Gibbons* (Baltimore, 1911), pp. 154-160.

[38] Browne, *op. cit.*, pp. 368-369.

[39] *Ibid.*, p. 370.

[40] *Ibid.*, p. 373.

[41] By 1895 it was clear to Daniel de Leon and others of his kind that radicalism was beaten in both the Knights of Labor and the American Federation of Labor. Cf., Selig Perlman, *A History of Trade Unionism in the United States* (New York, 1922), p. 210; Commons, *op. cit.*, 217-225.

[42] Cf., John Talbot Smith, "The 8-hr. Law," *Catholic World*, XLIII (December, 1886) 397-406; Abell, *loc. cit.*, 470-472; John G. O'Shea, "Labor's Discontent," *American Catholic Quarterly Review*, VII (October, 1882), 700-712. Terence V. Powderley was asked to speak on the labor question at the first lay congress at Baltimore in 1889, but he refused. Cf., Browne, *op. cit.* p. 337. For the work of Father Cornelius O'Leary in the Gould strike see Browne, *op. cit.*, pp. 188-189.

[43] Joseph Husslein, S.J., *Social Wellsprings* (Milwaukee, 1940), I, 168. This edition of the Encyclical is used throughout.

[44] *Ibid.*, 175. [47] *Ibid.*, 168. [50] *Ibid.*, 191. [53] *Ibid.*, 203.
[45] *Ibid.*, 177. [48] *Ibid.*, 189. [51] *Ibid.*, 197.
[46] *Ibid.*, 178. [49] *Ibid.*, 189. [52] *Ibid.*, 198.

[54] John A. Ryan, "The Church and the Workingman," *Catholic World*, LXXXIX (September, 1909) 781.

[55] *Ibid.*

[56] *Ibid.*

[57] For a discussion of this phase of the Church's problems, cf., Aaron I. Abell, "Origins of Catholic Social Reform in the United States: Ideological Aspects," *Review of Politics*, XI (July, 1949), 294-309.

[58] Commons, *op. cit.*, IV, 129-151.

[59] R. J. Holaind, S.J., "The Encyclical *Rerum Novarum*," *American Ecclesiastical Review*, V (August, 1891), 89.

[60] Cf., Francis W. Howard, "Social Science an aid in the Ministry," *American Ecclesiastical Review*, XII (April, 1895), 293-300.

[61] Paul Stroh, C.SS.R., *The Catholic Clergy and American Labor Disputes: 1900-1932*, (Unpublished Doctoral Dissertation, Catholic University, 1939), pp. 38-48; Theodore Roosevelt, "The Coal Miner at Home," *The Outlook*, XCVI, 899-908.

[62] Cf., Abell, "The Reception of Leo XIII's Labor Encyclical in America 1891-1919," *Review of Politics*, VII (October, 1945), p. 475; William J. Onahan, "Columbian Catholic Congress at Chicago," *Catholic World*, LVII (August, 1893), 604-608.

[63] "For a Catholic Social Movement," *The Review* (later the *Catholic Fortnightly Review*), IX (1902), 168.

[64] *Ibid.*, 330.

[65] *Ibid.*

[66] . . . dasz wir die in jenem Rundschreiben niedergelegten Grundsaetze und Verhaltungsmassregeln nach allen unsern Kraeften zur Anwendung bringen und ihnen auch in den weiteesten Kreisen bei Andern zur Anergennung und Ausfuehrung verhelfen wollen, in der festeten Ueberzeugung, dasz nur durch Festhaltung jener Prinzipien die Loesung dieser hochwichtigen Zeitfrage gefunden

werden kann. *Verhandlungen der Fuenften Allgemeinen Versammlung Katholiken deutscher Zunge der Vereinigten Staaten von Nord-Am.* (Buffalo, 1891), p. 85.

[67] *Infra.,* pp. 29-30.

[68] "Who is the 'Father of Federation,' " *Bulletin of the American Federation of Catholic Societies,* XII (July, 1917), 2. This reference will be cited as *Bulletin* hereafter.

[69] *Constitution and By-Laws,* p. 2.

[70] *Catholic Fortnightly Review,* IX (1902), 4.

[71] *Sacred Heart Review,* XXXII (August 13, 1904), 97.

[72] Kerby to Dietz, November 14, 1910. The Dietz Papers, Library of the German Catholic Central Verein, (St. Louis). Hereafter cited as C-V. This evaluation of Father Dietz is drawn from his *Diary,* his private correspondence, interviews with his students and with his brother, the Reverend Frederick C. Dietz, M.M., who lived with Father Peter Dietz in Oberlin, Ohio.

NOTES TO CHAPTER TWO

[1] Cf., *Elyria Daily Chronicle,* September 5, 1905. The same paper announced the coming of Debs to address the Socialists who have a "full ticket in the field" for the coming municipal election.

[2] *Ibid.*

[3] "The Social Question in its Bearing Upon the Clerical Profession." Dietz Family Papers.

[4] *Ibid.*

[5] *Ibid.*

[6] Foster Rhea Dulles, *Labor in America* (New York, 1949), p. 195; Commons, *op. cit.,* 129-137.

[7] Dulles, *op. cit.,* p. 194.

[8] *Ibid.,* p. 183; Selig Perlman, *A History of Trade Unionism* (New York, 1922), pp. 198-205.

[9] Fine, *op. cit.,* p. 216.

[10] Victor Cathrein, S.J., *Socialism: Its Theoretical Basis and Practical Application* (New York, 1904), p. 92.

[11] Joseph Husslein, S.J., *The Church and Social Problems* (New York, 1912), p. 201.

[12] The weekly publication *Appeal to Reason,* and the dailies *New York Call,* Berger's *Milwaukee Leader* and *Social Democratic Herald,* were the best known. By 1912 there were five English and eight foreign language dailies; two hundred and sixty-two English and thirty-six foreign language weeklies; ten English and two foreign language monthly publications. A complete list is given in *Year Book of American Labor* (New York, 1916), I.

[13] "Spread of Socialism in Our Colleges and Universities," III (November,

[14] *Ibid.,* p. 166.

[15] *Year Book of American Labor, op. cit.,* 157.

[16] Fine, *Labor and Farmer Parties in the United States* (New York, 1928), 242.

[17] Cf., VI, 1-6.

[18] Cf., IV (June, 1911), 12.

[19] Cf., a Brochure of the school dated, April 12, 1913. C-V.

[20] *Year Book of American Labor, op. cit.,* 95.

[21] "The American Federation of Labor," *Central Blatt and Social Justice,* II (December, 1909), 11. This will be cited hereafter as *C.B. & S.J.*

[22] *Ibid.*

[23] David Goldstein, *Autobiography of a Campaigner for Christ* (Boston, 1936), pp. 23-24.

[24] See, for example, *The Catholic World,* LXXXVII (April, 1908), pp.

100-103; *ibid.*, (July, 1908), pp. 544-547; *ibid.*, LXXXIX (September, 1909), pp. 828-829; *ibid.*, pp. 833-834.

[25] Goldstein, *Autobiography.* . . , *op. cit.*, p. 33.

[26] *Catholic Fortnightly Review*, XVI (September, 1909), 534.

[27] Cf., *Ibid.*, (January, 1909), p. 12; 90.

[28] "Can a Catholic be a Socialist?" *Ibid.*, pp. 70-73; 322-327.

[29] "The Church and the Workingman," *Catholic World*, LXXXIX (September, 1909), p. 282.

[30] "Social Reform Through Legislation," *Ibid.*, p. 441; 442. For the entire discussion cf., pp. 433-444; 608-614.

[31] *Ibid.*, p. 442.

[32] *Catholic Fortnightly Review*, XIII (November, 1906), 698.

[33] Dietz to Peter J. Muldoon, January 5, 1916. (Copy) C-V.

[34] *Ibid.*

[35] *C. B. & S. J.*, II (February, 1910), 12.

[36] *Ibid.*

[37] *Ibid.*

[38] *Ibid.*

[39] *Bulletin of the American Federation of Catholic Societies*, III (July-August, 1909), 8.

[40] *Ibid.*, II (July, 1909), 9.

[41] Cf., Offizieller Bericht ueber die Dreiundfuenfzigste General-Versammlung des Deutschen Roemisch-Katholischen Central Vereins, pp. 17-18.

[42] *Central Blatt*, I (March, 1909), 3.

[43] ". . . um mehrere Vorschlage des Clevelander Komites in Erwaegung zu ziehen." *Ibid.*

[44] *Ibid.*

[45] Cf., Dietz to Muldoon, January 5, 1916. (Copy) C-V. The name of the magazine was changed to *Social Justice Review* in 1940, and after that year was largely English.

[46] *Central Blatt*, I (March, 1909), 3.

[47] The school was never built, but the fund now subsidizes the activities of the Central Bureau. The plan for a school has been abandoned but the Bureau hopes to revive the Social Studies courses to explain the theories of Solidarism. Confirmed in a conference with Mr. Kenkel on May 7, 1949.

[48] "The Social Problem: A Supplement," March 16, 1908. Dietz Family Papers.

[49] Cf., *C. B. & S. J.*, II (December, 1909); (January, 1910).

[50] *Ibid.*, (September, 1909), 11.

[51] Cf., *C. B. & S. J.*, II (September, 1909), 11-12. A footnote, 11: "The Editor alone is responsible for the views expressed in this program. It does not proceed from official sources."

[52] *Ibid.*, p. 12. Note the similarity between this program and that proposed for his "Militia of the Divine Will," *Supra.*, pp. 8-9.

53 *C. B. & S. J.*, II (October, 1909), 9-10.

54 *Ibid.*, 10.

55 *Ibid.*, 8.

56 *Ibid.*, V (November, 1912); (December, 1912), 178, 198.

57 "Two Important Points in the Social Program of the Central Verein," *C. F. R.*, XVI (March, 1909), 132.

58 *Ibid.*

59 *Ibid.*

60 "Der Soziale-Kursus zu Belleville," *C. B. & S. J.*, II (March, 1910), 17.

61 *Ibid.*

62 *C. B. & S. J.*, IV (June, 1911), 59; *America*, IX (June 21, 1913), 263.

63 Goldstein, *Autobiography of a Campaigner for Christ, op. cit.*, especially 64, 117.

64 For a further development of this idea see, *Infra.*, pp. 212-214.

65 *Social Justice Review*, L (December, 1947), 288.

66 See Abell, "The Reception of Leo XIII's Encyclical in America, 1891-1919," *Review of Politics*, VII (October, 1945), 490.

67 Charles Howard Hopkins, *The Rise of the Social Gospel in American Protestantism, 1865-1915* (Yale Studies in Religious Education, XIV, New Haven, 1940), pp. 280-317.

68 *Bulletin*, V (September-October, 1911), 21.

69 "Social Service," *America, VII* (May, 1912), 137.

70 See Chapters V and VI for a detailed account of, Father Dietz's work as secretary.

71 "Our Catholic Charities," *Catholic World*, C (November, 1914), 151.

72 "Fundamental Relations of Charity," *Ibid.*, XCIX (April, 1914), 36.

73 *Proceedings* (Washington, 1910), p. 173.

74 *Ibid.*, 176.

75 *Bulletin*, VIII (May, 1914), 6.

76 David Goldstein, "Report before the Conference of the Social Service Commission," (Baltimore, 1914) cf., Minutes of the Conference, pp. 19-21. Central Verein Papers.

77 *Bulletin*, VIII (May, 1914), 6.

78 Charles Fay, "Socialism and the Immigrant," *Bulletin*, X (November, 1915), 4.

79 *America*, X (December, 1913), 280.

80 Richard Dana Skinner, "The Eunomic League," *America*, X (May, 1914), 584.

81 *Common Cause*, I (March, 1912), 89.

82 *Ibid.*, p. 90.

83 See Chapter VII for his American Academy of Christian Democracy.

88 *America*, VIII (October, 1914), 16.

[84] John A. Ryan, *Social Doctrine in Action,* (New York, 1941), p. 78.

[85] "A Course of Social Service at the Salesianum," *C. F. R.,* XVI (1911), 736.

[86] Thomas T. Woodlock, "The School for Social Studies," *Common Cause,* I (January, 1912), 83-85.

[87] *America,* VIII (November, 1912), 136.

[88] *America,* VIII (October, 1914), 16.

[89] *Bulletin,* IX (October, 1914), 11. This was Father Siedenberg's report at the Baltimore convention of the American Federation of Catholic Societies. *Infra.,* p. 129.

[90] "Labor Legislation," a typed sheet in the Dietz Family Papers.

[91] *Ibid.*

[92] "The Present Outlook," *C. B. & S. J.,* II (February, 1910), 11.

[93] A handbill announcing his candidacy. C-V. Two delegates were elected from ten candidates. Father Dietz was fourth highest. Cf., *Elyria Evening Telegram,* Nov. 9, 1911.

[94] Ryan, *Social Doctrine in Action, op. cit.,* pp. 121-123.

[95] *Bulletin,* XI (April, 1916), 2; XII (April, 1917), 2.

[96] Stroh, *op. cit.,* pp. 69-75.

[97] John E. Sexton, *Cardinal O'Connell* (Boston, 1926), p. 154.

[98] Secretary's Report to the Semi-Annual Conference of the Social Service Commission, Chicago, Illinois, February 12, 1913. C-V.

[99] "When will the Catholic Social Movement Come?" *Bulletin,* XI (February, 1916), 1.

[100] *Ibid.*

NOTES TO CHAPTER THREE

[1] *Supra.*, p. 17.

[2] Glennon to G. Gramann, president of the society, May 19, 1909. C-V. (Copy)

[3] *Social Service,* I (May, 1911), 59.

[4] *Central Blatt and Social Justice,* II (December, 1909), 9.

[5] *Social Service, loc. cit.,* 60.

[6] *Ibid.*

[7] *Ibid.,* 62.

[8] *Ibid.,* 64.

[9] C-V.

[10] *Social Service, loc. cit.,* 72. Other members of the Directorate were: Denis Hayes, president of the Association of Glass Bottle Blowers, John Alpine, president of the International Association of Plumbers and Steamfitters, David Carey, chairman of Separate School Board of Toronto, Roady Kenehan, treasurer of the State of Colorado, Michael J. Hallinan of the Boot and Shoe Workers, James Creamer, vice-president of the Virginia State Federation of Labor, John Moffit, president of the International Association of Hatters, T. V. O'Connor, International president of the Longshoremen, and John Golden, International secretary of the United Brotherhood of Carpenters and Joiners. *Ibid.*

[11] "The Constitution of the Militia of Christ," p. 2.

[12] *Ibid.,* 6. One-third were retired each year.

[13] *Ibid.,* 8.

[14] *Social Service, loc. cit.,* 73.

[15] *Ibid.*

[16] C-V. Some of these rules were: Have a personal program of social service; read and study your social literature; talk it over with God in prayer and meditation; be generous with your money and resources; attend the meetings of your societies and unions; accept committee-work and delegations; in the absence of leadership, qualify for it; use the privilege and fulfill the duty of citizenship.

[17] *Social Service, loc. cit.,* 74-75.

[18] Achatz to Dietz, March 11, 1911. C-V.

[19] *Social Service,* I (August, 1911), 118.

[20] *Ibid.,* (May, 1911), 75.

[21] "Christian Manifesto," p. 16.

[22] Falconio to Dietz, March 21, 1911. C-V.

[23] Blenk to Dietz, January 25, 1911. C-V.

[24] Grace to Dietz, January 30, 1911. C-V.

[25] Fox to Dietz, February 10, 1911. C-V.

PETER E. DIETZ, LABOR PRIEST

²⁶ Donahue to Dietz, February 13, 1911. C-V.

²⁷ Harty to Dietz, April 8, 1911. C-V. To these names cited could be added the following: Bishop James A. McFaul, Trenton, N. J., January 27, 1911; Bishop Joseph M. Koudelka, Cleveland, Ohio, February 3, 1911; Bishop Joseph Schrembs, Grand Rapids, July 13, 1911; Bishop John E. Gunn, Natchez, Miss., December 26, 1911; Archbishop William O'Connell, Boston, (Martha M. Avery to Dietz, March 21, 1911); Bishop J. F. Regis Canevin, Pittsburgh, Pa. (McArdle to Dietz, January 17, 1911).

²⁸ Bishop Shanahan was correct on the heraldry question. Later Father Dietz wrote to an authority on heraldry, Pierre de Chaignon la Rore, Cambridge, Mass., who wrote a detailed criticism of the coat of arms. "The chief trouble with your shield," he wrote, "is that it tries, and in a very arbitrary manner, to expose a vast deal of doctrine, etc., instead of merely identifying the society in simple appropriate terms." (June 20, 1913) The shield bore in its three fields a crown, a mailed arm and a dove. The first bore the dual symbolism of the Kingdom of the Father in the Trinity of the spiritual order and the "steward-ship of capital" in the "Trinity of Human Interests;" the mailed arm symbolized the "Executive power of the Son" and the "Dignity of Labor;" the Dove repre-sented the "unitive Fusion of the Holy Spirit" and the "Prosperity of the Commonwealth." This explanation was printed on the inside cover of each issue of *Social Service* and on the Militia of Christ circular sent out from Oberlin.

²⁹ Ryan to Dietz, February 18, 1911. C-V.

³⁰ Ryan to Dietz, March 25, 1911. C-V.

³¹ Cf., "Have we any Catholic Solutions of Social Problems?" *Social Service,* I (November, 1911), 147-152.

³² Maeckel to Dietz, October 11, 1911. C-V. See also his article, "Christian Democracy," *Social Service,* I (November, 1911), 160-163, signed "By a Jesuit."

³³ White to Dietz, February 2, 1911. C-V.

³⁴ "Rome has Spoken," *C. B. & S. J.,* V (March, 1913), 270.

³⁵ Husslein to Dietz, January 12, 1912. C-V.; February 22, 1912. C-V.; *America,* V (September, 1911), 550.

³⁶ Neill to Dietz, February 28, 1911. C-V.

³⁷ *Ibid.*

³⁸ Connelly to Dietz, January 18, 1912. C-V.

³⁹ Bonaparte to Dietz, March 4, 1911. C-V. (Charles Bonaparte was the grandson of Jerome Bonaparte and Elizabeth Patterson.) Regarding this matter of his forced resignation, Mitchell wrote to Father Dietz: "It is needless to say that I feel very keenly the injustice done me by the majority of the delegates. . . They did not even give me an opportunity to speak in my own behalf. However, I have the consolation of believing that the action of the Convention does not accurately reflect the wishes of the men at home, although it is just as binding upon me as though it were the result of a popular vote." Mitchell to Dietz, February 8, 1911. C-V.

⁴⁰ *Ibid.*

⁴¹ Smith to Dietz, July 5, 1911. C-V.

⁴² *Ibid.,* March 10, 1911.

⁴³ *Ibid.,* September 20, 1911. C-V. In 1914, Smith attended the con-vention of the A. F. of L. in Philadelphia and addressed the delegates.

⁴⁴ Mitchell missed his train on this visit because he was so interested in the

conversation they were having he gave little attention to the time. Cf., Mitchell to Dietz, June 1, 1911. C-V.

[45] June 1, 1911. C-V. It is interesting to recall that Mitchell had been a Catholic only five years when he wrote this letter.

[46] Mitchell to Dietz, August 1, 1912. C-V.

[47] Cf., for example, Golden to Dietz, August 30, 1912; O'Connor to Dietz, May 3, 1911. C-V.

[48] Cf., John A. Voll, Vice-President of Glass Bottle Blowers Association, February 4, 1911; P. J. Flannery, International President of Brotherhood of Railroad Freight Handlers, February 3, 1911; Patrick McGowan, Recording Secretary of Amalgamated Association of Iron and Steel Workers of North America, March 11, 1911. C-V.

[49] May 30, 1911. C-V.

[50] "Organized Intolerance," *Milwaukee Leader,* June 14, 1913.

[51] Quoted in *Social Service,* I (August, 1911), 126.

[52] Father Gilbert Jennings to Dietz, March 16, 1911. Dietz Family Papers. Bishop Horstmann died suddenly in 1908. His death was a personal loss to Father Dietz, especially since his successor was never friendly to him. Cf., Dietz to Schrembs, October 24, 1922. C-V. (Copy)

[53] Glennon to Dietz, January 7, 1911. C-V.

[54] Ryan to Dietz, March 15, 1911. C-V.

[55] *Ibid.,* March 25, 1911.

[56] Glennon to Dietz, March 18, 1911. C-V.

[57] Gibbons to Dietz, August 12, 1911. C-V.

[58] Shahan to Dietz, July 17, 1911. C-V.

[59] Glennon to Dietz, August 7, 1911. C-V.

[60] July 18, 1911. C-V.

[61] Fanning to Dietz, February 15, 1911. C-V.

[62] Farelly to Dietz, July 8, 1911. Dietz Family Papers.

[63] Falconio to Dietz, September 29, 1911. Dietz Family Papers.

[64] Koudelka to Dietz, January 6, 1912. Bishop J. M. Koudelka had belonged to the Cleveland Diocese also, but had difficulties with the Bishop, and removed to Milwaukee. Cf. Koudelka to Dietz, February 1, 1912. Dietz Family Papers.

[65] Messmer to Dietz, January 20, 1912. Dietz Family Papers.

[66] Report of the Secretary of the Social Service Commission, August, 1912 to August, 1913. C-V.

[67] Dietz to Mitchell, December 30, 1911. Quoted from Reverend John P. Boyle, "Peter E. Dietz and the American Labor Movement," unpublished Master's essay, Catholic University of America, Department of Economics, 1948, pp. 56-57.

[68] *Ibid.*

[69] September 5, 1911. C-V.

[70] *Ibid.,* December 30, 1911.

[71] Cf., Brochure announcing Collins' lecture Tour. C-V.

[72] Collins to Dietz, March 27, 1911. C-V.

[73] Cf., *supra,* p. 52.

[74] Collins to Dietz, October 19, 1911. C-V.

[75] Dietz to Heckenkamp, January 14, 1913. C-V. (Copy)

[76] Keates to Muldoon, December 25, 1912. C-V. His plan was to organize

a "Catholic Laymen's Guild" to train men for the platform to address schools, societies, religious institutions, and the like.

[77] Joseph Meyung, Journeyman Barber's International Union, Cincinnati, to Dietz, July, 1913. C-V.

[78] Dietz to Keates, March 19, 1914. C-V. (Copy)

[79] "Socialism and Social Service," a pamphlet, April 28, 1912, p. 3.

[80] *Morning Star,* Diocesan paper of New Orleans, April, 1912.

[81] Smith to Clarke, May 18, 1912. C-V.

[82] Downing to Dietz, July 27, 1912. C-V.

[83] Downing to Dietz, January 25, 1912. C-V.

[84] Rombouts to Dietz, August 1, 1912. C-V.

[85] Charles Denechaud, former member of the Social Service Commission, was then President of the American Federation of Catholic Societies.

[86] Dietz to Blenk, February 7, 1913. C-V. (Copy)

[87] Gassler to Dietz, April 22, 1913. C-V.

[88] *Catholic Fortnightly Review,* XX (1913), 362.

[89] July 21, 1913. C-V.

[90] Report of the Secretary of the Social Service Commission.

[91] *Bulletin,* VI (June, 1912), 8.

[92] March 19, 1913. C-V.

[93] January 12, 1913. C-V.

[94] Victor Hoppe, Milk Driver's Union, to Dietz, January 29, 1914. C-V.

[95] *Milwaukee Leader,* I (October 1, 1912)

[96] *Ibid.*

[97] Quoted in *Bulletin,* VI (October, 1912), 17.

[98] *Ibid.*

[99] Dietz to Keates, February 26, 1913. C-V. (Copy)

[100] April 4, 1913. C-V.

[101] *Catholic Citizen,* Milwaukee, March 29, 1913, p. 3.

[102] *Ibid.,* September 6, 1913.

[103] Moeller to Meyung, July 24, 1913. C-V.

[104] Dietz to Budenz, February 17, 1913. C-V.

[105] Besides being Associate Editor of *The Carpenter,* his union paper, he was Vice-President and State Organizer of the Indiana Federation of Catholic Societies, President of his Conference of St. Vincent de Paul Society, on three important committees of Young Men's Institute, and had privately organized a group of young men in a Guild of St. Charles Borromeo for apologetical work. Budenz to Dietz, February 28, 1913. C-V.

[106] Budenz to Dietz, February 28, 1913. C-V.

[107] Budenz to Dietz, April 28, 1913. C-V.

[108] Budenz to Dietz, December 14, 1913. C-V.

[109] Dietz to O'Connell, March 15, 1913. C-V. (Copy)

[110] Supple to Dietz, Roxbury, Mass., March 8, 1913. C-V.

[111] Dietz to Supple, April 10, 1913. C-V. (Copy)

[112] May 5, 1914.

[113] Messmer to Dietz, April 12, 1912. Dietz Family Papers.

[114] February 8, 1913. C-V. (Copy)

[115] Dougherty to Dietz, October 26, 1912. C-V.

NOTES TO CHAPTER THREE

[116] J. M. Conley, Editor of *Labor Leader*, Dubuque, Iowa, to Dietz, November 16, 1914. C-V.

[117] May 18, 1914. C-V. (Copy)

[118] Dietz to J. F. Burns, Secretary of Structural Iron Workers Union, January 29, 1915. (Copy)

[119] Dietz to Wilde, March 13, 1915. C-V. (Copy)

[120] Resolution dated August 31, 1915. C-V.

[121] *Ibid.*

[122] Dietz to the Grand Knights, September 21, 1915. C-V. (Copy)

[123] Dietz to Van Nistelroy, February 11, 1914. C-V. (Copy)

[124] Walker to Mahoney, October 15, 1913, C-V.

[125] *Newsletter*, December 20, 1913. C-V.

[126] Dietz to Van Nistelroy, January 20, 1914. C-V. (Copy)

[127] Other demands were granted but not the one big point for which the miners struck—union recognition. Cf. Commons, *History of Labor in the United States: 1896-1932*, IV, 248-253.

[128] *Newsletter*, January 15, 1914.

[129] *Ibid.*

[130] Hogan to Dietz, December 29, 1913. C-V.

[131] Dietz to Hogan, January 19, 1914. C-V. (Copy)

[132] *Ibid.*

[133] Dietz to O'Connell, January 4, 1914. C-V. (Copy)

[134] McArdle to Dietz, May 8, 1911. C-V.

NOTES TO CHAPTER FOUR

[1] Dietz to Whalen, February 4, 1913. C-V. (Copy) Cardinal Gibbons had requested that Dr. Kerby be present. Denis Hayes was ill and John Mitchell was not available.

[2] Copy found among the Mitchell papers, Mullen Library. Quoted by Father John P. Boyle, *op. cit.*, pp. 62-63. The paper was dated November 21, 1921, Rochester, New York.

[3] Dietz to Glennon, February 8, 1913. C-V. (Copy) The two who refused were John C. White of the Miners, and Edward F. Ward of the Brewery Workers.

[4] *Ibid.*

[5] Dietz to Gibbons, March 27, 1913. C-V. (Copy)

[6] *Ibid.*

[7] *Ibid.*

[8] *Ibid.*

[9] The Cardinal was to be contacted by a New York Committee appointed by Father D. J. McMahon, cf., Dietz to McMahon, February 4, 1913. C-V. (Copy)

[10] Glennon to Dietz, February 10, 1913. C-V.

[11] Dietz to Glennon, February 17, 1913. C-V. (Copy)

[12] Glennon to Dietz, February 20, 1913. C-V.

[13] Kerby to Dietz, July 7, 1913. C-V.

[14] Dietz to O'Connell, January 13, 1915. C-V. (Copy) Dietz to Muldoon, July 28, 1916. C-V. (Copy). Archbishop O'Connell prepared a statement on the relations of the Church to labor but advised the Cardinal against issuing it at that time. Cf. Ellis, *op. cit.*, I, pp. 537-538.

[15] Dietz to Muldoon, January 26, 1914. C-V. (Copy)

[16] *Ibid.*

[17] *Ibid.*

[18] Dietz to Muldoon, February 18, 1914. C-V. (Copy)

[19] *Ibid.*

[20] *Ibid.*

[21] Dietz to O'Connell, April 16, 1914. C-V. (Copy)

[22] *Ibid.*

[23] *Ibid.*

[24] *Ibid.*

[25] *Ibid.*

[26] *Ibid.*

[27] Dietz to O'Connell, January 4, 1915. C-V. (Copy)

[28] *Ibid.*

[29] *Ibid.*

[30] Some of these were Charles Denechaud at Atlanta, Georgia; Bishop John P. Carroll at Seattle, 1913; and Walter George Smith at Philadelphia, 1914.

[31] *Bulletin,* VI (December, 1912), 8.

[32] *Report of the Proceedings* of the A   , 1912, p. 254.

[33] *Ibid.*

[34] *Newsletter,* November 22, 1913.

[35] Quoted in *Newsletter,* No. 45, n.d., p. 2.

[36] *Ibid.*

[37] John S. O'Connell, Secretary-Treasurer of New York Typographical No. 6 to Dietz, March 3, 1914. C-V.

[38] *Ibid.*

[39] Norman J. Ware, *Labor in Canadian Relations* (Toronto, 1937), pp. xvi-xviii.

[40] Arthur Saint-Pierre, *L'Organization Ouvriere* (Montreal, 1913), p. 31.

[41] Arthur Saint-Pierre, *La Fédération Americaine du Travail* (Montreal, 1914), p. 2.

[42] Cf., Ware, *op. cit.,* p. xvi; Dietz to Right Reverend Belineau, Manitoba, n.d. C-V. (Copy)

[43] William Engelen, S.J., "Rome has Spoken," *C. B. & S. J.,* V (January), 1913), p. 219.

[44] Saint-Pierre, *op. cit.,* p. 23.

[45] *Ibid.,* p. 22.

[46] *Ibid.,* pp. 24-25. Neither the *American Federationist,* official magazine of the A. F. of L., volumes XVII (1910) to XX (1913), nor the *Report of Proceedings* (1910-1913) make any reference to this pamphlet.

[47] *Ibid.,* p. 31. "Jugée du point de vue moral et religieux, elle ne merite en aucune façon le sympathie et l'encouragement des ouvriers Catholiques."

[48] Tobin to Dietz, Dec. 13, 1913. C-V.; Duffy to Morrison, Jan. 6, 1914. C-V. (Copy).

[49] Dietz to Cardinal O'Connell, January 4, 1914. C-V. (Copy)

[50] April 9, 1912. C-V.

[51] April 11, 1912. C-V. (Copy)

[52] Tobin to Dietz, December 13, 1913. C-V.

[53] *Ibid.*

[54] Dietz to O'Connell, January 4, 1914. C-V. (Copy)

[55] Saint-Pierre to Dietz, January 9, 1914. C-V.

[56] Saint-Pierre to Dietz, February 23, 1915. C-V.

[57] Dietz to Germain, July 5, 1916. C-V. (Copy). Father Germain had written Father Dietz asking information about the following: the part taken by the A. F. of L. in the dynamiting of the *Times* in Los Angeles; the support by Gompers of recognition of Carranza; the attitude of the A. F. of L. on Socialism. Cf., June 19, 1916. C-V.

In reply, Father Dietz disavowed any connection with the dynamiting, explaining the autonomy of the individual unions; he suggested that Gompers' support of Carranza might possibly be due to the fact that Gompers had joined the Freemasons; lastly, he did not deny there were Socialists in the Federation, but insisted that the philosophy of the A. F. of L. was not anti-Christian.

[58] Dietz to Gompers, March 21, 1920. C-V. (Copy)

[59] John Voll to Dietz, April 7, 1920. C-V.; Tobin to Dietz, April 16, 1920. C-V.

[60] Moeller to Bruchesi, May 26, 1920, C-V. (Copy). Father Dietz had

moved his school from Hot Springs to Cincinnati in 1917.

[61] Bruchesi to Fortin, June 20, 1920. C-V. (Original)

[62] Dietz to Woll, July 5, 1920. C-V. (Copy)

[63] *Ibid.*

[64] June 21, 1920. C-V. (Copy)

[65] Father John O'Rourke to Dietz, July 15, 1920. C-V.

[66] A Memorandum of an Indianapolis Conference dated September 28, 1920, indicates that Matthew Woll, Daniel Tobin, and Jacob Fisher were the three. C-V.

[67] September 25, 1920. C-V. (Copy)

[68] Dietz to Matthieu, September 29, 1920. C-V. (Copy)

[69] Memorandum, September 28, 1920. C-V.

[70] . . . si, d'une part, les représendants de la Fédération Américaine du Travail veulent prendre leur parti sans discussion du fait de l'existence de la Confédération Nationale des Travailleurs Catholiques du Canada, et si, d'autre part, ils veulent bien faire connaitre quelles questions ils voudraient discuter au cours de cette conference. C-V.

[71] Undated communication, possibly a night letter to Roy. C-V.

[72] Dietz to Golden, May 24, 1921. C-V. (Copy); Tobin to Dietz, December 20, 1920. C-V.

[73] Dietz to Tobin, May 25, 1921. C-V. (Copy)

[74] Gompers to Duffy, July 11, 1921. C-V. (Copy); Woll to Dietz, August 3, 1921. C-V. Woll to Gompers, August 3, 1921. C-V. (Copy)

[75] *Ibid.* Efforts to determine whether this pamphlet was ever written have proved unsuccessful. Cf., Reverend Gerard Dion, Department of Industrial Relations, Laval University, Quebec, to author, December 6, 1949; Reverend M. Herbert Delaney, vice-chancellor, Archdiocese of Toronto, to author, December 30, 1949; Woll to author, January 3, 1950.

[76] Dietz to McNeil, October 3, 1921. C-V. (Copy)

[77] Woll to Dietz, November 8, 1921. C-V.

[78] For good surveys of the social movement in the various countries, cf., Henry Somerville, *The Catholic Social Movement* (London, 1933); Parker T. Moon, *Labor Problems and the Social Catholic Movement in France* (New York, 1921), p. 319ff.; Theodore Brauer, "The Catholic Social Movement in Germany," *The Catholic Social Year Book* (Oxford, 1932); Karl Waninger, Trans. by Charles Plater, S.J., *Social Catholicism in England* (St. Louis, 1923); P.J.-S. Serrarens, *Le Syndicalisme Catholique en Hollande* (Montreal, 1920).

[79] Theodore Brauer, *op. cit.*, pp. 33-34.

[80] *Bulletin,* IV (November, December, 1910), 5.

[81] Karl Waninger, *op. cit.*, pp. 181-182.

[82] John Price, *The International Labour Movement* (London, 1945), pp. 16-19.

[83] *Report of Proceedings* of the A. F. of L., St. Louis, 1910, p. 125; 1920, p. 132.

[84] *Ibid.,* Rochester, 1912, p. 26.

[85] *International News-Letter,* December 24, 1913. C-V.

[86] *Ibid.*

[87] Burns to Dietz, May 22, 1913. C-V.

[88] *Ibid.*

[89] *Newsletter,* (October 24, 1913).

[90] Burns to Dietz, November 24, 1913. C-V.

[91] *Ibid.*

[92] Brauer to Dietz, April 28, 1911. C-V.

[93] Brauer to Dietz, August 8, 1913. C-V.

[94] Brauer to Dietz, February 28, 1914. C-V.

[95] Burns to Dietz, November 24, 1913. C-V.; Brauer to Dietz, May 26, 1914. C-V.

[96] Dietz to O'Connell, April 16, 1914. C-V. (Copy)

[97] Dietz to Burns, n.d. C-V. (Copy)

[98] Dietz to Muldoon, January 5, 1916. C-V. (Copy)

[99] "Scouting for Social Service," *Bulletin,* X (February, 1915), 3.

[100] *Ibid.*

[101] *Ibid.*

[102] Dietz to His Holiness Benedict XV, Pentecost, 1915. C-V. (Copy)

[103] Dietz to Honorable Robert Lansing, Secretary of Foreign Affairs, September 26, 1918. C-V. (Copy)

[104] Copy at C-V. There is no evidence that the Holy Father answered the letter.

[105] Dietz to Burns, May 25, 1919. C-V. (Copy)

[106] *Report of Proceedings,* Montreal, 1920, pp. 131-154.

[107] *Ibid.,* p. 150.

[108]. *Ibid.*

[109] *Ibid.,* p. 154.

[110] Tobin to Dietz, April 16, 1920. C-V.

[111] Dietz to Woll, April 14, 1920. C-V. (Copy)

[112] Dietz to Woll, April 23, 1920. C-V. (Copy)

[113] *Ibid.*

[114] *Ibid.*

[115] *Ibid.*

[116] *Ibid.*

[117] Dietz to Muldoon, April 15, 1920. C-V. (Copy)

[118] *Ibid.*

[119] *Ibid.*

[120] Muldoon to Dietz, April 18, 1920. C-V.

[121] Burns to Dietz, June 29, 1920. C-V.

[122] Brauer to Dietz, June 17, 1921. C-V.

[123] Appleton to Gompers, April 15, 1920, quoted in *Report of the Proceedings* (Montreal, 1920), pp. 164-165.

[124] Dietz to Brauer, August 24, 1920. C-V. (Copy)

[125] Dietz to Brauer, May 15, 1921. C-V. (Copy)

[126] Brauer to Dietz, June 17, 1921. C-V.

[127] Dietz to Kenkel, August 8, 1921. C-V. (Copy)

[128] Dietz to Brauer, September 15, 1921. C-V. (Copy)

[129] David Dubinsky, "Rift and Realignment in World Labor," *Foreign Affairs,* XXVII (January, 1949), 233-245; "World Labor's New Weapon," *Ibid.,* XXVIII (April, 1950), 451.

130 *La Confédération Internationale des Syndicats Chrétiens, 1946-1949.* Huis van den Arbeid, Utrecht: 1949. p. 3.

131 *Official Report of the Free World Labour Conference and the First Congress of the International Confederation of Free Trade Unions.* McIntosh and Ireland, London: 1949. p. 18.

132 *Ibid.*, p. 64. The vote on the resolution was 46-8., *Ibid.*, p. 67.

133 "Christian Unions go it Alone," *America*, LXXXIII (June 3, 1950), p. 258.

134 P. J-S. Serrarens, secretary-general of I.F.C.T.U., to author, October 1, 1950. Serrarens has held the office of secretary-general since 1920.

NOTES TO CHAPTER FIVE

[1] For the origin of Federation see pp. 18-19.

[2] *C.F.R.*, IX (1902), 3; *Bulletin,* VI (November, 1912), 1.

[3] *Constitution and By-Laws,* (1911), p. 7.

[4] *Supra.,* p. 29.

[5] Dietz to Mitchell, December 30, 1911. Quoted in Boyle, *op. cit.*

[6] Matre to Dietz, September 22, 1911. C-V.

[7] Cavanaugh to Dietz, September 4, 1911. C-V.

[8] Hagerty to Dietz, December 6, 1911. C-V.

[9] *Ibid.*

[10] *Ibid.*

[11] *Newsletter,* No. 29, n.d.

[12] Messmer to Dietz, April 12, 1912. C-V.

[13] *Ibid.*

[14] *Ibid.*

[15] *Ibid.*

[16] *Supra.,* pp. 29-30.

[17] *Supra.,* pp. 45-47.

[18] "What shall our Catholic Societies do?" pp. 18-22. For the full text of the questionnaire see Appendix, 270-271.

[19] Report of the Secretary of the Social Service Commission, August, 1912-August, 1913. C-V.

[20] *Ibid.*

[21] *Ibid.*

[22] Letter was dated August 1, 1912. C-V.

[23] Tobin to Dietz, August 2, 1912. C-V. Heckenkamp to Dietz, August 3, 1912. C-V.

[24] Tobin to Dietz, August 2, 1912. C-V.

[25] Golden to Dietz, August 14, 1912. C-V.

[26] Bonaparte to Dietz, August 7, 1912. C-V.

[27] Parn to Dietz, August 10, 1912. C-V.

[28] Kerby to Dietz, October 8, 1912. C-V.

[29] Muldoon to Cavanaugh, August 6, 1912. Papers of the Reverend John W. Cavanaugh, Archives of the University of Notre Dame.

[30] Report of the Secretary, August, 1912-August, 1913. The first annual convention of the Catholic Press Association was held in Columbus, Ohio, in 1911. Here a permanent organization was completed. *Catholic Citizen,* LI (June 15, 1912), Milwaukee.

[31] Dietz to Zenkert, Reform Press, New York, February 5, 1913. C-V. (Copy)

[32] Becker to Dietz, February 19, 1913. C-V.

[33] Dietz to Muldoon, January 18, 1913. C-V. (Copy)

[34] Dietz to Muldoon, June 20, 1914. C-V. (Copy)

[35] Heckenkamp to Dietz, July 20, 1915. C-V.

PETER E. DIETZ, LABOR PRIEST

36 Becker to Dietz, March 27, 1913. C-V.

37 Phillips to Dietz, February 28, 1913. C-V.

38 Zenkert to Dietz, February 23, 1913. C-V.

39 O'Neill to Dietz, January 21, 1913. C-V.

40 Dietz to Heckenkamp, March 25, 1913. C-V. (Copy)

41 February 6, 1914. C-V.

42 *Ibid.*

43 Dietz to Noll, May 15, 1914. C-V. (Copy)

44 Dietz to Noll, June 10, 1914. C-V. (Copy)

45 April 21, 1916. C-V.

46 Smith to Dietz, July 14, 1916. C-V.

47 Marie Louise Points to Dietz, August 10, 1916. C-V.

48 Tierney to Dietz, July 11, 1916. C-V.

49 April 22, 1916.

50 Glennon to Dietz, February 22, 1916.

51 *Newsletter,* January 26, 1915.

52 *Ibid.*

53 *Ibid.*

54 *Ibid.*

55 *Ibid.*

56 *Ibid.*

57 McFaul to Dietz, February 8, 1915. C-V.

58 O'Connell to Dietz, February 4, 1915. C-V.

59 Dietz to Muldoon, February 10, 1915. C-V. (Copy) Other bishops responding were: Regis Canevin, February 12, 1915; Austin Dowling, January 29, 1915; Joseph Busch, January 31, 1915; Vincent Wehrle, February 1, 1915; Eugene Garvey, n.d.; Leo Haid, February 2, 1915; Joseph Schrembs, February 3, 1915; J. Henry Tihen, n.d.; Cornelius Van de Ven, February 2, 1915. All C-V.

60 Willis to Dietz, July 11, 1913. C-V.

61 Report of the Secretary, August, 1912-August, 1913. C-V.

62 Dietz to Muldoon, June 6, 1914. C-V. (Copy)

63 *Ibid.*

64 Heckenkamp to Dietz, March 3, 1915. C-V.

65 Heckenkamp to Dietz, March 17, 1915. C-V.

66 Francis Matre to Dietz, October 24, 1913. C-V.

67 Dietz to Muldoon, February 10, 1915. C-V. (Copy)

68 R. J. Hennessey, District Deputy, to Dietz, October 31, 1912. C-V.

69 Carey to Dietz, October 10, 1913. C-V.

70 *Catholic Citizen,* March 16, 1912.

71 *Ibid.,* June 29, 1912.

72 Constitution, C-V.

73 *Ibid.*

74 Messmer to Dietz, February 27, 1913. C-V.

75 Dietz to Shea, March 15, 1913. C-V. (Copy)

76 Kerby to Dietz, April 3, 1913. C-V.

77 Kerby to Dietz, February 12, 1915. C-V. By 1915 only 10 dioceses had sent in complete information; 53 dioceses were incomplete and 32 had sent no

data. Of the more than 1000 institutions in charge of religious, 530 sent information. A last effort made in June, 1914, by a personal letter to 526 institutions asking for a simple directory blank to be filled out and returned brought a response from only 38. Cf., *Newsletter,* (February 16, 1915). After World War I the task was resumed and completed.

[78] *Supra.,* pp. 8-9.

[79] O'Neill to Dietz, n.d. C-V.

[80] *Ibid.*

[81] *Ibid.*

[82] Watts to Dietz, May 30, 1913. C-V.

[83] *Ibid.* Christopher Watts eventually secured a position on the staff of *The Lamp,* a publication of the monks of Graymoor Abbey. Watts to Dietz, August 23, 1913. C-V.

[84] O'Neill to Dietz, n.d. C-V.

[85] Goldstein to Dietz, May 25, 1913. C-V.

[86] See Chapter VII.

[87] Messmer to Dietz, January 2, 1913. C-V.

[88] *Bulletin,* VIII (March, 1914), p. 5.

[89] *Ibid.*

[90] Kliefoth to Carey, November 9, 1914. C-V.

[91] Dietz to Muldoon, January 6, 1915. C-V. (Copy)

[92] Constitution, p. 11.

[93] Dietz to Neill, May 7, 1914; C-V. (Copy); Dietz to Amberg, May 18, 1914. C-V. (Copy)

[94] Dietz to Hagerty, October 14, 1914. C-V. (Copy)

[95] Muldoon to Dietz, n.d. C-V.

[96] Duffy to Dietz, July 20, 1911. C-V.

[97] *Proceedings* of the Second General Conference of the Social Service Commission, August 11, 1913. pp. 11-16.

[98] Duffy to Dietz, February 5, 1915. C-V.

[99] O'Connell to Dietz, February 9, 1915. C-V.

[100] Green to Dietz, February 9, 1915. C-V.

[101] Hayes to Dietz, February 12, 1915. C-V.

[102] Dietz to Hagerty, March 12, 1915. C-V. (Copy)

[103] "The Immigration Problem," *Bulletin* X (October, 1915), 1, 4. Quoted in Abell, "The Catholic Church and Social Problems in the World War I Era," *Mid-America,* XXX (July, 1948), 146.

[104] *Newsletter,* July 19, 1915.

[105] Dietz to Matre, April 6, 1916. C-V. (Copy)

[106] Dietz to Ryan, March 29, 1916. C-V. (Copy)

[107] *Ibid.*

[108] Ryan to Dietz, April 1, 1916. C-V.

[109] Matre to Dietz, April 6, 1916. C-V. Did Father Dietz have a slip of memory? A letter from Mr. Kenkel (March 17, 1914) questions the reason for the resolution of the Executive Board asking all affiliated societies to take up the protest. "I suppose you know my position on that question," Kenkel wrote, "and it seems to me that you too cannot have endorsed this resolution unqualified. . . . To my mind the resolution was inopportune."

[110] Dietz to Ryan, April 13, 1916. C-V. (Copy)

[111] Ryan to Dietz, April 15, 1916. C-V.

[112] *Ibid.*

[113] Dietz to Muldoon, January 14, 1915. C-V. (Copy)

[114] Cavanaugh to Dietz, January 15, 1915. C-V.; Heckenkamp to Dietz, January 16, 1915; Hayes (night letter) to Dietz, January 19, 1915. C-V.

[115]

God bless us, united in worship and song,
And pledge us, Thy workers, to right every wrong;
With faith and with love, with a will and with might
We go forth to champion the weak and the right.

We'll boast not of progress in thunderous peals,
Till out from the frenzy of industry's wheels
The voice of the worker in pitiful cry,
No longer will pierce thru the Christ-heart on high.

In mine, mill and work-shop, on rail-road and farm,
Wherever earth yields to the working-man's arm;
In commerce and labor, on land and on sea,
To sanctify labor our motto shall be.

The cross is our emblem, our pride and the hope,
Of laymen and women, priest, bishop and pope;
In wealth and in poverty, Catholic and true,
Obeying Christ's Vicar, 'all things we renew.'

Then, forward in service, brave soldiers of Christ,
While weaklings forsake Him by false-hood enticed;
Though forests be riven and mountains brought low
To craft, God and country, we'll render our vow.

[116] Cf., copy of the Memorial, C-V.

[117] Cavanaugh to Dietz, January 19, 1915. C-V.

[118] Hayes to Dietz, (night letter) January 19, 1915. C-V.

[119] Duffy to Dietz, September 10, 1915. C-V.

[120] Gompers to Dietz, September 25, 1915. C-V. The complete text of the letter appears in the Appendix, pp. 272-275.

[121] Dietz to Morrison, October 1, 1915. C-V. (Copy)

[122] Gillen to Dietz, March 21, 1913. C-V.

[123] Gillen to Dietz, March 6, 1913. C-V.; Dietz to Gillen, March 21, 1913. C-V. (Copy)

[124] Gillen to Dietz, March 28, 1913. C-V.

[125] Gillen to Dietz, October 7, 1916. C-V.

[126] Macfarland to Dietz, December 22, 1911. C-V.

[127] Macfarland to Dietz, January 2, 1912; January 10, 1912. C-V.

[128] *Newsletter,* January 5, 1915; *Catholic Citizen,* January 23, 1915.

[129] Macfarland to Dietz, December 14, 1914. C-V.

[130] *Newsletter, loc. cit.*

[131] Dietz to Ward, October 5, 1915. C-V. (Copy)

[132] Ward to Dietz, October 5, 1915. C-V.

[133] Low to Dietz, October 7, 1913. C-V.

[134] Jeremiah Jenks, chairman of the Executive Committee, to Dietz, March

NOTES TO CHAPTER FIVE

4, 1914. C-V.; James L. Phillips, executive secretary, to Dietz, n.d. C-V.

135 Owen R. Lovejoy, general secretary, to Dietz, May 6, 1915. C-V.; Dietz to William Swift, January 19, 1916. C-V. (Copy)

136 Clinton Woodruff to Dietz, February 28, 1914; J. W. Beatson to Dietz, October 10, 1914; Nathaniel Pratt to Dietz, August 3, 1916. Secretaries respectively of the above named organizations. All at C-V.

137 Beatson to Dietz, October 14, 1914. C-V.

138 Taylor to Dietz, January 8, 1913. C-V.

139 Taylor to Dietz, January 15, 1913. C-V. Pauline Martin entered the convent to work with foundlings. Cf., Dietz to Taylor, March 9, 1913. C-V. (Copy)

140 Dietz to Muldoon, January 7, 1913. C-V. (Copy)

141 Taylor to Dietz, October 9, 1912. C-V.

142 "Views of Catholic Societies," *Survey*, XXIX (October 19, 1912), 84.

143 *Ibid.* These were resolutions to "further the abolition of unnecessary labor on Sunday; urging the religious care and human peace of the world; and demanding a living wage, reasonable hours of labor, protection of life and limb, abolition of child labor, just compensation for injury, proper moral and sanitary conditions in the home, shop, mine and factory; sympathizing with organized effort and conservative trade unions, recommending cooperation with other institutions providing for the welfare of the more handicapped members of society, the immigrant, the colonist, the unorganized worker and the helpless; endorsing social study circles, lecture conferences, institutes for merchants and mechanics, and the study of co-operative movements especially among foreigners."

144 *Bulletin,* VI (September, 1912), 17.

145 *Ibid.*

146 Taylor to Dietz, March 6, 1913. C-V.

147 *Bulletin,* VIII (January, 1914), 7-8; *Survey,* XXXI (January 31, 1914), 521-22.

148 Taylor to Dietz, February 11, 1915. C-V.

149 Dietz to Taylor, February 17, 1915. C-V. (Copy)

NOTES TO CHAPTER SIX

[1] Plater to Dietz, July 24, 1913. C-V.

[2] *Ibid.*

[3] Plater to Dietz, October 25, 1913. C-V.; Dietz to Plater, February 11, 1914. C-V. (Copy) See also *Catholic Social Year Book* (London, 1913), pp. 115-118 and Charles Plater, S.J., *The Priest and Social Action* (London, 1914), especially pp. 127-128; 140-144.

[4] Crawford to Dietz, January 15, 1914. C-V.

[5] Cf., Circular letter to priests, June 19, 1914. C-V.

[6] Dietz to Guillen, July 2, 1915. C-V. (Copy)

[7] *Ibid.*

[8] Guillen to Dietz, July 16, 1915. C-V.

[9] Kenkel to Muldoon, September 25, 1912. C-V.

[10] Cavanaugh to Dietz, October 19, 1912. C-V.

[11] *Ibid.,* Hagerty to Dietz, October 19, 1912. C-V.

[12] Heckenkamp to Dietz, September 15, 1913. C-V.

[13] Heckenkamp to Dietz, May 26, 1914. C-V.

[14] Kliefoth to Matre, December 17, 1914. C-V.

[15] "Central Verein and the American Federation of Catholic Societies." C-V.

[16] Kliefoth to Dietz, November 6, 1914. C-V.

[17] Dietz to Henry Grammling, M.D., February 1, 1915. C-V. (Copy); Federation Committees Address to Archbishop Messmer, January 22, 1916. C-V.

[18] Dietz to Frey, January 28, 1915. C-V. (Copy)

[19] Dietz to Frey, March 12, 1915. C-V. (Copy)

[20] Dietz to Kenkel, March 1, 1915. C-V. (Copy)

[21] Dietz to Kenkel, August 8, 1921. C-V. (Copy)

[22] Quoted in Kenkel to Dietz, August 24, 1921. C-V.

[23] Dietz to Muldoon, June 5, 1914. C-V. (Copy)

[24] Proceedings of the Social Service Commission, Baltimore, 1914.

[25] *Ibid.*

[26] "A Question of Increasing Productivity," *Newsletter,* April 11, 1916.

[27] The organizations represented were: Catholic Knights and Ladies of America; Catholic Ladies Benevolent Association; Catholic Ladies of Columbus; German Roman Catholic Knights of St. George; Catholic Order of Foresters; Massachusetts Catholic Order of Foresters; Western Catholic Union; Catholic Knights of America; Knights of St. John; Knights of Father Matthew; Irish Catholic Benevolent Union. Cf. *Bulletin,* IX (November, 1914), 3.

[28] Heckenkamp to Dietz, September 15, 1913. C-V.

[29] *Ibid*

[30] *Ibid.*

[31] Dietz to Heckenkamp, May 23, 1914. C-V. (Copy) The circular letter was dated May 27, 1914. C-V.

[32] *Minutes* of the conference. C-V.

[33] *Ibid.*, see Abell, "Labor Legislation in the United States: The Background and Growth of Newer Trends," *Review of Politics*, X (January, 1948), 35-41, on this movement.

[34] *Bulletin*, IX (November, 1914), 3.

[35] *Ibid.*

[36] *Minutes* of the conference.

[37] *Ibid.*

[38] Report of the Secretary of Social Service Commission, August 17, 1915-July 23, 1916. C-V.

[39] "A Proposed Catholic Federation for Women," *Bulletin*, VI (September, 1912), 9.

[40] *Ibid.*

[41] Lydia Pease to Dietz, August 4, 1913; August 18, 1913; August 25, 1913. Sophie Koehler to Dietz, July 19, 1913; July 28, 1913. C-V.

[42] *Bulletin*, VII (September, 1913), 20.

[43] Report of Secretary of the Social Service Commission, August 17, 1915-July 23, 1916. C-V.

[44] *Ibid.*

[45] Matre to Dietz, September 15, 1916. C-V.

[46] The *Newsletter* was dated September 11, 1916.

[47] Muldoon to Dietz, September 15, 1916. C-V.

[48] Dietz to Peter Gans, M.D., October 29, 1914, Louisville. C-V. (Copy)

[49] Matre to Kliefoth, December 21, 1914. C-V.

[50] Heckenkamp to Dietz, October 20, 1916. C-V.

[51] Messmer to Dietz, January 9, 1915. C-V.

[52] Dietz to Muldoon, January 5, 1916. C-V. (Copy)

[53] Dietz to Hagerty, September 5, 1916. C-V. (Copy)

[54] Heckenkamp to Dietz, August 29, 1916. C-V.

[55] Report of the Secretary, August 17, 1915-July 23, 1916; Dietz to Hayes, February 13, 1915. C-V. (Copy)

[56] Dietz to Heckenkamp, July 16, 1915. C-V. (Copy)

[57] Dietz to Heckenkamp, April 8, 1916. C-V. (Copy)

[58] See Chapter VII for a detailed account of the school.

[59] Daly to Matre, July 25, 1916. C-V.

[60] Dietz to Muldoon, August 3, 1916. C-V. (Copy)

[61] *Ibid.*

[62] Dietz to Charles Daly, August 9, 1916. C-V. (Copy)

[63] Dietz to Schrembs, September 6, 1916. C-V. (Copy)

[64] Schrembs to Dietz, September 11, 1916. C-V.

[65] No report of this committee is available.

[66] "The Catholic Federation of the United States," *Bulletin*, XII (November, 1917), 2. Bishop McFaul died June 16, 1917.

[67] "Democratic Control of United States Foreign Policy," *Bulletin*, X (February, 1915), 3.

[68] Dietz to Schrembs, May 28, 1915. C-V. (Copy)

[69] *Ibid.*

[70] Schrembs to Dietz, n.d. C-V.

71 Dietz to Gompers, February 9, 1917. C-V. (Copy)

72 *Ibid.*

73 April 10, 1917.

74 Quoted in Muldoon to Dietz, March 20, 1918. C-V.

75 *Ibid.*

76 August 20, 1916-August 26, 1917.

77 Heckenkamp to Dietz, September 3, 1918. C-V.

78 Muldoon to Dietz, December 28, 1917. C-V.

79 Cannon to Messmer, September 6, 1918. C-V. (Copy) The last issue of the *Bulletin* was dated November-December, 1919.

80 Cannon to Dietz, September 6, 1918. C-V.

81 Dietz to Muldoon, December 6, 1918. C-V. (Copy)

82 *Ibid.*, March 31, 1919. C-V. (Copy)

83 Dietz to Burns, May 25, 1919. C-V. (Copy)

84 Michael Williams, "Work of the National Catholic War Council," *N.C.-W.C. Bulletin,* I (June 1, 1919), 2.

85 *Ibid.*

86 *Ibid.;* The other two members were Archbishop Patrick J. Hayes and Bishop William T. Russell.

87 Dietz to Heckenkamp, February 17, 1919. C-V. (Copy)

88 Dietz to Muldoon, February 17, 1919. C-V. (Copy)

89 Dietz to Messmer, October 27, 1922. C-V. (Copy)

90 C-V. n.d.

91 Dietz to Muldoon, May 19, 1919, C-V. (Copy); Muldoon to Dietz, May 22, 1919. C-V.

92 *Infra.*, p. 202.

93 "Important Meeting at Notre Dame," *N.C.W.C. Bulletin,* I (August, 1919), 22.

94 *Ibid.; Bulletin* XIV (August-September, 1919), 1; Circular letter signed by the Committee, July 5, 1919. C-V. Other members on the Committee were Bishops Schrembs, Russell and Joseph Glass, C.M.

95 July 10, 1919. C-V.

96 *Infra.*, p. 180.

97 Dietz to Muldoon, September 8, 1919. C-V. (Copy)

98 *Ibid.*

99 *Ibid.*

100 *Ibid.*

101 *Ibid.*

102 "The Bishop's Pastoral Letter," *N.C.W.C. Bulletin,* I (November, 1919), 25; "The National Catholic Welfare Council," *Ibid.*, (January, 1920), 7; Augustin Dowling, "The National Catholic Welfare Conference," *Ecclesiastical Review,* LXXIX (October, 1928), 337-354.

103 "The National Catholic Welfare Council," *op. cit.* The other member of this committee was the Right Reverend Regis Canevin.

104 *Ibid.*, cf., *Supra.*, pp. 41; 128.

105 *Ibid.*, 8.

106 October 14, 1919. C-V.

[107] Dietz to Muldoon, October 25, 1919. C-V. (Copy)

[108] *Ibid.*

[109] *Ibid.*

[110] Circular letter signed by Bishop Muldoon, December 15, 1919. C-V.

[111] *Ibid.*

[112] The list of those present is among the Dietz papers at Central Verein: Fathers Siedenberg, S.J., J. O'Grady, John A. Ryan, Charles Moulinier, S.J., William Bolger, C.S.C., J. McGinn, S.J., Edward Garesche, S.J., William Kerby, John Burke, C.S.P., J. Husslein, S.J., C. Bruehl, E. O'Hara, Monsignor Splaine, Hagerty, Matre, Kenkel, David McCabe of Princeton, Carlton Hayes, Prof. Parkinson of Columbia, Neill, Gillespie.

[113] Selected were: Monsignor Splaine, Fathers Kerby, Bolger, O'Hara and Siedenberg, Neill, Hagerty, Kenkel, and Gillespie. Cf., *N.C.W.C. Bulletin,* I (March-April, 1920), 27.

[114] *Ibid.*

[115] *Ibid.*

[116] McGowan to Dietz, May 12, 1920. C-V.

[117] *Ibid.,* May 22, 1920. C-V.

[118] Tobin, Woll, Fischer to Hanna, September 28, 1920. C-V. (Copy)

[119] Dietz to Woll, October 15, 1920. C-V. (Copy)

[120] Woll to Dietz, November 3, 1920. C-V.

NOTES TO CHAPTER SEVEN

[1] *Supra.*, pp. 31-32.

[2] Dietz to Mitchell, December 30, 1911. Mitchell Papers, Mullen Library of the Catholic University of America, Washington, D.C.

[3] *Ibid.* Quoted in Boyle, *op. cit.*, p. 56.

[4] *Supra.*, p. 134. Callahan to Dietz, August 12, 1912. C-V. Father Callahan's Missionary District, which he covered on his horse "Rebel" included 34 Counties, 16,000 square miles.

[5] Callahan to Dietz, n.d. C-V.

[6] Byrne to Dietz, October 18, 1913. C-V.

[7] Byrne to Dietz, n.d. C-V.

[8] Callahan to Dietz, December 1, 1911. C-V.; January 16, 1912. C-V.; Dietz to Brewer, agent of the railroad, January 21, 1913; February 6, 1913. C-V. (Copies)

[9] Dietz to Callahan, January 9, 1913. C-V. (Copy)

[10] *Ibid.* Thomas F. Ryan, a convert, had donated the money for the Cathedral of Richmond, Va., building and furnishings. Cf., *Catholic Who's Who.*

[11] *Ibid.*

[12] Dietz to Flaherty, February 5, 1913. C-V. (Copy); Dietz to Blenk, February 7, 1913. C-V. (Copy); Dietz to O'Connell, March 15, 1913. (Copy). Apparently none of these responded to Dietz's request.

[13] Dietz to Ryan, April 30, 1913. C-V. (Copy)

[14] *Ibid.*

[15] Ryan to Dietz, May 3, 1913. C-V.

[16] Bruehl to Dietz, July 17, 1913. C-V.

[17] Hagerty to Dietz, December 27, 1913. C-V.

[18] Muldoon to Dietz, n.d. C-V.

[19] *Ibid.*

[20] Muldoon to Dietz, November 10, 1913. C-V.

[21] Callahan to Dietz, n.d. C-V.; Kliefoth to Dietz, November 19, 1914. C-V.

[22] Dietz to Safford, May 19, 1914. C-V. (Copy)

[23] Dietz to Safford, February 24, 1915. C-V.; Dietz to Heckenkamp, July 16, 1915. C-V. (Copies)

[24] Dietz to Safford, February 24, 1915. C-V. (Copy)

[25] Dietz to Messmer, February 26, 1915. C-V. (Copy)

[26] Dietz to Muldoon, March 31, 1915. C-V. (Copy)

[27] Muldoon to Dietz, March 31, 1915. C-V.

[28] Dietz to Safford, March 19, 1915. C-V. (Copy)

[29] *Ibid.*

[30] Haid to Dietz, December 15, 1914. C-V.

[31] Dietz to Muldoon, May 21, 1915. C-V. (Copy)

[32] Dietz to Safford, May 22, 1915. C-V. (Copy)

[33] Dietz to Bruehl, May 21, 1915. C-V. (Copy)

[34] Dietz to Muldoon, August 2, 1915. C-V. (Copy)

[35] *Report,* October, 1914-August, 1915. This is the only reference to Mrs. Safford as "Katherine." Father Dietz addressed her as Mrs. Bessie Safford.

[36] *Ibid.*

[37] Dietz to Muldoon, September 7, 1915. C-V. (Copy)

[38] *Ibid.*

[39] Muldoon to Dietz, January 3, 1916. C-V.

[40] Dietz to Muldoon, January 5, 1916. C-V. (Copy)

[41] Muldoon to Dietz, January 18, 1916. C-V.

[42] *Ibid.*

[43] Dietz to Haid, August 26, 1915; Dietz to Sister Mary Benedicta, R.S.M., August 26, 1915. C-V. (Copies)

[44] Father J. K. Budds to Dietz, September 7, 1914. C-V.

[45] Theresa Dietz to author, February 19, 1948.

[46] Dietz to Heckenkamp, October 25, 1915. C-V. (Copy)

[47] *Announcements of the American Academy of Christian Democracy for Women* (1916-1917), p. 8.

[48] This cross was carried up the mountain in parts by Father Dietz and the girls.

[49] Dietz to Haid, October 23, 1915. C-V. (Copy)

[50] Dietz to Muldoon, November 3, 1915. C-V. (Copy)

[51] Dietz to Haid, October 23, 1915. C-V. (Copy)

[52] *Ibid.* Mrs. Safford later donated land for a tuberculosis sanitarium. Cf., Haid to Dietz, April 21, 1916. C-V.

[53] *Ibid.;* Haid to Dietz, October 27, 1915. C-V.

[54] Dietz to Domenico Puliafito, May 30, 1915. C-V. (Copy) This Southern Normal College was run by a corporation that had taken over the Hotel in Hot Springs. It closed after a few months. Dietz to Alexander, July 13, 1916. C-V. (Copy)

[55] Dietz to Hastings, July 9, 1915. C-V. (Copy); Hastings to Dietz, July 12, 1915. C-V.

[56] Dietz to Haid, October 1, 1915. C-V. (Copy)

[57] Kerby to Dietz, November 14, 1915. C-V.

[58] Kerby to Dietz, November 8, 1915. C-V.

[59] Bruehl to Dietz, May 30, 1916. C-V.

[60] *Ibid.*

[61] Dietz to Alexander, July 13, 1916. C-V. (Copy)

[62] *Ibid.*

[63] Dietz to Haid, December 29, 1915. C-V. (Copy)

[64] Quoted in *Announcements. . . ,* p. 18.

[65] *Ibid.,* p. 19.

[66] *Ibid.*

[67] Father Corrigan was made domestic prelate in 1929, appointed Rector in 1936, and consecrated bishop in 1940. *Catholic Who's Who.*

[68] Corrigan to Dietz, December 18, 1915. C-V.

[69] *Ibid.*

[70] Corrigan to Dietz, n.d.

71 Corrigan to Dietz, April 18, 1916. C-V.

72 Corrigan to Dietz, June 13, 1916. C-V.

73 *Ibid.*

74 Brock to Dietz, January 15, 1916. C-V.

75 O'Connell to Dietz, February 16, 1917. C-V.

76 Corrigan to Dietz, December 18, 1915. C-V.

77 Kerby to Dietz, December 13, 1915. C-V.

78 *Ibid.*

79 *Ibid.*

80 *Announcements,* p. 9.

81 *Ibid.,* pp. 10-11.

82 *Ibid.,* p. 11.

83 *Ibid.,* p. 12.

84 Hanley to author, February 3, 1948.

85 Dietz to Kelleher, October 25, 1916. C-V. (Copy)

86 Kelleher to Dietz, September 22, 1916. C-V.

87 Dietz to Kelleher, October 25, 1916. C-V. (Copy)

88 *Announcements,* p. 8.

89 Dietz to Frances Bradley, December 13, 1916. C-V. (Copy)

90 Theresa Dietz to author, March 7, 1948. Miss Dietz wrote: "Bishop Walsh of Maryknoll saw my ring in 1916, liked it, and ordered the rings for the Maryknoll Sisters from the same company—a little incident which carries for us some significance."

91 Theresa Dietz to author, February 9, 1948. Significantly the "Gift" drawn by Father Dietz was "Fortitude."

92 Two issues of this magazine are available, January, 1917 and July, 1917. C-V.

93 Three "volumes" of these minutes and resolutions are among the papers at C-V.

94 *Supra.,* p. 226.

95 Newspaper clippings from the Brooklyn *Tablet,* n.d.; *True Voice,* a Nebraska paper, n.d.; Denver *Catholic Register,* January 11, 1917.

96 *Tablet,* n.d.

97 "Minutes of the Public Morality Committee, W.C.N.," December 12, 1916. C-V.

98 Veronica Hanley to author, February 3, 1948.

99 Corrigan to Dietz, February 11, 1916. C-V.

100 Hanley to author, February 3, 1948.

101 *Ibid.*

102 The ledger is among the Dietz Family Papers.

103 Corrigan to Dietz, September 26, 1916. C-V.

104 *Ibid.* All did not agree with Father Corrigan on this "unusual activity." The Reverend Paul L. Blakely, S.J., deplored the neglect of "one highly necessary modern faculty." Cf., "A Neglected Faculty," *America,* XIII (September 4, 1915), 526. This was the tenor also of a paper read by the Reverend J. W. Maguire, C.S.V., before the Catholic Education Association in 1916. Cf. "Why Sociology should be taught in our Catholic Colleges," *The Catholic Educational Association Bulletin,* XIII (November, 1916), 108-113. Yet schools of Sociology had been established at the Catholic University, Loyola University, Fordham, the

University of Notre Dame, Duquesne, St. John's College, Toledo, Canisius College, and St. Viator's.

[105] Susan Frawley Eisele to author, November 2, 1949. Mrs. Eisele, wife of Albert Eisele, poet and short story writer, won the award for the best country columnist in the United States in 1936. She and her husband (now deceased) wrote a syndicated column, "Countryside," which appeared in twenty-six Minnesota, Iowa, and South Dakota papers.

[106] Ellen Blake to Dietz, December 31, 1917. C-V.

[107] Theresa Dietz to author, March 7, 1948.

[108] Winters to Dietz, November 19, 1916. C-V.; W. E. Walsh of St. Vincent de Paul Society, to Dietz, February 6, 1917. C-V.; Dietz to Walsh, February 20, 1917. C-V. (Copy)

[109] Linthicum to Dietz, October 6, 1917. C-V.

[110] Hanley to Dietz, September 22, 1916. C-V.

[111] Hanley to Dietz, March 26, 1920. C-V.

[112] Theresa Dietz to author, May 7, 1948. At that time Veronica Hanley was active in the National Council of Catholic Women of the Columbus diocese.

[113] Sister Mary Regina to Dietz, January 20, 1917. C-V.

[114] Sister Mary Celestine to Dietz, March 1, 1919. C-V.

[115] Morrison to Dietz, October 1, 1920. C-V.

[116] Hourigan to Dietz, November 28, 1922.

[117] Kuhlman to Dietz, August 4, 1918. C-V.

[118] Interview with Miss Kuhlman at the Central Bureau, St. Louis, in the spring of 1949.

[119] Dietz to Gavisk, May 17, 1916. C-V. (Copy)

[120] Alexander to Dietz, February 12, 1916. C-V.

[121] *Ibid.,* February 14, 1916.

[122] Dietz to Haid, July 5, 1916. C-V. (Copy)

[123] *Minutes* of the Social Service Commission, New York, August 19-23, 1916.

[124] *Ibid.*

[125] Dietz to Haid, September 7, 1916. C-V. (Copy)

[126] Haid to Dietz, November 6, 1916. C-V.

[127] Dietz to Haid, March 19, 1917. C-V. (Copy)

[128] Dietz to Gavisk, June 3, 1916. C-V. (Copy)

[129] Gavisk to Dietz, June 16, 1916. C-V. (Copy)

[130] Dietz to Chartrand, June 28, 1914. C-V. (Copy)

[131] Chartrand to Dietz, June 28, 1916. C-V.

[132] Dietz to Chartrand, June 30, 1916. C-V. (Copy); July 25, 1916; Dietz to Muldoon, July 25, 1916. C-V. (Copy); Chartrand to Dietz, July 27, 1916. C-V.

[133] Coakley to Dietz, June 24, 1916. C-V.

[134] Dietz to Dewe, July 5, 1916. C-V. (Copy)

[135] Dewe to Dietz, July 9, 1916. C-V.

[136] Dietz to Moeller, January 12, 1917. C-V. (Copy)

[137] Moeller to Dietz, January 15, 1917. C-V.

[138] Dietz to Moeller, January 22, 1917. C-V. (Copy)

[139] February 10, 1917.

[140] Patrick Browne to Dietz, February 17, 1917. C-V.; H. F. Hillenmeyer to Dietz, February 13, 1917. C-V.

[141] *Supra.*, p. 158

[142] Hoban to Dietz, February 13, 1917. C-V.

[143] March 12, 1917.

[144] Blandina to Dietz, March 13, 1917. C-V.

[145] Dietz to Moeller, March 19, 1917. C-V. (Copy)

[146] Safford to Dietz, n.d. C-V.

[147] Dietz to Safford, March 31, 1917. C-V. (Copy)

[148] Dietz to Haid, March 19, 1917. C-V. (Copy)

[149] Haid to Dietz, March 24, 1917. C-V.

NOTES TO CHAPTER EIGHT

[1] Dietz to Kuhlman, May 7, 1917. Kuhlman correspondence (1917-45) loaned to the author.

[2] *Ibid.*

[3] *Catholic Telegraph* quoted in *The White Cross Nurse* (July, 1917).

[4] *The White Cross Nurse* (July, 1917).

[5] *Announcement* of Seventh Course.

[6] *Ibid.*, Cf., also, Dietz to Muldoon, June 8, 1917. C-V. (Copy)

[7] *Announcement,* etc.

[8] "Who makes Bolshevism in Cincinnati?" *The New Republic,* XVIII (April 19, 1919), 365.

[9] *Ibid.* This couple represented a National Council organized in 1916 by Mr. and Mrs. Phillips, with Gifford Pinchot as its first president. The Council of thirty or more voted $135,000 to carry out this experiment. *Ibid.*

[10] The nine groups represented were: physicians, clergymen, teachers, social workers, nurses, recreation workers, business men, trade unionists and members of the local bureau of information. *Ibid.*, 366.

[11] Gressle to Dietz, June 20, 1917. C-V.

[12] *Ibid.*

[13] Phillips to Dietz, September 26, 1917. C-V.

[14] Clipping from the Cincinnati *Catholic Telegraph,* n.d.

[15] *The New Republic, loc. cit.*, 367. About a year later Mayor Galvin condemned the social unit as the "most dangerous type of Socialism." *Ibid.*

[16] Dietz to Moeller, June 24, 1917. C-V. (Copy)

[17] Phillips to Dietz, January 3, 1918. C-V.

[18] Anna Hourigan was assistant director and Catherine Quinlan acted as secretary.

[19] Report of the secretary, August 20, 1916-August 26, 1917. C-V.

[20] *Ibid.*

[21] July 14, 1917. C-V.

[22] Circular letter, August 5, 1917. C-V.

[23] *Ibid.*

[24] Report of the Committee on Education and Entertainment. C-V.

[25] Report of the Committee on Charities and Social Service. C-V.

[26] *The Cincinnati Enquirer,* September 2, 1923, gave the name as "Seck," but the deed in the Dietz Family Papers reads "Feck."

[27] Anna Hourigan and Leopoldina Krautgartner were there at the time. Cf. Theresa Dietz to author, February 13, 1948.

[28] Dietz to Very Reverend James A. Walsh, M.M., September 1, 1922. C-V. (Copy)

[29] Dietz to Moeller, October 14, 1918. C-V. (Copy); Very Reverend Frederick C. Dietz, M.M. to author. August 28, 1950.

[30] *Supra.*, pp. 231-2.

[31] Muldoon to Noll, April 27, 1918. C-V. (Copy)

[32] Noll to Dietz, May 2, 1918. C-V.

[33] Dietz to Moeller, January 7, 1919. C-V. (Copy)

[34] Others of the contributors were: T. J. Duffy, chairman of the Industrial Commission of Ohio. January 6, 1919; John Golden, president of United Textile Workers, January 3, 1919; Peter Collins, January 11, 1919; James Maloney, January 2, 1919; John Voll, December 26, 1918. All C-V.

[35] Dietz to Moeller, January 7, 1919. C-V. (Copy)

[36] Moeller to Dietz, January 11, 1919. C-V.

[37] Ibid.

[38] Albens to Dietz, February 9, 1919. C-V.

[39] Dietz to Muldoon, March 31, 1919. C-V. (Copy)

[40] Ibid.

[41] John P. Frey to author, October 13, 1948.

[42] May 26, 1919, signed by Adolph Kummer, president. C-V.

[43] From May 31, 1919 to July 7, Father Dietz spoke to twelve local unions about the Academy. The letters are among his papers. C-V.

[44] Dietz to Muldoon, July 3, 1919. C-V. (Copy)

[45] This apparently refers to the Militia of Christ.

[46] Dietz to Muldoon, July 3, 1919. C-V. (Copy)

[47] C-V.

[48] Dietz to Muldoon, July 3, 1919. C-V. (Copy)

[49] Ibid.

[50] Dietz to Muldoon, April 15, 1920. C-V. (Copy) The "Clifton School," opened November, 1918, had two hundred and fifty graduates by 1920. Cf., National Catholic Welfare Bulletin, I (February, 1920), 27.

[51] McCarthy to Dietz, December 3, 1919, C-V.; December 19, 1919. C-V.

[52] Woll to Dietz, January 10, 1919; September 19, 1919. C-V.

[53] Announcement of the Tenth Social Institute. C-V.

[54] Dietz to Moeller, January 29, 1920. C-V. (Copy)

[55] Dietz to Moeller, July 9, 1920. C-V. (Copy)

[56] Ibid.

[57] Moeller to Dietz, April 3, 1920. C-V.

[58] Ibid.

[59] Porter to Dietz, December 4, 1920. C-V.; Keller to Dietz, February 10, 1921. C-V.

[60] Dietz to Muldoon, May 19, 1919. C-V. (Copy)

[61] "Priest settles strike," Catholic Telegraph, May 1, 1919.

[62] April 16, 1919. The material on this whole matter is contained in typewritten sheets among the Dietz papers. C-V.

[63] Ibid.   [64] Ibid.

[65] Frey to author, October 13, 1948.

[66] LeBlond Company to H. Chapman, one of the strikers, May 20, 1920. C-V.

[67] Dietz to LeBlond, May 20, 1920. C-V. (Copy)

[68] LeBlond to Dietz, June 8, 1920. C-V.

[69] Ibid.

[70] Dietz to LeBlond, December 30, 1920. C-V. (Copy)

[71] Dietz to LeBlond, December 21, 1921. C-V. (Copy)

[72] Ibid.   [73] Ibid.

74 Dietz to LeBlond, December 30, 1921. C-V. (Copy)

75 *Ibid.*   76 *Ibid.*

77 *Ibid.*   78 *Ibid.*   79 *Ibid.*

80 Dietz to LeBlond, July 7, 1920; August 16, 1920. (C-V. (Copies)

81 LeBlond to Dietz, December 29, 1921. C-V.

82 "The Industrial Council of Cincinnati." This is a hand written sheet dated December 25, 1919. C-V.

83 Steinkamp to L. H. Van Matre, November 23, 1920. C-V.

84 *Constitution* of the Industrial Division of the Cincinnati Chamber of Commerce, p. 9. Dietz Family Papers.

85 In a pencil written speech Father Dietz quotes the various members who spoke at this meeting, attaching names to each quotation. According to the records this speech was never given. Dietz Family Papers.

86 *Ibid.*

87 *Constitution,* pp. 3-4.

88 *Ibid.,* p. 9.

89 The letter was dated November 29, 1920. C-V.

90 Voll to Dietz, December 30, 1920. C-V.

91 *Catholic Telegraph-Register,* October 31, 1947; Dietz to Abell, May 8, 1945; Frey to author, October 13, 1948.

92 Moeller to Dietz, December 4, 1920. C-V. For other incidents preceding this letter, cf., *Infra.,* pp. 192-193.

93 December 14, 1920. C-V. (Copy)

94 Drackett to Dietz, December 23, 1920. C-V.

95 "Builders Guild of Cincinnati," a typed sheet dated December 8, 1921. C-V. This article was published in *The American Federationist,* XXIX (March, 1922), pp. 188-190, under the same title.

96 Dietz to Moeller, November 30, 1920. C-V. (Copy); Dietz to Abell, May 8, 1945.

97 Circular letter, n.d., of Ohio State Federation of Labor to local unions and delegates attending the 38th Annual Convention of the Ohio State Federation of Labor.

98 *Ibid.*

99 *Ibid.*

100 Field to Dietz, December 13, 1921. C-V.

101 "Builders Guild. . . ," *loc cit.*

102 Frey to Gompers, April 14, 1922. C-V. (Copy); Reverend Charles Knapp, Wellington, Texas, to author, March 3, 1948.

103 Dietz to Moeller, November 30, 1920. C-V. (Copy)

104 Paul Knapp of Upholsterer's Union, to author, February 23, 1948.

105 Circular letter of Ohio State Federation of Labor, n.d. C-V.

106 *Ibid.*

107 New York *Sun,* March 10, 1922. There were then sixty-one Labor Colleges in nineteen states according to a questionnaire of the Workers' Education Bureau. C-V.

108 Frey to Gompers, April 14, 1922. C-V. (Copy) Professor A. C. Forsberg of Carroll College wrote Gompers for information on the Labor College. Gompers asked Frey for details.

109 *Ibid.*

110 *Ibid.*

111 This letter has no date. Doran was checking the article in the New York *Sun*.

112 Rudolph Hynicka, chairman of the Hamilton County Central Committee of the Republican Party to George B. Christian, secretary to Senator Harding, March 18, 1921. C-V. Of incidental interest is Dietz's sending the *Life of St. Stephen Harding* to the Senator. Christian to Dietz, January 6, 1921. C-V.

113 Dietz to Moeller, November 8, 1920. C-V. (Copy)

114 Hynicka to Christian, March 18, 1921. C-V.

115 "My Country 'Tis of Thee," a typed paper in the Dietz Papers dated October 22, 1920. See Appendix, pp. 276-277, for full text. Father Dietz submitted the article to Michael F. Girten, president of the Central Verein, for his opinion. Girten could see nothing in it "that should cause any difficulty for anybody. . . . There are thousands and thousands of regular real Americans who understand you because they feel just as you do." Girten to Dietz, November 1, 1920. C-V.

116 *Ibid.*

117 Moeller to Dietz, December 4, 1920. C-V.; Dietz to Moeller, December 8, 1920. C-V. (Copy)

118 *Supra.*, pp. 187-188.

119 December 8, 1920. C-V. (Copy)

120 Moeller to Dietz, December 15, 1920. C-V.

121 Dietz to Moeller, January 10, 1921. C-V. (Copy)

122 Dietz to Messmer, November 15, 1921. C-V. (Copy)

123 There is no evidence among the Dietz papers that this building was planned.

124 Dietz to Messmer, November 15, 1921. C-V. (Copy)

125 Dietz to Moeller, April 7, 1922. C-V. (Copy)

126 Kerby to Dietz, April 28, 1922. C-V. Dr. Kerby conferred with Monsignor Bernardini, who was associated with the office of the Apostolic Delegate.

127 *Ibid.*

128 Dietz to Moeller, April 30, 1922. C-V. (Copy)

129 Moeller to Dietz, May 6, 1922. C-V.

130 Messmer to Brossart, May 26, 1922. C-V. (Copy) John Frey claims that he requested Archbishop Messmer to do something about Father Dietz's permission to say Mass, when Dietz came to Frey "with tears in his eyes." Cf., Frey to author, October 13, 1948.

131 Brossart's secretary to Messmer, June 5, 1922. C-V.

132 Moeller to Dietz, November 22, 1922. C-V.

133 Dietz to Moeller, July 10, 1922. C-V. (Copy); Frey to author, October 13, 1948.

134 This was the last convention Father Dietz attended. He was proud to have the honor of opening the convention with a prayer. It was the first time a Catholic priest had done so. Cf., Appendix, p. 278.

135 June 16, 1922. C-V. (Copy)

136 Moeller to Tobin, June 18, 1922, from Homburghoe, Germany. C-V. (Copy)

137 Committee to Hickey, June 17, 1922. C-V. (Copy)

138 *Supra.*, p. 180.

139 Duffy, Woll, Tobin to Messmer, June 24, 1922. C-V. (Copy)

140 Moeller to Tobin, August 5, 1922. C-V. (Copy)

[141] Tobin and Woll to Messmer, April 20, 1923. C-V. (Copy)

[142] Dietz to Schrembs, November 17, 1921. C-V. (Copy); Schrembs to Dietz, October 25, 1922. C-V.

[143] Schrembs to Dietz, October 25, 1922. C-V.

[144] An extensive correspondence was carried on over a position for Father Dietz, between Rudolph Hynicka and George Christian. Even the consular service in Bavaria, Spain or Italy was considered. President Harding did consult with the State Department about it, but nothing came of it. Cf., Hynicka to Christian, March 18, 1921; Christian to Hynicka, November 26, 1921; Hynicka to Christian, n.d.; Hynicka to Dietz, May 8, 1922. All C-V.

[145] Messmer to Lenroot, April 19, 1921. C-V. (Copy)

[146] *Supra.*, p. 182; Dietz to Boyle, August 4, 1922. C-V. (Copy)

[147] Boyle to Dietz, September 8, 1922. C-V.

[148] Boyle to Dietz, October 18, 1922. C-V.

[149] Dietz to Boyle, February 6, 1923. C-V. (Copy)

[150] Dietz to Messmer, October 2, 1922. C-V. (Copy)

[151] Dietz to Messmer, October 2, 1922. C-V. (Copy)

[152] Messmer to Dietz, October 18, 1922. C-V.

[153] *Ibid.*

[154] *Ibid.*

[155] *Ibid.*

[156] *Ibid.*

[157] Woll to Tobin, January 5, 1923. C-V. (Copy)

[158] Dietz to Ryan, February 5, 1923. C-V. (Copy). A copy of this letter was sent to Archbishop Messmer asking him to write to Ryan also. Dietz to Messmer, February 5, 1923. C-V. (Copy)

[159] Dietz to Ryan, February 5, 1923. C-V. (Copy)

[160] *Ibid.*

[161] Dietz to Moeller, April 9, 1923. C-V. (Copy)

[162] "Pointed Opinion," *Catholic Bulletin,* XI, 1922.

[163] *Ibid.*

[164] Wey to Moeller, January 16, 1923. C-V. (Copy)

[165] Wey to Messmer, January 16, 1923. Copy in Wey's handwriting. C-V.

[166] Messmer to Dietz, April 20, 1923. C-V.

[167] Walsh to Dietz, August 28, 1922. C-V.; Dietz to Moeller, November 30, 1922. C-V. (Copy); Moeller to Dietz, December 5, 1922. C-V.

[168] Dietz to Noll, April 18, 1923. C-V. (Copy); Noll to author, December 6, 1948.

[169] Dietz to Moeller, April 9, 1923. C-V. (Copy)

[170] Moeller to Dietz, November 22, 1922. C-V.

[171] Tobin and Woll to Messmer, April 20, 1923. C-V. (Copy)

[172] *Supra.*, p. 180.

NOTES TO CHAPTER NINE

[1] Messmer to Dietz, April 23, 1923. C-V.

[2] *Herald-Citizen,* February 12, 1949, Milwaukee.

[3] *Ibid.*

[4] Brochure commemorating the fortieth jubilee of Father Dietz's ordination. Dietz Family Papers.

[5] *The Milwaukee Journal,* April 5, 1925. Dietz Family Papers.

[6] Dietz to Stritch, December 4, 1931. Dietz Family Papers. (Copy)

[7] Neary to Dietz, March 7, 1924. C-V.

[8] Conboy to Dietz, February 20, 1924. C-V. Father Dietz bought an Essex.

[9] *Herald-Citizen, loc. cit.*

[10] Since 1935 the school has been in charge of the School Sisters of St. Francis.

[11] Brochure commemorating. . . .

[12] *Ibid.*

[13] Dietz to Kuhlman, n.d. Kuhlman Correspondence.

[14] Dietz to Kuhlman, November 22, 1929. Kuhlman Correspondence.

[15] Dietz to Monsignor Bernard G. Traudt, diocesan administrator, December 10, 1929. Dietz Family Papers. (Copy)

[16] *Ibid.*

[17] *Ibid.*

[18] Circular letter to parishioners on the occasion of the 40th anniversary, sent by officers of parish organizations, December 10, 1944. Dietz Family Papers.

[19] Dietz to Mother Domitilla, I.H.M., August 17, 1929. Dietz Family Papers. (Copy)

[20] *Ibid.*

[21] Dietz to Stritch, December 4, 1931. Dietz Family Papers. (Copy). Archbishop Messmer died August 4, 1930 and was succeeded by the Most Reverend Samuel Stritch.

[22] Report of a Committee of three to a meeting of trustees, officers, and directors of the parish and the credit committee of the Credit Union, October 12, 1931. C-V.

[23] Dietz to Stritch, September 21, 1931. Dietz Family Papers. (Copy)

[24] Report of Committee of three. . .

[25] Dietz to Stritch, December 4, 1931. Dietz Family Papers. (Copy)

[26] Dietz to Stritch, December 4, 1931. Dietz Family Papers. (Copy)

[27] Dietz to Stritch, December 21, 1930. Dietz Family Papers. (Copy)

[28] McGuire to Dietz, October 25, 1934. C-V.

[29] Ohl to Dietz, March 20, 1935. C-V.

[30] O'Neill to author, December 9, 1949.

[31] *Ibid.*

[32] Dietz to Kuhlman, September 26, 1929. Kuhlman Correspondence.

[33] March 20, 1926. C-V.

[34] Sister Mary Irmtrudis Fiederling, O.S.F., *Adolph Kolping and the Kolping Society* (Washington, 1941), p. 22.

[35] Henry Somerville, *The Catholic Social Movement* (London, 1933), pp. 56-60; Fiederling, *op. cit.,* pp. 8-22.

[36] Somerville, *op. cit.,* p. 62.

[37] *Catholic Herald,* May 20, 1926. Milwaukee.

[38] Dietz to Kuhlman, May 20, 1926. Kuhlman Correspondence.

[39] Heuser to Dietz, July 3, 1927. Dietz Family Papers.

[40] *Catholic Herald, loc. cit.*

[41] *Ibid.*

[42] Arthur J. Straus Company to Dietz, October 31, 1927. Dietz Family Papers.

[43] Interview with Humphrey Desmond, Milwaukee, December, 1948. Since the Society was never affiliated with the national headquarters at Chicago, no records are available there. Cf., Hans Dexl, national secretary, to author, December 14, 1949.

[44] Dietz to Joseph Uihlein, April 18, 1934. C-V. (Copy)

[45] Messmer to Dietz, January 6, 1927. C-V.

[46] William M. Lamers, director, Marquette University School of Speech, November 14, 1923. Dietz Family Papers.

[47] Schuler to Dietz, July 1, 1927. Dietz Family Papers.

[48] Quinn to Dietz, February 19, 1929. Dietz Family Papers.

[49] *Ibid.*

[50] Walsh to Dietz, April 3, 1929. Dietz Family Papers.

[51] Frey to Dietz, January 29, 1924. Dietz Family Papers.

[52] Frey to Dietz, June 9, 1930. Dietz Family Papers.

[53] Husslein, *Social Wellsprings, op. cit.,* p. 189.

[54] These Articles of Federation were adopted at the first national convention in 1940. Regarding the relationship between A.C.T.U. and the Militia of Christ, John Cort, associate editor of *The Labor Leader,* A.C.T.U.'s organ, writes: "I can say that there was no connection between Father Dietz's group and the A.C.T.U. In fact, I did not even know about the group until last year. Then we were very much surprised to learn that there had been an organization so much like our own in its purposes so long ago." Cort to author, October 1, 1948.

[55] *Ibid.* See also the *Constitution* of the Militia of Christ, p. 5.

[56] John C. Cort, "Catholics, Communists, and Unions," *The Sign,* November, 1948, p. 15.

[57] Deverall to Dietz, September 9, 1938. C-V. Richard Deverall later served as director of Labor Education in Japan under General MacArthur.

[58] Deverall to Dietz, n.d. C-V.

[59] Erbacher to Dietz, August 16, 1939. C-V.

[60] *Ibid.*

[61] Dietz to Erbacher, September 29, 1939. Loaned by Father Erbacher to author.

[62] *Supra.*, pp. 182, 201.

[63] A typed sheet. C-V.

[64] *Ibid.*

[65] *Ibid.*

[66] *Ibid.*

[67] Clippings from an unidentified newspaper. C-V.

[68] *Ibid.*

[69] Dietz to Kuhlman, November 4, 1926. Kuhlman Correspondence.

[70] Husslein, *op. cit.*, p. 191.

[71] *Ibid.*

[72] Wolfe to Dietz, September 10, 1934. C-V.

[73] Wolfe to Dietz, January 10, 1935. C-V.

[74] Wolfe to Dietz, September 15, 1936. Dietz Family Papers.

[75] *Telegraph Herald,* October 12, 1936.

[76] *Ibid.*

[77] Dietz to Cicognani, October 3, 1936. Dietz Family Papers.

[78] *Ibid.*

[79] *Ibid.*

[80] *Ibid.* A few days later Father Dietz received a notification from the secretary that his letter had been received and contents "duly noted." **Binz to Dietz, October 13, 1936. C-V.**

[81] May 17, 1937. C-V.

[82] Paul Tanner, secretary to Archbishop Stritch, to Dietz, June 20, 1937. C-V.

[83] Dietz to Archbishop McNicholas, O.P., July 31, 1937. C-V. (Copy)

[84] *Ibid.*

[85] Dietz to Kuhlman, July 30, 1937. Kuhlman Correspondence.

[86] Monsignor Frank Thill, chancellor, to Dietz, January 1, 1937. C-V.

[87] *Ibid.*

[88] *Ibid.*

[89] *Ibid.*

[90] *Ibid.*

[91] Dietz to McNicholas, January 2, 1937. C-V. (Copy)

[92] *Ibid.*

[93] *Ibid.*

[94] McNicholas to Dietz, January 8, 1937. C-V.

[95] *Ibid.*

[96] Dietz to McNicholas, January 11, 1937. C-V. (Copy)

[97] McNicholas to Dietz, January 14, 1937. C-V.

[98] Dietz to McNicholas, July 31, 1937. C-V. (Copy)

[99] *Ibid.*

[100] Freking to Dietz, September 3, 1937. C-V. Monsignor Freking's first contact with Father Dietz was while he was a student of Sociology at Xavier

University in 1920-21. He heard Dietz preach on *Rerum Novarum* in St. Paul's Church. After that he used to visit Father Dietz at Crusade Castle to hear his views on labor. Freking to author, November 23, 1949.

[101] Freking to Dietz, January 17, 1938. C-V.

[102] Dietz to Abell, May 8, 1945. Father Dietz was sixty years old.

[103] Frederick Dietz, M. M. to Abell.

[104] Theresa Dietz to author, April 12, 1949.

NOTES TO CHAPTER TEN

[1] *Social Service,* I (May, 1911), 61.

[2] Murray to author, December 28, 1949. See Appendix, pp. 279-281, for excerpts from letters of other leaders who knew and appreciated Father Dietz.

APPENDIX I

Father Dietz and Professor James Hagerty prepared the following questionnaire for members of the American Federation of Catholic Societies. Its two-fold purpose was to obtain data on the local activities and to suggest possible lines of social action for the members to follow.

AN EXAMINATION OF THE SOCIAL CONSCIENCE

This questionnaire is addressed to our Catholic societies in particular. If read at the regular meetings of County and State Federations, much good will result. Any data forwarded to this office will serve a valuable purpose for the Social Service Commission.

EDUCATION

Are your organizations interested in the social welfare of children and young people? Are the playgrounds of the community ample for their needs? What objections are there, if any, to their places of amusement? Have your organizations created or helped to complete the parish libraries? Do these libraries contain the proper books for children and young people? Are these libraries known and patronized? Is there any instruction in the domestic sciences—cooking, sewing, etc.? What opportunities are there for industrial education? For the learning of a trade? Do your local high-schools afford industrial and domestic education? What is their attitude toward children from the parochial schools? Have your organizations a plan to help the immigrants? Have you established settlements and social centers for them where they may learn the English language, American history, the structure and functions of government? Where they may have meeting rooms for their social betterment under Catholic auspices?

JUSTICE AND CHARITY

a) *The Industrial Relations.*

Is your organization doing anything to establish happier relations between the employer and the employed? Are peaceful methods pursued in industrial disputes? Do you use your influence in the direction of conciliation? Are the factories, workshops, department stores, etc., in your community, sanitary and properly inspected? Are the safeguards against injury adequate? Is there a legal or private compensation in case of accident? Are the wages sufficient for a decent livelihood? Do your organizations influence employers to introduce a measure of welfare work? Do you know and help enforce the child labor laws of your state? Are your organizations doing anything to increase the wages of girls in shops and factories? Do you know that they often work a whole week for the wages that a man gets in a single day? Have you reflected upon the possible effect on their morals? Is there a working girls' home in your community? Are there any labor or trade unions in your city? Do you attend the meetings of the local and central bodies? What is the attitude of the employers towards the unions? Are the labor leaders honest, able and prudent men? Do Socialists exercise great influence in your local central bodies? Whose fault is it? Are you obliged to subscribe to Socialist papers and to assist Socialist undertakings?

b) *Community Welfare.*

Have your organizations taken any interest in public health? The problem of clean streets and alleys, garbage removal, human housing, light, ventilation, sanitary plumbing? Have you got a city market? Is there any milk inspection and supervision over foods and markets? Is there a way to bring down the high cost of living? Have your societies assisted toward the improvement of health ordinances? Have you any agency whereby to counteract the loan shark? To give legal advice gratis to the poor? To protect them against exorbitant

APPENDIX I

prices, rent, and extortion of every kind? Are your organizations in co-operation with the juvenile court, where it exists? If so, in what way? If it does not exist, are you ready to urge the establishment of one? Are there within the limits of your organization or federation any public hospitals, orphan asylums, alms-houses, jails and penitentiaries, placing-out agencies and similar institutions? Is the proper separation of sexes provided for? Do the Catholic inmates receive the visits and attentions of Catholics? Are they supplied with religious instruction, religious articles and reading? What opportunities have they for attendance at Catholic worship? Do the members of your organizations assist the priests in these works? How many free beds for the poor have been provided in the Catholic hospitals? Is there a free dispensary? Is it possible to secure nurses for poverty cases at home? Is your city well governed? What interest are your societies taking in local good government? Do the public officials fulfill their obligations to the citizens? Do they invite public meetings and discussions on civic problems? Do you take any part, individually or collectively, in these efforts for civic government? Do the departments issue annual reports to the public? Have your organizations studied the methods of securing state legislation in the interest of the people? Have they taken part in movements that tend to protest against excessive labor, work in dangerous and evil surroundings, work unsuited to age or sex? In fact, against exploitation of every kind? Is your society, besides being a Catholic society, a civil force as well? Why should it not be the finest civic institution in your community?

PUBLIC MORALS

What is your organization doing to prevent the giving of immoral plays? The presentation of immoral pictures in the nickel-shows and penny-arcades? Is your organization doing anything to prevent the display of indecent posters on billboards and immoral advertising in newspapers? What is your society doing in co-operation with city officials toward the punishment of men who insult girls and women on the streets? Toward driving immoral women from the streets? Toward the supervision of dance halls? Toward the carrying out of the liquor laws and ordinances against lotteries and gambling devices? Have you moulded public opinion upon the subject of literature in the public libraries? Have you succeeded in securing a proper censorship? Have your organizations aroused the public conscience of the community on the divorce evil and similar issues?

THE PRESS

Have your organizations taken official note of the intellectual and moral tone of the secular press in your home community? Are you concerned at all about the daily reading of the members of your family? Do you attempt to overcome prejudice, to correct misrepresentation, to nail lies, to furnish correct information, to reach the responsible editors? Is the Catholic press of your community properly supported? Do you subscribe for it? Do your organizations welcome representatives of the Catholic press in your meetings? Do you refuse patronage to unfair and un-Christian newspapers and periodicals? Is the Socialist press active in your community? What are Socialists doing to circulate their literature? Would some of their methods deserve to be imitated?

ORGANIZATION

What Catholic societies, agencies, institutions exist in your community that are interested in social service? Would you be ready to furnish us their names and addresses? Apart from organizations, what Catholic individuals are particularly interested? Are any new organizations needed? If so, of what character? Have you a city or county federation? Does it hold regular meetings? What progress is it making? Have regular committees been appointed to these and similar works? Do you co-operate with non-Catholic endeavors along parallel lines? Have you any volunteer workers in the field? Will you introduce them to us? Are your organizations able to secure lecturers? What are the topics desired?

271

APPENDIX II

In January, 1915, Father Dietz addressed a Memorial to the Executive Council of the American Federation of Labor suggesting ways in which closer relations could be established between that organization and the American Federation of Catholic Societies. The following letter is Gompers' reply:

September 24, 1915.

REVEREND SIR:

The communication you addressed to the Executive Council of the American Federation of Labor under date of January 12, 1915, was duly received and considered by us. At the meeting of the Executive Council held January 11-16, it was there decided that copies of your letter should be furnished to each member of the Council so that we might have the opportunity of giving it better thought between that and the present meeting held at the office of the American Federation of Labor this week. We beg to assure you that nothing but the importance of your letter and the desire to give it the best consideration, interfered with an earlier response.

At our present meeting, which began Monday, we have given the subject of your letter the fullest consideration and our best thought, and feel that our response should be as full, free, and candid as the thought, suggestion and proposition which you have submitted to us. At the outset one may be permitted to say all you have done, all that your commission has done, in furtherance of the great underlying principles and high ideals for which the American Federation of Labor stands, are fully appreciated.

You say that there has been some criticism of the fraternal delegateship of your Commission at the Philadelphia American Federation of Labor Convention, and add that whether just or unjust, need not be considered but that it has raised the question, "how it might be possible to make the relation more vital, definite and progressive." It is difficult to understand how the relations between our two great bodies can become more vital, definite, and progressive by our entering into the agreement you propose.

We are sure it is not the disposition of the American Federation of Labor to decry, criticize or minimize that which your commission has done or aims to do, but we are strongly of the opinion that the greatest definite, vital relations between your Commission and the American Federation of Labor will result when each is free to express itself fully upon the fundamental principles upon which our respective organizations are based.

At this point it is interesting to note that at one of the early conventions of the American Federation of Labor, the following was unanimously adopted:

> Resolved, we deplore the introduction of any sectarian or captious side issues among the working people. Such movements divide labor's forces, produce bitter antagonisms as they produce religious bigotry, provoke rancorous intolerance, and divert the working people from working out their own emancipation.

> Resolved, That we here and now reaffirm as one of the cardinal principles of the labor movement that the working people must unite and organize, irrespective of creed, color, sex, nationality or politics.

That declaration has been reaffirmed and emphasized at nearly every convention by the American Federation of Labor, and adherence to it faithfully enforced. You can readily see therefore how important it is, in view of the above quoted declaration, for the American Federation of Labor to seriously

272

consider the subject of entering into an agreement such as you suggest and to carry into effect the propositions you make.

It is true as you say that no subsidiary national movement can afford to isolate itself in the nation, and that "neither the American Federation of Labor nor the American Federation of Catholic Societies can fulfill its mission unless properly related with the other forces that constitute American Society." But Sir, there may be a common polity; there may be sympathetic co-operation among the forces that constitute American society without the necessity of these forces entering into an agreement for the accomplishment of that purpose.

While it is true as you say that the American Federation of Labor aims to better the material, intellectual, and moral interests of the American working people, it is an error to state that special emphasis is placed upon the material, for as sure as cause is related to effect, the intellectual and moral development of the working people is essentially dependent upon their material well-being. The very fact as you point out that the aim of the American Federation of Catholic Societies is primarily concerned with religion, is in itself a bar to the American Federation of Labor to enter into such an agreement with a religious body as you propose.

There is much common ground for co-operation, but we submit that the co-operation can best be furthered by each pursuing its own course, free to dissent from any matter upon which in the judgment of each body freedom of expression and action may be necessary.

In urging the agreement you submit the following:

> There would be unanimity of opinion upon policies resulting from the principle that the state shall not do for associations and unions, what they ought to do for themselves without state aid: e.g., hours of labor, minimum wage, social insurance, etc., etc.
>
> 2) Industrial education without discrimination against the parochial school system would be to the point on the score of compromise.
>
> 3) There could be no compromise on policies that would adopt fundamental tenets of Marxism, prohibition by legislation, or any other proposition socially unsound.

In regard to some of these proposals which you mention there can be no adverse criticism from your Commission or from any body of America's workers and citizenship. Upon others there are wide and diverse opinions. You know, as all the world knows, that the American Federation of Labor has rung true in every proposition for the development of independent character, manhood, and citizenship of the people of our country. Indeed the Constitution of the American Federation of Labor, Section 8, of Article 3, declares that

> Party politics, whether they be Democratic, Republican, Socialistic, Populistic, Prohibition, or any other, shall have no place in the Conventions of the American Federation of Labor

and we submit that it is scarcely just to our movement that we should enter into an agreement specifically including propositions barred by our Federation's Constitution.

You propose that the American Federation of Catholic Societies send delegates to the Conventions of the American Federation of Labor and vice versa. That proposition is not within the power or the province of the Executive Council to carry into effect.

The American Federation of Labor, as its name implies, is not an organization, but a federation of trade and labor unions. The power of its government is vested in the rank and file, the constituent unions making up the American Federation of Labor. The American Federation of Labor is not, as many have mistakenly designated it, the parent organization of the trade union movement; trade unions are the parents of the American Federation of Labor.

PETER E. DIETZ, LABOR PRIEST

With the exception of the trade union movements of foreign countries, no organization or association has ever been invited by the American Federation of Labor to send fraternal delegates. These associations or commissions which have sent fraternal delegates, have found a cordial reception at our conventions, a kindly greeting, and an interesting and sympathetic audience. May we not entertain the hope that nothing shall occur in the future to impair these pleasant and interesting proceedings?

And it is necessary to say that it is not within the province or power of the Executive Council or the American Federation of Labor itself to provide for the exhange of fraternal delegates for city, central and state federations of labor.

The American Federation of Labor has always been open and frank in its every declaration and every act. It declares the views and voices the needs, the sentiments the hopes and the aspirations of the toiling masses of America. It has never denied or shrunk from the frankest relations with all bodies of men as well as with individuals. It seeks the sympathetic cooperation of all in the effort which the organized labor movement is making to rid the toilers of the hardships and the evils resulting from modern industry. It insists that the hours of daily labor shall be normal and not overburdensome; that the wages of the toilers as the reward for the services which they give to society, and without which civilized life would be impossible, shall be ample. It strives for a better life for the masses of our people that they shall have the opportunity to cultivate the best that is in them and make for a more virile manhood, a more beautiful womanhood, and a happier childhood. In that great work, than which there is not greater in the interests of society, humanity and civilization, there is no more powerful force and agency than the much misunderstood and misrepresented organized labor movement of America.

We invite criticism and gladly welcome sympathetic and honest counsel.

There can be no dissent from the suggestion that each shall review with perfect freedom the work of the other, nor can the American Federation of Labor be justly accused of at any time refusing to act in accord with the rules of courtesy or procedure, but the exercise of that courtesy has been and must remain the development of our inner and better selves rather than to be made a subject of agreement.

The trade unions of America, the American Federation of Labor, have not been accused by those who know our movement as lacking virility, character and manhood. There is not a proposition within the realm of practicability or possibility that shall make for the protection and advancement of the right, the interests, and the welfare in their broadest sense of the working people of America, but what the American Federation stand staunch and true in the effort to accomplish it and such is not the purpose not only of this Executive Council and of the American Federation of Labor in its convention assembled, but deep down in the hearts of the great rank and file of our federated unions is imbedded the will and the desire to be true to ourselves, and to each other, true to historic struggles of the masses, for justice, for right, and for freedom, but also to be true to the countless millions yet unborn who shall await and meet the great heritage which the great labor movement of our time will hand down to them.

It is known not only from your own observation, but from the experience of all who have participated in our proceedings, and understand our movement, that we have received fraternal delegates from Churches other than the Catholic, and from philanthropic associations, and that these representatives have been accorded courteous greetings and kindly, sympathetic reciprocal expressions and treatment.

Were it possible for the American Federation of Labor to enter into an agreement as you suggest and propose, it would not dare refuse to enter into similar agreements with the other bodies and churches equally as is suggested and proposed by you. And pray, Sir, where would our activities lead; whither would we be drifting?

274

APPENDIX II

The trade unions constituting the American Federation of Labor are made up of men and women of all religious denominations and persuasions. No one who has been in the great struggle can fail to have a keen understanding of what it has meant to unite men and women of labor with all their deep religious, national and political feelings, and to bring them into some form of co-operative and sympathetic action in order that they may unite as workers in defense of their rights, and their interests against encroachments of employers, private and corporate, and try to secure for the great mass of workers some little hope in their hearts and light in their lives.

There may be here and there employers who give preference to workers of their own nationality, politics, or religious faiths, but the rule, the general, aye, the nearly universal rule is, that the first consideration of employers is—how can they get the most out of the workers for as little compensation as possible, and the questions of the religion, nationality, and politics are driven to the background. If there be one lesson to the toilers more trenchant than another, it is that they must stand united for the principles of fraternity, sympathetic cooperation, and solidarity in furtherance of their rights and protection of their rights and welfare.

We trust therefore that the American labor movement as understood and carried on by the American Federation of Labor be left free from the influences, policies, and tactics which have to their great detriment divided the workers in several other countries.

In no country on the face of the globe do the employers as a rule feel so little obligation to the workers as do the employers of our country. In no country on the face of the globe is wealth and power so concentrated as it is in corporate and vested interests of the United States. In no country on the face of the globe is the unity and solidarity of the working people so essential to the protection and the welfare of the toilers as it is in our own country.

We are firmly persuaded that after giving the above your earnest consideration, you will agree that the ground we have taken is one calculated to serve the best interests of all, a position from which the American Federation of Labor cannot depart.

With assurances of high regard, we have the honor to remain,

> Yours very respectfully.
> The Executive Council of the A. F. of L.
> (Signed)
> Frank Morrison   Samuel Gompers

APPENDIX III

Father Dietz wrote this article on the League of Nations and published it in the Cincinnati *Times-Star*. It annoyed Archbishop Henry Moeller exceedingly and he asked Father Dietz not to publish further articles without ecclesiastical censor.

"MY COUNTRY 'TIS OF THEE"

Cardinal Gibbons ordained me. I am proud of it and of him, but I do not believe in the "League to Enforce Peace." A priest is out of place on a police force; he is out of place in an army or navy except as a chaplain; he is out of place in President Wilson's League of Nations; he is out of place wherever force is requisite for primary sanction.

In the public prints of the day Cardinal Gibbons is made to lend the weight of his personal and ecclesiastical influence to a piece of political propaganda for "the League of Nations." The Pope is quoted in favor of a league of nations, not "The League of Nations." But the innuendo of the report compels the reader to see capital letters only.

Are good, honest folks to be deceived? Does [sic] the Cardinal and the Pope incline toward Wilson's League or Harding's Association? That is the question.

When I became a priest, I graduated from the ordinary pursuits of men and I was dedicated to bring "peace to men of good will"—not a peace of this world, not a peace by force, but a "peace such as the world cannot give."

I am not now going back to the ordinary pursuits of life, either as a Democrat or as a Republican. I shall vote, yes; I am a citizen—sovereign, church and country alike tell me, and I wish to vote intelligently.

If to vote is a mere privilege I might persuade myself to renounce this privilege too. In a democracy, however, a vote is a service, rather than a privilege. I am determined, therefore, to contribute what little sovereignty I have to Christianize democracy; my ballot will bring peace to men of good will only; such, at least, is my intention.

Let whoever will vote for political purposes that are based upon "force," whether they look to their interests through militarist or capitalist or diplomatist or any other kind of eyes. Democratic government is forever built upon the "free consent of the governed" and for all time to come "good-will" alone can fashion the nexus of free consents.

I am strong for any kind of an association that will engender good will and free consents among the peoples of the earth. "The League of Nations" is not, however, of this "Mother" and it doesn't care for mother's milk.

Someone has well said: "I do not know what precise language will make 'The League of Nations' finally acceptable throughout the world; I do not know behind what web of words, or texture or rhetoric the selfish interests of the leading European nations will be concealed; I do not know with what fantoms of phrases, or artifices of speech the real intent of the League will be disguised; I do not know with what honeyed locutions and sugared ambiguities its sinister purposes will be obscured; I do not know with what vacuities of eloquence and bombastic expostulations of benevolence its hypocrisies will be glossed over, nor with what diplomatic verbiage its insincerities will be camouflaged—but this I do know, that beneath the splendor of its verbal draperies the cloven hoof will protrude and the spangled veil of phrases will not be able to conceal the hideous countenance of the beast. This I do know that within the velvet glove of mellifluous speech will be concealed the mailed fist of FORCE."

Just before the war President Wilson splendidly announced that: "The essential principle of peace is the actual equality of nations in all matters of right and principle." "A league of honor, a partnership of democratic nations. Intrigue would eat its vitals away; the plottings of inner circles, who could plan what they would and render account to no one, would be a corruption center at its very best."

276

And now after all that has happened and of which we are but faintly informed, the President asks the People to accept the "Covenant," inseparable from the Peace of Versailles, in the name of the "Five High Contracting Parties," of which he is one. If America's representative, I ask, were not one of the "high contracting parties" what American would ever give a moment's thought, not to mention blind faith, to a contract that would make a democratic partnership of the world forever impossible? But now "it is bone of our bone and flesh of our flesh" and our wrestling is with flesh and blood as well as "with the evil spirits on high."

Today the political atmosphere of the world is opaque—full of mists and vapors. The sun of justice may have dawned and it may be high in the heavens; we can't see it; it has no-where broken through and we can't walk in the light. The world magnates have been compelled by the exigencies of our political campaign to let through a little "open diplomacy." What has come through can only make me fearful and cautious of what is concealed. That is as far as I will go.

I am no lion-tamer and I won't put my head into his paws. I don't want my country to be committed to any league just now, certainly not to "The League of Nations," if I can help it.

There is no Irish blood in me, but with all my heart I want an Independent Ireland. Yet if Ireland could be freed today through the instrument of the "League of Nations," through political expedience, her freedom would be the price of treason to the world—the thirty pieces of silver—if it served to strangle the undeveloped and weak national entities and political aspirations still unborn. Irish generosity and sacrifice is made of other stuff.

The international gunmen tell us to throw up our hands. They'll get no "cameraderie" from me. Oceans of British supremacy and a battleship on every wave—militarism triumphant on the face of the earth—a "Pax Romana" blood-red; shall I underwrite this crucified peace built upon dishonorable repudiation of all the idealism that surged behind the "Four Minute-Men," the "Liberty Bonds," conscription and the cheerful suppression of cherished American Liberties?

No, neither Pope, nor Cardinal, nor Bishop is asking me to sign on the dotted line; they're not asking anybody to sign. Political sovereignty is sacredly enshrined in the Constitution of Christianity itself. Shame to the citizen whose partisanship and ballot is predetermined by unworthy motive or by the hope of mere political reward or because his brother or uncle is washing windows in the City Hall. Much has been written, much has been said; interpretations and reservations are in the air; documents are plentiful and the pages of history are open; choose, choose wisely for your country, for humanity and for God.

I am for international peace and comity; yes, with Washington and Lincoln and Harding; yes, and when the election is decided, eternal vigilance again must be the price of liberty and so on forever until liberty rests securely not upon "Force," but upon the unshakeable foundation of "Good Will": Christianity.

This is the paramount issue; the other issues can wait; the American people will cope with them as they come. I am a Republican today and if on the morrow of the election this allegiance shall conflict with another more dear to me I shall rebel against the Republican Party and every decent American will respect me for it.

My national and international program is based upon Christian foundation; devoted to the ideals and institutions of American democracy; herein lies the test of my political faith; the trial of patriotic service. "If we should" in the words of Thomas Jefferson, "wander from them in moments of error or alarm, let us hasten to retrace our steps and regain the road which alone leads to peace, liberty and safety."

May the breath of the Holy Spirit sweep over our American People and renovate the face of the earth.

AMERICAN ACADEMY OF CHRISTIAN DEMOCRACY
Cincinnati, Ohio, October 22, 1920.

APPENDIX IV

Father Dietz attended his last convention of the American Federation of Labor in June, 1922, at Cincinnati, Ohio. He opened the Convention with the following prayer. Father Dietz was the first priest to be given this privilege.

You have come together in this city, trade union representatives from all over the land, to exercise the rights and to share the responsibilities of the great American Union Parliament. You stand ready, in the name of God, to begin. For you and for your constituents I appeal to the God who rules the universe to witness the justice of your cause and the rectitude of your intentions. I appeal to Him to preside in your councils, to supply your defects, to bless all your efforts for the preservation and extension of the liberties and prosperities of the American people.

Great deeds do not come from indecision or inaction. Your purpose is to decide and to act. Power without truth and wisdom, even though supported by majorities leads but to anarchy. God gives to you His inspiration, His truth and His guiding power: The freedom to fulfill your human destinies, the liberty to serve mankind cannot be achieved and preserved without vigilance. May God keep you, as you have been, the minute-men of American liberties!

The noblest purposes are wrecked through imprudence; prudent men abide both the time and the circumstance. God grant that more and more there shall arise from your ranks the ablest statesmen of the future! Justice is the foundation of empire, without it no law will stand and no government is secure. This justice we implore at Thy hands, Supreme Judge of the world! Fortitude is the finest test of mankind; to suffer and to wait while the ends of justice are in the balance, to be strong in adversity, this fortitude, oh God do Thou bestow upon Thy servants here assembled that they may go forth once more, bearing aloft the burdens of men with spirit unbroken! Men have been strong in defeat and weak in victory.

To be temperate, to be magnanimous when victory comes, when you shall wipe away the tears of the fatherless and widows, when the weak and needy shall be lifted up from their loneliness,—the fruits of victory long delayed—unto that day, Oh loving Father, prepare in our hearts the virtue of victory!

We pray Thee, Father, through Christ Our Lord, to stir up in this assembly the spirit of wisdom and of understanding, the spirit of counsel and fortitude, the spirit of knowledge and of godliness, the spirit of fear of the Lord! Come, Thou Holy Spirit and fill our hearts that we may be created anew to renovate the face of the earth. Give us peace in this Thy day, remove from us the rumors, the tumults, the agonies of civil and industrial strife, and make Thou, O God secure the borders of the nations.

Go now to your tasks, ye men of labor, with the hope of all these things in your hearts. God and all men are with you. The blessing of the Almighty, The Father, The Son and The Holy Spirit descend upon you and abide with you forever. Amen.

APPENDIX V

A number of the friends of Father Dietz in the early days have recalled their impressions of him and have written their evaluation of his work in the light of an historical perspective of some twenty-five years. Excerpts from these letters follow:

THE MOST REVEREND BISHOP J. H. SCHLARMAN
BISHOP OF PEORIA

"My close friendship with Father Dietz began in 1908, when he sponsored a Social Institute at Oberlin, Ohio, where he was then pastor. Somehow, we became close friends immediately and that friendship lasted till his death. To my mind, Father Dietz was a dreamy introvert. On my fairly frequent visits with him I just took it for granted that during the first half hour I had to do the talking. As the night wore on the hours did not count—Father Dietz would spin out his dreams in a fascinating way. . . .

With all his dreaming, he was a profound scholar of the Encyclicals of Leo XIII and Pius XI. He hated hypocrisy and sham and was not afraid to unmask it. That passionate attachment to reality and truth frequently involved him in newspaper controversies."

(July 6, 1949)

REVEREND RAYMOND A. McGOWAN
DIRECTOR OF THE DEPARTMENT OF SOCIAL ACTION
NATIONAL CATHOLIC WELFARE CONFERENCE

"Father Dietz was not made director of the Social Action Department, but he was put on the early committee which advised its work. Dr. John Ryan was made director largely because of his pre-eminence in the field at that particular time and because he lived in Washington."

[Of his work, Father McGowan writes]
"It was pioneer and great work."

(November 30, 1949)

RIGHT REVEREND MONSIGNOR EDWARD A. FREKING

NATIONAL SECRETARY-TREASURER CATHOLIC STUDENTS' MISSION CRUSADE

"The thinking of Father Dietz at that time [1920-1921] was well in advance of his day and his sermons met with a lot of discussion. St. Paul's Church packed every time he talked because the working men wanted to hear the Church's doctrine on social problems. . . . I know of no priest before or since who has had such an influence on the labor movement directly."

(November 23, 1949)

PHILIP MURRAY
PRESIDENT OF THE CONGRESS OF INDUSTRIAL ORGANIZATION

"The split within the labor movement following the 1935 AFL convention was caused by the failure of the then dominant group of leaders to recognize this need. Father Dietz was wise in his observation that such a lack was a structural weakness in the AFL. There is no reason why craft unionism and industrial unions cannot exist and co-operate within a single national federation for such purposes as are of general and mutual advantage. Neither is there any reason why they could not usefully co-operate in an industry council scheme; each in its proper place according to function.

PETER E. DIETZ, LABOR PRIEST

Father Dietz was equally keen in his judgment of men and their motivation. He strongly voiced the rights of labor to organize and bargain collectively. This he did at a time when few public figures were willing to do so. He preached well on the dignity of the worker and the doctrine of labor and management co-operation. The need for improved wages, working and living standards were stressed by him as labor rights. His was one of the clear voices of the Church for social justice through union organization. In this field he was a pioneer."

(December 28, 1949)

MATTHEW WOLL

SECOND VICE PRESIDENT OF THE AMERICAN FEDERATION OF LABOR

"I can say to you honestly and truthfully that Father Dietz well understood the cause of organized labor as represented by the A. F. of L. and that he was extremely sympathetic to its objectives and that he attempted to further the interests of organized labor and its objectives on every possible occasion.

He was well liked by all who knew him and they considered him a friend indeed. It was unfortunate we were unable to retain him in his position in Cincinnati, but we did everything possible within our power to prevent his being sent back to Milwaukee. Unfortunately, we failed in our efforts."

(January 3, 1950)

DANIEL J. TOBIN

GENERAL PRESIDENT OF THE INTERNATIONAL BROTHERHOOD OF TEAMSTERS
FIFTH VICE-PRESIDENT OF THE AMERICAN FEDERATION OF LABOR

"I would not say that Father Dietz was radical either in his views or in his methods. He was progressive and he was ahead of his time. He was sincerely desirous of helping the under-dog. He understood the benefits and the good that trade-unions were doing for the masses of the working people who were organized. . . .

I would say that Father Dietz made many friends amongst non-Catholics for the Catholic Church by his sincerity and his interest in the labor movement. Today we have very, very many Catholic Priests that are, in my judgment, much more radical than Father Dietz was and I think some of those Priests have changed their views against labor because of the early work of Father Dietz. . . . I am happy to say there has been a substantial change on the part of the Clergy, favorable to labor since the days of Father Dietz."

(October 13, 1948)

JOHN P. FREY

PRESIDENT OF THE METAL TRADES DEPARTMENT OF THE AFL

"I became acquainted with Father Peter E. Dietz shortly after he entered the priesthood. He was making special studies of industrial conditions, the social problems which arose from these, and the trade union movement. . .

From the beginning a personal friendship developed between Father Dietz and myself, and I came to learn not a little relative to his spiritual and intellectual life, although I was not of the same religious faith, having been born and brought up in the Methodist Church. . .

[*Regarding the petition to Archbishop Moeller, Frey wrote:*]

280

APPENDIX V

The first three signatures were Thirty-Second Degree Masons; the next three were members of the Roman Catholic Church; the next three were Jews, and this standing of religious affiliations was carried throughout the hundreds of signatures signed to the petition. Of course, the signers did not state what their religions were, but I had prepared a separate list so that the Archbishop could know those who were Protestant, those who were Catholic, those who were Jews.

A committee presented this petition to the Archbishop, but it failed to change his attitude, and so the project which had become so dear to Father Dietz was abandoned, with the regret of many in the Roman Catholic hierarchy in this country, as well as the leaders of the trade union movement who had seen in Father Dietz a man equipped to give the trade union movement, services which no one else at that time was competent to supply.

He felt that for reasons known to the Almighty only, a discipline had been placed upon him, a discipline he must submit to for his spiritual welfare. This is a point of view which I can understand, but it is something which, with my convictions, I am glad I never submitted to for I cannot agree that we should remain silent when we believe injustice is being done."

(October 13, 1948)

BIBLIOGRAPHY

Most of the material for this study was taken from two collections of Dietz papers. In 1944, at the request of Frederick P. Kenkel, director of the Central Bureau of the German Catholic Central Verein, Father Dietz sent the larger and more significant collection to the Verein's library at 3835 Westminster Place, St. Louis, Mo.

Father Dietz had made a cursory sorting of the papers but it took several months of sorting and filing before they were ready to use. Consisting almost entirely of letters, these papers now fill seven metal book files arranged in the following categories: The Militia of Christ, Labor, The American Federation of Catholic Societies, The Social Service Commission, The American Academy of Christian Democracy, The White Cross Nurses, and Miscellaneous. This last file contains recent correspondence and materials on other interests of Father Dietz not closely related to the other six divisions. Father Dietz kept duplicates of the letters he wrote and these are quite complete from 1911 to 1922. Volumes of the *Newsletter*, stapled according to years, are also a part of this collection.

The second more personal collection was loaned by the Reverend Frederick C. Dietz, M.M. of Maryknoll, New York. It includes the intimate family letters and other personal ones from friends and parishioners. Besides these letters there are several notebooks of class notes, quotations from European and American authors on politics and the social question, outlines of classes Father Dietz taught, and sermon notes. The most valuable part of this collection, however, is the two volume *Diary*, begun when Father Dietz was twenty-three years old (1901) with a flashback to his childhood. Covering the years spent in Europe and America up to the time of ordination (1904) it provides an important supplement to the letters of that period. Isolated entries after 1904 bring the *Diary* to 1908.

BOOKS

Brooks, Graham. *The Social Unrest.* New York: Macmillan, 1903.

Brophy, Sister Mary Liguori, B.V.M. *The Social Theories of the German Roman Catholic Central Verein.* Washington: 1941.

Browne, Henry J. *The Catholic Church and the Knights of Labor.* Washington: Catholic University Press, 1949.

Cathrein, Victor, S.J. *Socialism: Its Theoretical Basis and Practical Application.* New York: Benzigers, 1904.

The Catholic Social Year Book. Oxford: The Catholic Social Guild, 1932.

Chaplin, Ralph. *Wobbly: The Rough-and Tumble Story of an American Radical.* Chicago: University of Chicago Press, 1948.

Coleman, McAlister. *Eugene V. Debs.* New York: Greenburg Publishers, 1930.

Commons, John R. and Associates. *History of Labor in the United States.* 4 vols. New York: Macmillan, 1935. Vols. III and IV.

Dulles, Foster Rhea. *Labor in America.* New York: Crowell, 1949.

Elder, Benedict. *A Study of Socialism.* St. Louis: Herder, 1915.

Ellis, John Tracy. *Life of James Cardinal Gibbons.* 2 vols. Milwaukee: Bruce, 1952.

Ely, Richard T. *The Labor Movement in America.* New York: Crowell, 1886.

Fiederling, Sister M. Irmtrudis, O.S.F. *Adolf Kolping and the Kolping Society of the United States.* Washington: 1941.

Fine, Nathan. *Labor and Farmer Parties in the United States.* New York: Rand School of Social Science, 1928.

Galenson, Walter. *Rival Unionism in the United States.* New York: American Council on Public Affairs, 1940.

BIBLIOGRAPHY

Ginger, Ray. *The Bending Cross.* New Brunswick: Rutgers University Press, 1949.

Glueck, Elsie. *John Mitchell: Miner.* New York: The John Day Co., 1929.

Goldstein, David. *Autobiography of a Campaigner for Christ.* Boston: Boston Catholic Campaigners for Christ, 1936.

—— and Avery, Martha Moore. *Socialism: The Nation of Fatherless Children.* Boston: Thomas F. Flynn, 1903.

Hopkins, Charles H. *The Rise of the Social Gospel in American Protestantism.* New Haven: Yale University Press, 1940.

Husslein, Joseph, S.J. *The Church and Social Problems.* New York: America Press, 1904.

—— *Social Wellsprings.* Milwaukee: Bruce, 1940.

Ireland, John. *The Church and Modern Society.* 2 vols. St. Paul: Pioneer Press, 1905.

Markham, S. F. *A History of Socialism.* London: A & C Black, 1930.

Ming, John, S.J. *The Characteristics and the Religion of Modern Socialism.* New York: Benzigers, 1908.

Moon, Parker T. *Labor Problems and the Catholic Social Movement in France.* New York: Macmillan, 1921.

Murrett, John C. *Tar Heel Apostle.* New York: Longmans, Green, 1944.

Perlman, Selig. *History of Trade Unionism.* New York: Macmillan, 1922.

Plater, Charles, S.J. *The Priest and Social Action.* London: Longmans, Green, 1914.

Price, John. *The International Labor Movement.* London: Council for Public Affairs, 1945.

Ryan, John A. *Social Doctrine in Action.* New York: Harpers, 1941.

Sexton, John E. *Cardinal O'Connell.* Boston: Pilot Press, 1926.

Somerville, Henry. *The Catholic Social Movement.* London: Burnes, Oates and Washbourne, 1933.

Spalding, Henry S., S.J. (ed.) *Social Problems and Agencies.* New York: Benzigers, 1925.

Spalding, John L. *The Religious Mission of the Irish People and Catholic Colonization.* New York: Catholic Publishing Society, 1880.

—— *Socialism and Labor and Other Arguments.* Chicago: McClurg, 1902.

Stang, Wm., S.J. *Socialism and Christianity.* New York: Benzigers, 1905.

Walsh, J. Raymond. *Labour's Battle in the U.S.A.: The Fight for Industrial Unionism.* London: Allen & Unwin, 1938.

Waninger, Karl. *Social Catholicism in England.* Translated by Charles Plater, S.J. St. Louis: Herder, 1923.

Will, Allen, S. *Life of James Cardinal Gibbons.* 2 vols. Baltimore: John Murphy, 1911.

Ware, Norman J. *Labor in Canadian Relations.* Toronto: Ryerson, 1937.

Year Book of American Labor. New York: Rand School of Social Science, 1916.

PAMPHLETS

Dietz, Peter E. *The Christian Manifesto.* Milwaukee: Militia of Christ Series No. 2, 1912.

—— *Need of an Organized Christian Force in the American Labor Movement.* Milwaukee: Bulletin No. 6, n.d.

—— *What Shall Our Catholic Societies Do?* Milwaukee: Bulletin No. 3, 1912.

Saint-Pierre, Arthur. *La Fédération Américaine du Travail.* Montreal: Secretariat de L'Ecole Sociale Populaire, 1914.

———— *L'Organization Ouvriere.* Montreal: Secretariat de L'Ecole Sociale Populaire, 1913.

Serrarens, P. J-S. *Le Syndicalisme Catholique en Hollande.* Montreal: 1920.

Stone, N. I. *The Attitude of the Socialists Toward the Trade Union.* An address delivered at the National Convention of the Socialist Labor Party at Rochester, New York, 1900.

MAGAZINE ARTICLES

Abell, Aaron I. "The Catholic Church and Social Problems in the World War I Era," *Mid-America,* XXX (July, 1948), 139-151.

———— "Labor Legislation in the United States: The Background and Growth of Newer Trends," *The Review of Politics,* X (January, 1948), 35-60.

———— "Origins of Catholic Social Reform in the United States: Ideological Aspects," *The Review of Politics,* XI (July, 1949), 294-309.

———— "The Reception of Leo XIII's Labor Encyclical in America. 1891-1919," *The Review of Politics,* VII (October, 1945), 464-495.

Achatz, Raymond. "Social Service in the Non-Catholic Universities," *Social Service,* I (August, 1911), 118-119.

America II (1909) to XVII (1917), *passim.*

Browne, Henry J. "Peter E. Dietz, Pioneer Planner of Catholic Social Action," *Catholic Historical Review,* XXXIII (January, 1948), 448-456.

Bruehl, Charles. "A Course of Social Science at the Salesianum," *Catholic Fortnightly Review,* XVIII (1911), 734-736.

Bulletin of the American Federation of Catholic Societies, III (1909) to XII (1917), *passim.*

Conway, John. "America's Workmen," *Catholic World,* LVI (January, 1893), 490-496.

Cort, John C. "Catholics, Communists, and Unions," *The Sign,* November, 1948, pp. 12-15.

Dietz, Peter E. "Builders Guild of Cincinnati," *The American Federationist,* XXIX (March, 1922), 188-190.

Dowling, Austin. "The National Catholic Welfare Conference," *Ecclesiastical Review,* LXXIX (October, 1928), 337-354.

Engelen, William, S.J. "Rome has Spoken," *Central Blatt and Social Justice,* V (January, 1913), 217-219; (March, 1913), 269-272.

Holaind, R. J., S.J. "The Encyclical Rerum Novarum," *American Ecclesiastical Review,* V (August, 1891), 83-93.

Howard, Francis. "Social Science as an Aid in the Ministry," *American Ecclesiastical Review,* XII (April, 1895), 293-300.

Keane, John J. "America as Seen from Abroad," *Catholic World,* LXVI (March, 1898), 721-723.

Kenkel, Frederick P. "Spread of Socialism in Our Colleges and Universities," *Central Blatt and Social Justice,* III (November, 1910), 165.

Kerby, William. "Aims in Socialism," *Catholic World,* LXXXV (July, 1907), 500-511.

———— "Fundamental Relations of Charity," *Catholic World,* XCIV (April, 1914) 29-41.

———— "Our Catholic Charities," *Catholic World,* C (November, 1914), 145-154.

———— "Principles of Social Reform," *Catholic World,* LXXX (January, 1905), 425-433; (February, 1905), 582-591; (March, 1905), 709-718.

Maguire, J. W. "Why Sociology Should be Taught in our Catholic Colleges," *The Catholic Educational Association Bulletin,* XIII (November, 1916), 108-113.

National Catholic Welfare Council Bulletin, I (1919-1920), *passim.*

BIBLIOGRAPHY

Onahan, William J. "Columbian Catholic Congress at Chicago," *Catholic World,* LVII (August, 1893), 604-608.

Roosevelt, Theodore, "The Coal Miners at Home," *The Outlook,* XCVI (December, 1910), 899-908.

Ryan, John A. "Can a Catholic be a Socialist?" *Catholic Fortnightly Review,* XVI (July, 1909), 70-73.

————— "The Church and the Workingman," *Catholic World,* LXXXIX (September, 1909), 776-782.

————— "Does the Catholic Church Condemn Modern Economic Socialism?" *Catholic Fortnightly Review,* XVI (July, 1909), 391-394.

————— "The Employer's Obligation to Pay a Living Wage," *Catholic World,* LXXVII (April, 1903), 44-59.

————— "Have we any Catholic Solutions of Social Problems?" *Social Service,* I (November, 1911), 147-152.

————— "Social Reform Through Legislation," *Catholic World,* LXXXIX (July, 1909), 433-444; 608-614.

————— "Two Important Points in the Social Program of the Central Verein," *Catholic Fortnightly Review,* XVI (March, 1909), 130-132.

————— "The Underpaid Laborers of America: Their Number and Prospects," *Catholic World,* LXXXI (May, 1905), 143-156.

Simmons, William I. "A Plea for the Wage-Earner," *Catholic World,* LVIII (December, 1893), 424-430.

Smith, John Talbot. "The Children at Work," *Catholic World,* XLIII (August, 1886), 619-625.

————— "The 8-hr. Law," *Catholic World,* XLIII (December, 1886), 397-406.

"Who Makes Bolshevism in Cincinnati?" *The New Republic,* XVIII (April 19, 1919), 365-367.

Woodlock, Thomas T. "The School for Social Studies," *Common Cause,* I (January, 1912), 83-85.

REPORTS AND PROCEEDINGS

La Confédération Internationale des Syndicats Chrétiens d'Amsterdam a Lyon 1946-1949, Utrecht: 1949.

Official Report of the Free World Labour Conference and of the First Congress of the International Confederation of Free Trade Unions, London: November-December, 1949.

Proceedings of the National Conference of Catholic Charities, Washington: 1910, 166-193.

Report of the Proceedings of the American Federation of Labor. (1910-1922), *passim.*

"Report of the Secretary of the Social Service Commission," (February, 1912-August, 1917).

Verhandlungen der Fuenften Allgemeine Versammlung Katholiken Deutscher Zunge der Vereinigten Staaten von Nord-Amerika, Buffalo: 1891.

Verhandlungen der Sechsten Deutsch-Amerikanischen Katholiken Versammlung, New York: 1892.

UNPUBLISHED MATERIAL

Boyle, John P. "Peter E. Dietz and the American Labor Movement," Unpublished Master's Thesis, Department of Social Science, The Catholic University of America, August, 1948.

Stroh, Paul, C.SS.R., "The Catholic Clergy and American Labor Disputes: 1900-1932," Unpublished Ph.D. Dissertation, Department of Economics, The Catholic University of America, 1939.